The *NEW* VEGETABLE & HERB EXPERT

Dr. D.G.Hessayon

All Editions & Reprints: 4,870,000 copies

Published 1997
by Expert Books
a division of Transworld Publishers Ltd

Copyright ©Dr. D. G. Hessayon 1997

The right of Dr.D.G.Hessayon to be identified
as author of this work has been asserted in accordance
with sections 77 and 78 of the Copyright Designs and
Patents Act 1988.

A catalogue record for this book is available from the British Library

TRANSWORLD PUBLISHERS LTD
61–63 Uxbridge Road, London W5 5SA

 Distributed in the United States
by Sterling Publishing Co. Inc.,
387 Park Avenue South,
New York, NY 10016–8810

Distributed in Canada by
Cavendish Books Inc.,
Unit 5, 801 West 1st Street,
North Vancouver, B.C. V7P 1A4

EXPERT BOOKS

Contents

Reproduction by Spot On Repro Ltd, Perivale, Middlesex
Printed and bound in Great Britain by Jarrold & Sons Ltd, Norwich

ISBN 0 903505 46 0

CHAPTER 1

GETTING STARTED

One of the important changes in gardening since World War II has been the resurgence of interest in growing vegetables at home. The concept that it is only for the poor or the country dweller has long been swept away with the realisation that home-grown produce beats the shop-bought equivalent in three vital ways. Firstly, you can harvest at the peak of tenderness and flavour instead of having to wait for maximum yields like the professional grower. You can also serve vegetables within an hour or two of picking and with sweet corn, beans, asparagus, etc. this can mean a new flavour experience for you. Finally, you can grow vegetables which do not appear in High St shops and you can sow top-quality varieties of ordinary vegetables which are not grown commercially.

You can save money by growing your own — it has been estimated that an expenditure of £1 on seeds, fertilizers, canes, etc. yields crops worth about £9 at shop prices. But saving money is not the main motive for many — it is just a bonus from a hobby which provides a special thrill from growing and then eating your own.

Most of the basic principles of vegetable growing have been with us for hundreds of years, but the subject doesn't stand still. There have been several important developments since the earlier edition of this book appeared. Interest in herbs continues to expand and specially-bred baby vegetables have made their appearance in seed catalogues. Until recently growing vegetables nearly always meant long rows of plants, but now the idea of growing in pots, raised beds and even in the flower bed and shrub border has taken root.

BUYING & STORING SEED

When you buy a packet of seeds your interests are protected by law — there are standards for purity and germination capacity, but you must still choose carefully. Order early and buy from a reputable supplier.

SEED TERMS

Open-pollinated seed Most of the varieties in the catalogues are of this 'conventional' or 'standard' type. No specialist hybridisation has been carried out and so it is generally the most economic. Remember, however, that new varieties cost more than old favourites.

F₁ hybrid seed A variety produced by the careful crossing of two pure-bred parents. Increased vigour and uniformity of height, shape etc. are the major characteristics and so an F₁ hybrid is often a good buy despite the higher price. One major drawback — the plants all tend to mature at the same time, which is good for the professional but bad for the amateur.

Pelleted seed Seed coated with clay or other material to make handling easier. Useful for tiny seeds as you can sow them at wide enough intervals so as to cut down or eliminate the need for thinning. Results are often disappointing as the soil around the seeds must be kept uniformly moist — if kept too dry or too wet germination will be poor.

Dressed seed Seed which has been coated with a fungicide or fungicide/insecticide before packing by the nurseryman.

Vacuum-packed seed Seed which has been packed into vacuum sealed foil sachets before being placed in the package. Such seeds maintain their viability longer than seeds packed in the ordinary way.

Chitted seed Seed which has been germinated by the grower and set out in waterproof sachets. Such seed must be planted immediately.

Saved seed Some seed is usually left over after sowing. Nearly all varieties can be saved for next year — see below.

Home-grown seed It is tempting to save seed from vegetables which have been left to form pods or seed-heads. In most cases it is not advisable. F₁ hybrids will not breed true and brassicas may well have been cross-bred and so produce worthless plants. Exceptions are peas, beans and onions — many champion onion growers insist on using their own seed.

The storage lives for vegetable seed listed in this book are for unopened packages kept under proper conditions — bad storage will cut down viability quite drastically. Tightly close opened packages and place in a jar with a screw top. Place the container in a cool, dry and dark place.

CROP ROTATION

You should not grow a vegetable in the same spot year after year. If you do then two basic problems are likely to arise. Firstly, soil-living pests and diseases which thrive on the crop will steadily increase and may reach epidemic proportions. Secondly, continuous cropping with the same vegetable may lead to the levels of soil nutrients becoming unbalanced. Crop rotation is the answer, and the standard 3 year plan is shown here. A strip of land at one end of the plot is sometimes used for permanent crops (asparagus, rhubarb, etc.) and is left out of the plan. Not everyone is able or willing to practise crop rotation, and unfortunately all idea of a rotation is abandoned. It would be much better to follow a very simple routine — roots this year, an above-ground vegetable next year and then back to a root crop … with the proviso that if a vegetable does badly one year then you should *never* follow it next year with one from the same group shown in the table below.

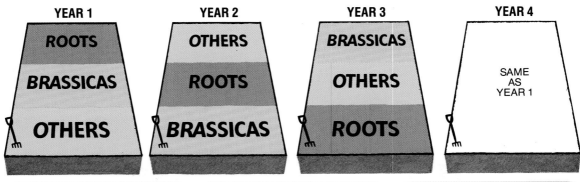

YEAR 1
ROOTS
BRASSICAS
OTHERS

YEAR 2
OTHERS
ROOTS
BRASSICAS

YEAR 3
BRASSICAS
OTHERS
ROOTS

YEAR 4
SAME AS YEAR 1

ROOTS
beetroot • carrot • chicory jerusalem artichoke • parsnip potato • salsify • scorzonera

Do not add manure.

Do not lime.

Star need Rake in a general-purpose fertilizer about 2 weeks before sowing or planting.

BRASSICAS
broccoli • brussels sprout cabbage • cauliflower • kale kohl rabi • radish swede • turnip

Add some well-rotted manure or compost at digging time if soil is known to be short of humus.

Star need Lime the soil unless you are sure it is already alkaline.

Star need Rake in a general-purpose fertilizer about 2 weeks before sowing or planting.

OTHERS
aubergine • bean • capsicum celeriac • celery • cucumber endive • leaf beet • leek lettuce • marrow • onion • pea spinach • sweet corn • tomato

Star need Add a liberal amount of well-rotted manure or compost at digging time.

Lime only if the soil is known to be acid.

Rake in a general-purpose fertilizer about 2 weeks before sowing or planting.

DIGGING

- Choose a spade which is suited to your height and strength. Keep the blade clean.
- Choose the right day. The ground must be neither frozen nor saturated. If possible pick a time of settled weather.
- Begin slowly. About 30 minutes is quite enough for the first day if you are not used to strenuous exercise.
- Insert the blade vertically, not at an angle. Annual weeds can be turned in but roots of perennial weeds should be removed.
- Leave the soil in lumps — frost will break down the clods during winter.
- Never bring subsoil to the surface — raw clay, chalk or sand will ruin the fertility.

Don't try to dig and make a seed bed in one operation. The time for digging is during a dry spell in late autumn or early winter if you plan to sow or plant in spring. Dig out a trench about 1½ ft wide and 1 spit (spade-depth) deep at the front of the plot and transport the soil to the back. Spread compost over the surface of the area to be enriched with humus (see 'crop rotation' above). Now begin to dig the plot — invert a 4–6 in. wide strip of soil into the trench in front. Move back, turning over each successive strip until a final trench is formed. Fill this with the soil brought over from the first trench. Once every 3 years some keen vegetable growers carry out double digging in order to break up the compacted layer below the depth of digging. This calls for forking over the bottom of each trench before turning over the soil from the adjacent strip.

MANURING

Manuring is the start of the gardening year. In autumn or early winter spread bulky organic matter over the surface at the rate of 10 lb per sq. yard (approximately 1 barrowload per 10 sq. yards). The area chosen should be for crops other than roots or brassicas, but *all* land can be enriched with well-rotted manure or old compost if it is starved of humus.

Animal manure is scarce and garden peat is expensive. The answer is to make as much compost as you can, using both garden and kitchen waste. Make sure some carbon-rich matter (straw, leaves, chopped newspaper, etc.) is present, and remember to keep the heat in and the rain out. Do not use lime but add a little soil between organic matter layers.

Where time allows, fork the organic layer into the surface before digging starts (see page 4). It is vital that this manuring routine is carried out so that part of the plot is enriched each year until the whole area has been treated. Its role is to improve the crumb structure and increase the water- and food-holding capacity.

LIMING

The addition of manure and fertilizer plus heavy cropping tend to increase the acidity of the vegetable plot. Never lime each year as a matter of routine — if you are following the standard crop rotation plan then lime only the land which is to be used for brassicas. This means that the land is limed once every 3 years — see page 4.

There is no need to guess the correct amount of lime to use these days. A simple pH kit will tell you the degree of acidity, and this reading plus the type of soil in question determines the application rate. This will be between ½–1½ lb per sq. yard — the experts recommend ground limestone rather than hydrated lime. If you don't want to go to the trouble of testing, use ½ lb per sq. yard.

Timing is all-important. If organic matter has not been added to the soil, sprinkle the lime over the freshly-dug surface — do not incorporate into the surface. If manure has been added, postpone liming until February. Lime likes to be alone, and that applies to fertilizers as well as manures. Feeding should take place either a month before or after the application of lime to the soil surface.

PREPARING THE SEED BED

A few vegetables are grown by planting rooted material. The roots of these transplants are either bare or contained in a soil ball, and examples are asparagus, rhubarb, globe artichoke and some herbs. There are other vegetables, especially half-hardy ones such as tomatoes and aubergines, which are first raised indoors under glass and then transplanted into the open garden when conditions are suitable. The pattern for most vegetables, however, is to sow seeds outdoors and then either leave them to grow where sown or else transplant them as seedlings to another spot where they grow to maturity. Either way, a seed bed is required.

Early spring is the usual time to start, but you must wait until the soil is workable. The surface will have started to change colour but it will still be moist just below this thin dry layer. Walk over the plot — if the soil sticks to your boots then it is still too wet.

The first job is to break down the clods which you brought up with the winter digging using a hand cultivator or a garden fork. Work on a push-pull principle to shatter the large lumps and roughly level the surface — do not let the prongs or tines go deeper than 6 in. below the surface. If the surface is still very uneven and clods are still present, repeat the cultivation at right angles. The next step is to apply a dressing of fertilizer to the surface. It is unwise to leave all of this dressing on the surface as in concentrated form it can damage the tiny roots of germinating seeds. To avoid this risk work the fertilizer into the top few inches with a hand cultivator.

Now you are ready to prepare the seed bed, and the rules have changed in recent years. The traditional way was to tread over the surface in order to consolidate the lower levels and to squash any remaining clods. The final step was to rake the surface smooth. Nowadays treading is frowned upon because it has been shown to damage the soil structure, so follow the new rules. Walk over the surface with a rake and use it to fill in the hollows and break down the mounds. Pick up debris and small stones. When you have finished this operation, use the rake in a push-pull fashion to produce a smooth and level seed bed with a crumbly surface. These crumbs must not be too small. A surface with the consistency of coarse breadcrumbs should be your goal — the larger the seed, the less the need for a fine 'tilth' (crumb structure).

SOWING SEED OUTDOORS

Not too early, not too deeply and not too thickly are the golden rules. Proper timing is extremely important. The calendars in this book will give you approximate times but your own soil and weather conditions must determine the precise time. Seeds will germinate only when the temperatures are high enough to allow growth to begin — sowing in wet and near-freezing soil is bound to lead to disaster.

Mark out the row with a length of taut string. With a stick, trowel or the edge of a hoe draw out the drill to the depth recommended for the vegetable to be sown. Feel the soil at the bottom of the drill — if it is dry, water gently through the rose of a watering can. Sow seed as thinly as you can along the row. Do not do this directly from the packet — place some seeds in the palm of your hand and gently sprinkle between thumb and forefinger. Fine seed should be mixed with sand before sowing.

When the drill has been sown, cover the seed by gently replacing the soil with the back of a rake. If you are not skilled at this operation it is better to forget the textbooks and push the soil back with your fingers. Firm gently but *do not water*. If the weather is dry then cover the surface with newspaper.

Large seeds such as sweet corn, marrow and broad beans are sown in the drill or in holes dug with a trowel or dibber at the stations where they are to grow. It is usual to sow 2 or 3 seeds at each station, thinning all but the strongest seedling after germination.

SOWING SEED INDOORS

1 **CONTAINER** Many types of container are suitable provided they have holes or cracks at the base for drainage. Avoid old wooden trays — disease organisms are difficult to remove by washing. Choose plastic — full trays are usually too large and a better choice is a 3½–5 in. half pot or a half tray. Large seeds can be sown into the cells of cellular trays or peat pots filled with compost.

2 **COMPOST** Use a seed or multi-purpose compost. Fill the container with compost and firm gently with a piece of board — the surface should be about ½ in. below the top of the pot or tray. Sprinkle with water the day before seed sowing.

3 **COVER** Do not cover very fine seed with compost. Other seeds should be covered with compost or vermiculite to a depth which is twice the diameter of the seed. Compost should be applied through a sieve to form a fine and even layer. Firm gently with a board after sowing. Put brown paper over the tray or pot and place a sheet of glass on top. Change the paper if it gets wet.

4 **WARMTH** Most seeds require a fairly warm temperature (65–70°F) for satisfactory germination. Heating a whole greenhouse in March or April can be wasteful — a thermostatically-controlled heated propagator is a better idea. For windowsill propagation you will need a centrally-heated room where the temperature can be kept in the 60–70°F range.

5 **LIGHT & WATER** As soon as the seedlings break through the surface, remove the paper and prop up the sheet of glass. After a few days the glass should be removed and the container moved to a bright but sunless spot. Windowsill pots or trays should be turned every couple of days. Never let the compost dry out. The safest way to water is to use a fine sprayer.

6 **PRICK OUT** As soon as the first set of true leaves has opened the seedlings should be pricked out into trays, small pots or 24-cell cellular trays (Propapacks) filled with Multicompost. The seedlings should be set 1–1½ in. apart in pots or trays. Keep containers in the shade for a day or two after pricking out. High temperatures are not required — 50–55°F is satisfactory. Water as necessary.

Correct stage for pricking out ▶

7 **HARDEN OFF** When the seedlings have recovered from the pricking out move, they must be hardened off to prepare them for the life outdoors. Increase ventilation and move to a cold frame. Keep the lights closed for a week or two and then open on dry and frost-free days. Later keep them open day and night for 7 days before planting out. Windowsill seedlings should be moved into an unheated room before being stood out for a few days prior to planting in the garden.

CHAPTER 2

HOME-GROWN VEGETABLES

Practically all of the vegetables which can be grown in the garden are described in this chapter. Some are universal favourites — lettuce, carrots, beetroot, etc. and others are much less popular. You will not find celeriac, kohl rabi nor aubergine on the average plot.

Out of this extensive list, ranging from artichoke, globe (page 8) to turnip (page 105) you are free to make your choice. To avoid disappointment take a little time and trouble when making your selection — you will need more than a pin and a coloured seed catalogue!

When making up your seed list the first consideration should be the likes and dislikes of the family. By all means try a row or two of an unknown vegetable, but it is silly to grow a crop which you *know* the family will leave on the plate. And yet there are people who grow broad beans every year "because everybody does" and the pods go to waste. Once you have an acceptable list read the notes on each vegetable in this chapter. Can you give it a suitable home? Cauliflower will fail in sandy, impoverished soil and sweet corn is a gamble in Scotland. Some may be just too much trouble for you — aubergine and capsicum need pampering and

globe artichoke needs space. Your list will now be further reduced, but you are left with far more types than you could possibly grow. So you must now make your personal selection from the vegetables which the family will like and which will succeed in your garden.

We really are creatures of habit — year after year we tend to pick the same ones. The top seven in the national seed list continue to be lettuce, runner beans, tomatoes, cabbage, peas, carrots and beetroot. Then we have a second division in the popular league — radishes, onions, brussels sprouts, broad beans and cauliflower. No doubt the major part of your own seed order is drawn from this group of favourites, and that is the way it should be. Do try some of the newer varieties, however, as improvements continue to appear.

Apart from choosing a new variety of an old friend you may wish to try a new vegetable. Unusual ones which can be bought as seed from most large nurserymen are described in this chapter — oddities which are listed in very few catalogues are included in the chapter on unusual vegetables. A plot made up entirely of the top seven plus potatoes or a plot full of out-of-the-way vegetables — it is entirely up to you.

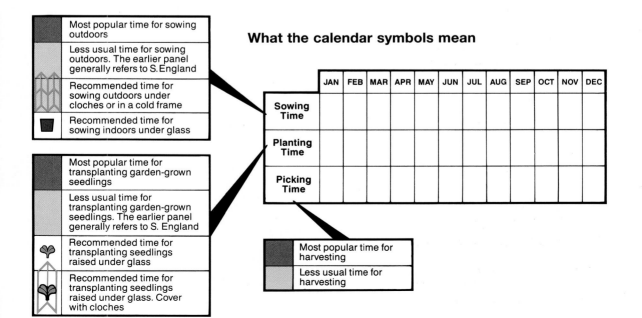

What the calendar symbols mean

	Most popular time for sowing outdoors
	Less usual time for sowing outdoors. The earlier panel generally refers to S. England
	Recommended time for sowing outdoors under cloches or in a cold frame
	Recommended time for sowing indoors under glass

	Most popular time for transplanting garden-grown seedlings
	Less usual time for transplanting garden-grown seedlings. The earlier panel generally refers to S. England
	Recommended time for transplanting seedlings raised under glass
	Recommended time for transplanting seedlings raised under glass. Cover with cloches

	JAN	FEB	MAR	APR	MAY	JUN	JUL	AUG	SEP	OCT	NOV	DEC
Sowing Time												
Planting Time												
Picking Time												

| | Most popular time for harvesting |
| | Less usual time for harvesting |

ARTICHOKE, GLOBE

This handsome, thistle-like plant is more at home in the herbaceous border than on a small vegetable plot. It grows about 4 ft high, its arching silvery leaves providing an attractive foil for the bright floral display. The globe artichoke, however, must never be allowed to bloom — the ball-like heads are removed for cooking just before the fleshy scales open. A fussy plant in many ways, requiring good soil, regular watering and feeding plus frost protection in winter, but the reward is a gourmet's delight. It will not last for ever — plant rooted suckers each spring so that mature specimens can be disposed of after a few years.

PLANT FACTS

Use offsets (rooted suckers) taken either from high-yielding plants in your own garden or bought from a garden centre. These offsets should be about 9 in. high and must have roots attached. Raising plants from seed is possible, but is not advisable.

¼ actual size

Seed sowing technique:	Sow thinly 1 in. deep in drills 1 ft apart. Thin to 9 in. Plant out in the following spring
Productive life:	4 years
Expected yield per mature plant:	10–12 heads
Approximate time between planting and cutting:	1½ years
Ease of cultivation:	Not easy — requires space and regular attention

SOIL FACTS

- Light or loamy soil in a sunny, sheltered location is needed — it is a waste of time to grow this crop in heavy clay. Good drainage is essential.
- Dig the soil in autumn and incorporate a liberal amount of compost or well-rotted manure. Rake in Growmore fertilizer shortly before planting.

PLANTING

36 in.

Plant firmly.
Remove tips of leaves.
Water in thoroughly

36 in.

2 in.

CALENDAR

	JAN	FEB	MAR	APR	MAY	JUN	JUL	AUG	SEP	OCT	NOV	DEC
Sowing Time												
Planting Time												
Cutting Time												

LOOKING AFTER THE CROP

- Keep the plants well watered until established. Apply a mulch around the stems in May.
- During the summer months hoe regularly and apply a liquid fertilizer at fortnightly intervals. Water thoroughly when the weather is dry.
- In late autumn cut down the stems and cover the crowns with bracken, leaves or straw. Remove this protective covering in April.

HARVESTING

- A few small heads will begin to form in the first year. Do not let them develop — cut off immediately and discard.
- Regular cropping begins in the season after planting. Remove the terminal bud ('king head') first. It should be large and swollen but still green and unopened. Leave 2 or 3 in. of the stem attached.
- Feed the plants after this initial cropping. Later in the season remove and cook the smaller secondary heads.

IN THE KITCHEN

Eating a globe artichoke may seem inelegant but it is a delicious vegetable, served hot or cold. The fleshy half-moon at the base of each cooked scale is chewed, after which the scale is placed back on the plate. When all the scales have been used in this way, the hairy centre ('choke') is removed. The fleshy heart ('fond') is then eaten with a knife and fork.

STORAGE Keep in a polythene bag in the refrigerator — heads will stay fresh for up to 1 week.

COOKING Cut off stalk, remove outer layer of scales and then wash thoroughly to remove insects. Boil in salted water for 30–40 minutes. To eat, remove each scale in turn and dip the base in melted butter, vinaigrette or hollandaise sauce.

VARIETIES

GREEN GLOBE: Large green heads — the variety you are most likely to find in the seed catalogues.
PURPLE GLOBE: Hardier than its green relative, but bottom of the ratings for flavour.
VERT DE LAON: This is the one to buy as offsets from your garden centre. Highly recommended.
CAMUS DE BRETAGNE: Large heads with an excellent flavour, but you will have to search for it. Not suitable for northern counties.
VIOLETTA DI CHIOGGIA: An excellent purple variety to raise from seed.

TROUBLES

PETAL BLIGHT

A serious but uncommon disease. Brown spots rapidly join together so that the head is ruined. Remove and burn affected tops.

APHID

Both blackfly and greenfly attack developing flower-heads. Spray with permethrin or heptenophos as soon as the first attacks are seen.

SLUGS

Young shoots are attacked during wet weather in spring. Sprinkle Slug Pellets around the plants.

1 in. = 2.5 cm, 1 ft = 30 cm, 1 oz = 28 gm, 1 lb = 450 gm

For key to symbols — see page 7

ARTICHOKE, JERUSALEM

You will find jerusalem artichokes in most text-books but in few gardens. The knobbly tubers are used as an alternative to potatoes — fine for slimmers but not to everybody's taste. Buy some and try them before planting a row. These grow-anywhere hardy plants will tower up to 10 ft or more — an excellent screen or windbreak but a line of them will form a light-robbing shield for lowly vegetables planted below. The name indicates the close relationship to the sunflower and not to the Middle East — it comes from the Italian word *girasole* (sun follower).

PLANT FACTS

Tubers bought from the greengrocer or supermarket can be used for planting. Choose roots which are the size of a small hen's egg.

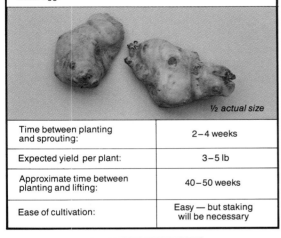

½ actual size

Time between planting and sprouting:	2–4 weeks
Expected yield per plant:	3–5 lb
Approximate time between planting and lifting:	40–50 weeks
Ease of cultivation:	Easy — but staking will be necessary

SOIL FACTS

- Not fussy at all, provided that the soil is neither very acid nor subject to prolonged waterlogging in winter. It is a useful plant for breaking up heavy land.
- Dig the soil in autumn or early winter and incorporate compost if the soil is short of humus.

PLANTING

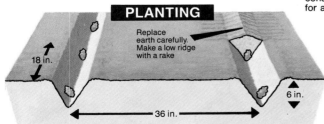

Replace earth carefully. Make a low ridge with a rake

18 in.

6 in.

36 in.

CALENDAR

	JAN	FEB	MAR	APR	MAY	JUN	JUL	AUG	SEP	OCT	NOV	DEC
Planting Time												
Lifting Time												

LOOKING AFTER THE CROP

- Use a hoe to earth-up the base of the stems when the plants are about 1 ft high. Water when the weather is dry.
- Insert a cane at each end of the row and run plastic-coated wire on either side of the plants. In this way they will be protected from the wind.
- During the summer months remove flower buds as they form and feed occasionally with a liquid fertilizer.

HARVESTING

- Cut down the stems to about 1 ft above the ground once the leaves have turned brown in autumn. Lift the tubers as required between October and early spring — cover the stem bases with straw or soil in severe weather.
- At the end of the season reserve some of the tubers for planting purposes. Make sure that *all* tubers have been removed from the soil — any left in the soil will grow as weeds.

IN THE KITCHEN

Boiled, fried, baked, roasted or stewed — jerusalem artichokes provide a novel alternative to potatoes. The gourmets praise creamed artichoke soup and also artichoke rissoles made by forming boiled and mashed artichokes into small balls or flat cakes which are then fried in deep fat.

STORAGE Keep in a polythene bag in the refrigerator — tubers will stay fresh for up to 2 weeks.

COOKING To prepare artichokes for boiling, scrub the tubers immediately after lifting and then boil in their skins in water containing a teaspoonful of vinegar. Cook for 20–25 minutes — peel before serving.

VARIETIES

The usual planting material is a white-skinned type bought from the greengrocer or supermarket, so the variety is not known. If you can, buy a named variety from your garden centre or nursery.

FUSEAU: This is the one to buy — long, white tubers with a far smoother surface than the ordinary variety. The plant is also more compact, reaching only 5–6 ft.

DWARF SUNRAY: White skin which does not need peeling. A free-flowering variety with a compact growth habit — worth considering for the flower border, but you will have to search for a supplier.

TROUBLES

SLUGS

Hollowed-out tubers generally indicate attack by slugs — sprinkle Slug Pellets around the growing plants to prevent trouble later on. Less likely causes of tuber damage are soil-living caterpillars — rake phoxim or diazonon into the soil before planting if you have had trouble in the past with root-eating grubs.

SCLEROTINIA ROT

The base of stems are attacked, and may show fluffy white mould. Black cyst-like bodies occur inside rotten stems. Lift and burn diseased plants immediately.

ASPARAGUS

The ferny foliage of asparagus is decorative in summer but should not be cut for flower arranging. The plants need all their green tissues in order to produce a plentiful supply of succulent young shoots ('spears') in the following spring. It is these spears which are cut and then cooked to produce a dish which is a far cry from the soggy dwarfs sold in tins. Old wives' tales abound — the ancients believed that the spears arose from rams' horns buried in the soil, and many a modern-day gardener still believes that wide spacing, an annual heavy dressing of manure and a regular sprinkling of salt are all essential for top yields. One of our oldest crops, but there are new varieties and new ideas. Grow it if you have free-draining soil, adequate land which can be tied up for a decade or more … and patience — you will have to wait two years for your first hearty meal!

PLANT FACTS

Use 1-year-old crowns. You can buy 2- or 3-year-old crowns but they can be temperamental. Asparagus can be raised from seed but it will be 3 years before regular cropping can begin.

¼ actual size

Seed sowing technique:	Sow thinly 1 in. deep in drills 1 ft apart. Thin to 6 in. when seedlings are 3 in. tall. Plant out largest plants in beds during the following spring
Productive life:	8–20 years
Expected yield per mature plant:	20–25 spears
Approximate time between planting 1-year-old crowns and regular cutting:	2 years
Ease of cultivation:	Not easy — requires thorough soil preparation, space and regular hand weeding

SOIL FACTS

- Good drainage is essential — the soil type is much less important. Pick a sunny spot, sheltered from strong winds, and dig thoroughly in the autumn — incorporate a liberal dressing of well-rotted manure or compost. Liming will be necessary if the soil is very acid.
- Remove the roots of *all* perennial weeds during soil preparation. Leave the soil rough after digging — fork over in March and rake in Growmore fertilizer.

PLANTING

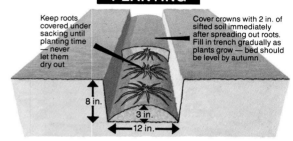

Keep roots covered under sacking until planting time — never let them dry out

Cover crowns with 2 in. of sifted soil immediately after spreading out roots. Fill in trench gradually as plants grow — bed should be level by autumn

8 in.

3 in.

12 in.

LOOKING AFTER THE CROP

- Keep the bed clean by hand weeding. Provide support for the stems if necessary and water during dry weather. Remove berries before they fall to the ground.
- In autumn cut down the ferny stems once they have turned yellow. The stumps should be 1–2 in. above the surface.
- Before the spears appear in spring make a ridge of soil over each row with a draw hoe. Apply a surface dressing of Growmore fertilizer.

HARVESTING

- Soon after planting the first spears will appear. On no account should these be cut — they must be left to develop into bushy fern-like stems.
- In the year after planting little or no cutting should take place. Some experts believe that the removal of a single spear per plant in May will do no harm — others believe that no growth at all should be removed at this stage.
- Cutting can begin in earnest in the second year after planting. As soon as the spears reach a height of 4–5 in. they should be severed about 3 in. below the soil surface. Use a long serrated kitchen knife or a special asparagus knife. Cut every day if necessary — never let the spears grow too tall before cutting.
- Stop cutting in early or mid June. All spears must now be allowed to develop into fern in order to build up their reserves for next year's crop.

- Plant crowns in early April if the soil is in good condition — delay for a couple of weeks if the weather is cold and wet. Trenches should be dug about 3 ft apart.
- Harvesting of the mature crop takes place over a 6–8 week period. To ensure the maximum harvest period, plant a mixed bed containing an early variety such as Connovers Colossal with a later variety such as Martha Washington.

CALENDAR

	JAN	FEB	MAR	APR	MAY	JUN	JUL	AUG	SEP	OCT	NOV	DEC
Sowing Time			█	█								
Planting Time				█	█							
Cutting Time					█	█						

1 in. = 2.5 cm, 1 ft = 30 cm, 1 oz = 28 gm, 1 lb = 450 gm

For key to symbols — see page 7

IN THE KITCHEN

Steaming is the classical method of preparing asparagus—it is then served hot with melted butter or cold with an oil-and-vinegar dressing. The golden rule is to avoid storing or cooking for too long — the cooked heads should be firm (not bending when held from the base) but not so firm as to be crunchy or leathery when eaten. There are other recipes — asparagus soup, asparagus soufflé, etc., but in practice there are usually not enough spears left over for such delights.

FREEZING Divide the spears into thick and thin stems. Wash thoroughly to remove grit and then tie into small bundles. Blanch (4 minutes for thick stems, 2 minutes for thin ones) and then freeze in a rigid container.

STORAGE The quality of asparagus deteriorates quickly with age. It should be cooked within an hour of cutting — it this is not possible put the spears in a polythene bag and keep in the refrigerator for up to 3 days.

COOKING Wash the spears and then use a sharp knife to peel away the skin below the tips. After shaving put the spears into a bowl of cold water until all of them have been prepared. The next step is to tie them into a bundle with soft string, one band close to the base and the other just below the tip. Trim the ends to provide a level base. Place and support the bundle upright in a pan of boiling salted water — the tips must be well above the level of the water. Cover the pan and boil gently for 10–15 minutes — drain carefully and serve. Don't throw the water away — use it for making soup.

VARIETIES

The variety you are most likely to be offered is Connovers Colossal. This old favourite produces large, fine-flavoured spears and is especially suitable for sandy soil. The other old variety, Giant Mammoth, is more suitable for heavy land. In both cases the male plants are more productive than the female, berry-bearing ones.

Several other varieties have been introduced in recent years. There is Regal which was bred in Britain but most of the others have come from either the U.S. or France. They are all-male hybrids, which means that no energy is wasted in seed production. This generally results in heavier crops, but you will have to start from crowns and not seed.

CONNOVERS COLOSSAL: The No.1 variety, available as seed or crowns. It is a thick-stalked type which crops early and is excellent for freezing.

FRANKLIM: You are more likely to find this all-male hybrid in the catalogues than any of the other new varieties of asparagus. The spears are thick and it is claimed that yields are heavy. You can cut some spears in the second year after planting.

MARTHA WASHINGTON: The best-known of the U.S. varieties, this type and Mary Washington are the 'old favourites' in America. A heavy cropper with long spears until early June — it is resistant to rust.

CITO: A French variety which has earned a good reputation in Britain. It is noted for its heavy crops of unusually long spears which appear early in the season. An all-male hybrid.

LUCULLUS: This was the first of the all-male hybrids and it has all the features of the newer varieties — long and straight spears with heavier crops than the old favourites.

LIMBRAS: Like Franklim this is an F_1 hybrid which produces only male plants. Seed is obviously not available — buy Limbras as 1-year old crowns in April.

Connovers Colossal

TROUBLES

ASPARAGUS BEETLE

Grubs and adult beetles attack both stems and foliage. Stems are eaten — leaves are stripped. Beetle is easily recognised by square orange markings on ¼ in. long black body. Spray with permethrin or derris at first sign of attack.

VIOLET ROOT ROT

Most serious asparagus disease. Roots covered with purplish mould — leaves turn yellow and die. If attack is severe make a new bed on a fresh site. Do not grow root vegetables on the affected area for at least 3 years. If not severe, isolate healthy plants by inserting corrugated plastic sheets vertically into the bed.

SPINDLY SPEARS

Thin shoots, about ⅛ in. across, are sometimes produced instead of typical thick spears. The most likely cause is prolonged cutting in the previous season. Spears should not be harvested after mid June. Other possible causes are cutting too soon after planting and failing to feed the bed.

SLUGS

Spears are gnawed, making them unfit for table use. Sprinkle Slug Pellets sparingly around the shoots.

FROST

Young shoots may turn black and die if a severe frost occurs in late spring. Destroy affected shoots. Cover bed with sacking if a hard frost is expected.

RUST

Reddish-brown spots appear on the leaves during the summer. Spraying is not effective so cut down and burn affected shoots as soon as the first spots are seen.

WIND ROCK

Roots are loosened if stems are left unsupported on an exposed site. This can lead to rotting, so some summer support should be provided if windbreaks are absent.

1 in. = 2.5 cm, 1 ft = 30 cm, 1 oz = 28 gm, 1 lb = 450 gm

AUBERGINE

The aubergine or egg plant is one of the new wave of vegetables which were once regarded as unusual but are now to be found on the shelves of supermarkets everywhere. It can be grown in a greenhouse as easily as the tomato, to which it is related, but outdoors it is much more of a gamble. In a long, hot summer it will grow and fruit satisfactorily in a sunny, sheltered spot, but in most years and in most areas this plant will fail without glass protection. It needs pampering — it is one for mild areas, and barn cloches or a cold frame will be needed. The prickly, shrubby plants bear attractive flowers followed by shiny fruits — usually oval but sometimes round, usually purple but sometimes white.

SEED FACTS

Actual size

Expected germination time:	14–21 days
Expected yield per plant:	4–5 lb
Life expectancy of stored seed:	5 years
Approximate time between sowing and picking:	20 weeks
Ease of cultivation:	Difficult outdoors — needs protection plus regular watering and feeding

SOIL FACTS

- For outdoor cultivation, well-drained fertile soil in a sunny, sheltered location is necessary. Add a general-purpose fertilizer before planting.
- In the greenhouse grow in 9in. pots filled with compost or plant in growing bags — 3 per bag.

SOWING & PLANTING

- Raise seedlings under glass at 60–70°F. Sow 2 seeds in a compost-filled peat pot — remove weaker seedling. Harden off before planting outdoors.

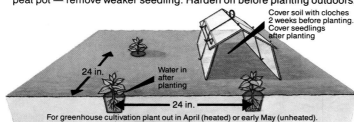

Cover soil with cloches 2 weeks before planting. Cover seedlings after planting

24 in.

Water in after planting

24 in.

For greenhouse cultivation plant out in April (heated) or early May (unheated).

LOOKING AFTER THE CROP

- Remove growing point when the plant is 12 in. high — stake stems.
- Mist plants regularly to keep down red spider mite and encourage fruit set. When 5 fruits have formed, remove lateral shoots and remaining flowers.
- Water regularly but do not keep the compost sodden. Add a potassium-rich soluble fertilizer with each watering once the fruit have begun to swell.

HARVESTING

- Cut each fruit once it has reached a satisfactory size (usually 5–6 in. long) but before the surface shine has gone. Dull fruit are usually over-ripe and bitter.

IN THE KITCHEN

Aubergines are a basic ingredient for *ratatouille* (French vegetable stew) and *moussaka* (Greek minced lamb stew). They can also be stuffed by cutting in half and filling the scooped-out middles with minced beef, but perhaps the best way to cook them is to fry thin slices, as described below, and serve as a hot vegetable.

STORAGE Keep in a polythene bag in the refrigerator — aubergines will stay fresh for up to 2 weeks.

COOKING Slice thinly and sprinkle salt on the cut surfaces to absorb the bitter juices and soften the flesh. Rinse after 20 minutes and then dry with absorbent kitchen paper. Lightly coat the slices with flour and fry until golden-brown.

VARIETIES

LONG PURPLE: The old favourite — no special advantages, but it has stood the test of time.
MONEYMAKER: A new favourite — this F_1 hybrid produces an early crop of good-sized fruits.
SLICE RITE: This is the variety to grow if you like giant vegetables, or you can try Black Enorma. Fruits can weigh 1 lb or more.
BONICA: An F_1 hybrid with a good reputation for reliability. Compact and bushy with large oval fruits.

TROUBLES

RED SPIDER MITE

Pale mottling occurs on the upper surface of the leaves. Tiny mites can be found on the underside. Spray thoroughly with malathion or derris — mist the leaves regularly with plain water.

APHID

Greenfly can be a nuisance on both the outdoor and greenhouse crop. The answer is to spray with permethrin or heptenophos as soon as the first attacks are seen.

WHITEFLY

A pest of the greenhouse crop — severe enough in some seasons to seriously weaken the plants. Not easy to control with chemical sprays — as an effective alternative hang up several yellow Greenhouse Flycatcher Cards.

CALENDAR

	JAN	FEB	MAR	APR	MAY	JUN	JUL	AUG	SEP	OCT	NOV	DEC
Sowing & Planting Time (Outdoor crop)			■		✿							
Sowing & Planting Time (Greenhouse crop)		■		✿✿								
Picking Time								▨	▨			

For key to symbols — see page 7

BEANS

We all know beans when we see them, and yet their classification is bewildering. Words like 'flageolet' and 'haricot' are used to describe both the maturity of the bean at cooking time and also the varieties which are favoured for producing seeds at these stages of maturity. American catalogues contain unfamiliar groupings such as 'snap', 'pole' and 'lima' — it would take a whole chapter to explain all the terms, but the chart below should help to clear up the major misunderstandings. Beans make up an invaluable group for the cook and also for the gatherer of odd facts — beans have been found alongside prehistoric man and yet our old favourite, the runner bean, was grown solely as an ornamental flower and not as a vegetable until late Victorian times.

FRENCH BEAN

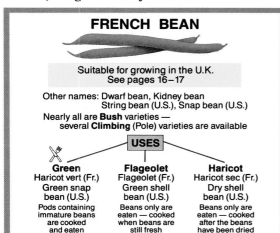

Suitable for growing in the U.K.
See pages 16–17

Other names: Dwarf bean, Kidney bean
String bean (U.S.), Snap bean (U.S.)
Nearly all are **Bush** varieties —
several **Climbing** (Pole) varieties are available

USES

Green
Haricot vert (Fr.)
Green snap
bean (U.S.)
Pods containing
immature beans
are cooked
and eaten

Flageolet
Flageolet (Fr.)
Green shell
bean (U.S.)
Beans only are
eaten — cooked
when beans are
still fresh

Haricot
Haricot sec (Fr.)
Dry shell
bean (U.S.)
Beans only are
eaten — cooked
after the beans
have been dried

BROAD BEAN

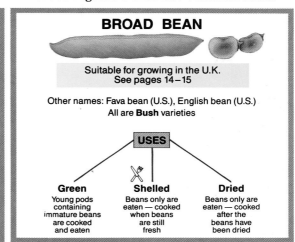

Suitable for growing in the U.K.
See pages 14–15

Other names: Fava bean (U.S.), English bean (U.S.)
All are **Bush** varieties

USES

Green
Young pods
containing
immature beans
are cooked
and eaten

Shelled
Beans only are
eaten — cooked
when beans
are still
fresh

Dried
Beans only are
eaten — cooked
after the
beans have
been dried

RUNNER BEAN

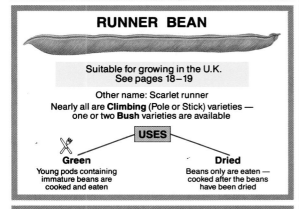

Suitable for growing in the U.K.
See pages 18–19

Other name: Scarlet runner
Nearly all are **Climbing** (Pole or Stick) varieties —
one or two **Bush** varieties are available

USES

Green
Young pods containing
immature beans are
cooked and eaten

Dried
Beans only are eaten —
cooked after the beans
have been dried

BEAN SPROUTS

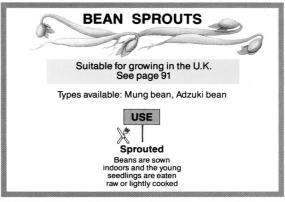

Suitable for growing in the U.K.
See page 91

Types available: Mung bean, Adzuki bean

USE

Sprouted
Beans are sown
indoors and the young
seedlings are eaten
raw or lightly cooked

SOYA BEAN

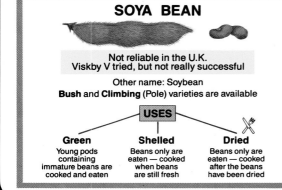

Not reliable in the U.K.
Viskby V tried, but not really successful

Other name: Soybean
Bush and **Climbing** (Pole) varieties are available

USES

Green
Young pods
containing
immature beans
cooked and eaten

Shelled
Beans only are
eaten — cooked
when beans
are still fresh

Dried
Beans only are
eaten — cooked
after the beans
have been dried

LIMA BEAN

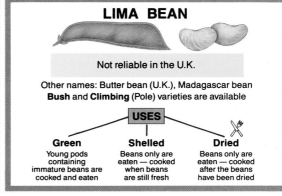

Not reliable in the U.K.

Other names: Butter bean (U.K.), Madagascar bean
Bush and **Climbing** (Pole) varieties are available

USES

Green
Young pods
containing
immature beans are
cooked and eaten

Shelled
Beans only are
eaten — cooked
when beans
are still fresh

Dried
Beans only are
eaten — cooked
after the beans
have been dried

Main use of home-grown produce

BEAN, BROAD

The broad bean is one of the most ancient and also one of the easiest vegetables in cultivation. From each seed about three or four square sectioned stems appear, the standard varieties growing about 4 ft tall and the dwarfs 12–18 in. The fragrant white-and-black flowers are followed by leathery pods, short and broad in some varieties — long and narrow in others. Within these pods are the broad beans — round or kidney-shaped, white or green depending on the variety chosen. Picking can begin as early as the end of May if you have pampered the crop, but even the maincrop sown in the ordinary way in early April will be ready in July — the first of the garden beans to grace your table. Yet the scientists tell us that it is not really a bean at all — it is closely related to a plant grown as cattle food!

SEED FACTS

Actual size

Points to watch for:		Discard all seeds which bear small, round holes
Expected germination time:		7–14 days
Approximate number per ounce:		15
Amount required for a 10 ft double row:		2 oz
Expected yield from a 10 ft double row:		20 lb
Life expectancy of stored seed:		2 years
Approximate time between autumn sowing and picking:		26 weeks
Approximate time between spring sowing and picking:		14 weeks
Ease of cultivation:		Easy

SOIL FACTS

- The ideal soil is rich and free-draining, but nearly every soil will produce an adequate crop, provided it is neither very acid nor waterlogged. Lime, if necessary, in winter.
- Pick a reasonably sunny spot which did not grow beans last year. Dig in autumn if the crop is to be sown in spring — add compost or well-rotted manure if the ground was not enriched for the previous crop. Apply a general-purpose fertilizer about 1 week before sowing.

SEED SOWING

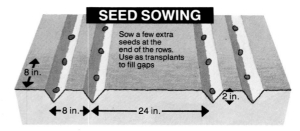

Sow a few extra seeds at the end of the rows. Use as transplants to fill gaps

8 in.

8 in. 24 in. 2 in.

LOOKING AFTER THE CROP

- Regular hoeing will probably be necessary to keep down weeds during the early stage of the crop's life, but watering should not be necessary before the flowers appear. If the weather turns dry when the pods are swelling it will be necessary to water copiously.
- Some form of support will probably be necessary for tall-growing varieties. Place a stout stake at each corner of the double row and then string between the posts at 12 in. intervals.
- Pinch off the top 3 in. of stem as soon as the first beans start to form. This will ensure an earlier harvest and also provide some degree of blackfly control. This serious pest *must* be kept down, so spray if attacks persist.
- After cropping has finished, dig the plants into the soil to provide valuable green manure.

HARVESTING

- When growing broad beans for the kitchen, remember that you are not trying to win a prize at the local show. Leaving the pods to reach their maximum size will provide an overwhelming flush of large and tough beans.
- Begin picking when the first pods are 2–3 in. long — cook them whole.
- The time to pick beans for shelling is when the beans have begun to show through the pod but before the scar on each shelled bean has become discoloured — it should still be white or green.

  Scar not black
- Remove each pod from the plant by applying a sharp downward twist.

- There are several ways of growing a crop which will be ready for picking in June. November sowing (Aquadulce or The Sutton) will provide beans in early June, but there can be serious losses in a severe winter. Only attempt autumn sowing if your plot is sheltered, free-draining and located in a mild area. It is a better plan to sow under cloches in February.
- Maincrop plantings begin in March and then at monthly intervals until the end of May to provide beans throughout the summer.

CALENDAR

	JAN	FEB	MAR	APR	MAY	JUN	JUL	AUG	SEP	OCT	NOV	DEC
Sowing Time												
Picking Time												

1 in. = 2.5 cm, 1 ft = 30 cm, 1 oz = 28 gm, 1 lb = 450 gm

For key to symbols — see page 7

IN THE KITCHEN

The broad beans offered for sale in many shops are well past their prime. The outer surface of the pods has often started to develop black blotches and the skin surrounding the beans has become too tough to be eaten. Do not let your garden crop reach this sorry state — cook the freshly-picked beans or store them for later use by freezing or drying. Salting consists of alternating layers of 3 lb of beans with 1 lb of salt in a large jar.

FREEZING An excellent vegetable for freezing — especially the green varieties. Wash the beans thoroughly and then blanch for 3 minutes. Freeze in polythene bags or rigid containers. Use within 12 months.

STORAGE Keep in a polythene bag in the refrigerator — broad beans will stay fresh for up to 1 week. Stored in a perforated basket in the kitchen they will keep for up to 3 or 4 days.

COOKING Treat small pods like french beans, cooking them whole and then slicing diagonally. More mature pods should be shelled and the young beans dropped into boiling salted water in a pan. Cook for about 10 minutes. Broad beans, a little melted butter and fried bacon — the combination recommended by the experts! If the beans have become too mature and each one bears a brown or black scar, remove the leathery skins after cooking but before serving. You can either serve them whole in their bright green or white underwear, or turn them into a purée or summer soup. The pods and beans are not the only part of the plant you can eat — the upper leaves can be cooked like spinach (see page 93).

VARIETIES

LONGPOD varieties

The long, narrow pods hang downwards, reaching 15 in. or more in length. There are 8–10 kidney-shaped beans within each pod — both green and white varieties are available. This is the best group for hardiness, early cropping, exhibiting and top yields.

AQUADULCE CLAUDIA (white): The broad bean which is the popular choice for autumn sowing. Tall, prolific, very hardy — an excellent bean for freezing.

IMPERIAL GREEN LONGPOD (green): This tall variety has few rivals for maximum yields and extra-long pods. It is a well-established favourite, but Relon may challenge its position.

RELON (green): A giant among broad beans — pod lengths over 20 in. with 10 beans per pod are claimed. Good for freezing — even better for the show bench.

IMPERIAL WHITE LONGPOD (white): According to some experts this old variety beats all others in yield and show-winning ability, but Hylon has appeared as a rival.

HYLON (white): One of the modern varieties which has staked a claim as the longest-podded broad bean.

WITKIEM VROMA (white): The Witkiem varieties are for sowing in early spring and for picking with the autumn-sown types.

BUNYARD'S EXHIBITION (white): Not the biggest nor longest nor most delicious. Just a completely reliable old favourite — good yields, good flavour, good for freezing.

MASTERPIECE LONGPOD (green): An early cropper with green beans and a fine flavour — highly recommended for freezing.

EXPRESS (greenish white): One of the fastest maturing of all broad beans — choose it if you intend to sow in early spring. Has earned a high reputation as a heavy cropper.

RED EPICURE (reddish brown): Quite, quite different to any other variety — the red beans turn yellow when cooked. The flavour is distinctive.

Hylon

WINDSOR varieties

The pods are shorter and broader than the Longpods. There are 4–7 round beans within each pod — both green and white varieties are available. This is the best group for flavour. They are not suitable for autumn sowing and they take longer to mature than Longpods.

GREEN WINDSOR (green): A heavy cropping variety renowned for its flavour. It has given rise to a host of descendants, all claiming to be a little better — Imperial Green Windsor, Unrivalled and so on.

JUBILEE MYSOR (white): This late-maturing variety has taken over from the old favourite White Windsor as the most popular white-seeded type. Excellent flavour and suitable for exhibition.

DWARF varieties

The dwarf, freely-branching bushes grow about 12–18 in. high, making them the ideal choice where tall growth is not required or the site is exposed. These are the broad beans to pick for growing under cloches.

THE SUTTON (white): The most popular of the Dwarf varieties — much praise has been heaped on its small shoulders. 'Ideal for small gardens' is the usual phrase.

BONNY LAD (white): Not much to choose between this variety and The Sutton, but it does grow rather taller (15–18 in. compared to 12 in.) and the beans are white-eyed.

The Sutton

TROUBLES

See pages 20–22

BEAN, FRENCH

Textbooks and seed catalogues sing the praises of french beans as a garden crop, but in Britain it is the runner bean which reigns supreme. For us the french bean is a stand-in crop until the long pods of the scarlet runners are ready, but in Europe it is the *haricot vert* which is queen throughout the summer. France, however, is only its adopted home — the plant is a native of S. America. The french bean is a half hardy annual which cannot stand frost. It likes warm conditions and hates heavy clay, and it is decorative enough to be grown in the flower garden. The standard varieties are bushy plants with 4–6 in. green pods following the white, pink or red flowers. There are variations — you can buy purple- and yellow-podded types as well as climbing varieties which may grow as tall as runner beans. In recent years there have been many introductions and also new ideas about spacing — today the recommendation is to plant the seeds much more closely than the older textbooks advise.

SEED FACTS

Actual size

Points to watch for:	Never plant before the recommended time — seed will rot in cold and wet soil
Expected germination time:	7–14 days
Approximate number per ounce:	60
Amount required for a 10 ft row:	½ oz
Expected yield from a 10 ft row (Bush varieties):	8 lb
Expected yield from a 10 ft row (Climbing varieties):	12 lb
Life expectancy of stored seed:	2 years
Approximate time between sowing and picking:	8–12 weeks
Ease of cultivation:	Easy

SOIL FACTS

- French beans will succeed in any soil provided it is neither very heavy nor acid. Lime, if necessary, in winter.
- Pick a reasonably sunny spot which is sheltered from high winds. The site should not have been used for beans last year. Dig in autumn and add compost or well-rotted manure. Prepare the seed bed about 2 weeks before sowing — apply a general-purpose fertilizer such as Growmore at this time.

SEED SOWING

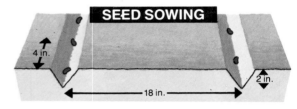

4 in.

18 in.

2 in.

LOOKING AFTER THE CROP

- Protect seedlings from slugs and hoe regularly to keep weeds down during the early stages of the crop's life.
- Support the plants with short twigs or pea sticks to prevent them from toppling over. Use twiggy branches or plastic netting for climbing varieties.
- Spraying the flowers is not necessary in order to ensure that they will set properly. Moisture at the roots, however, is essential to ensure maximum pod development and a long cropping period. Water copiously and regularly if the weather turns dry during or after the flowering period.
- Mulch around the stems in June. Once the pods have all been harvested, feed the plants with a liquid fertilizer. In this way a second crop can be obtained — smaller, of course, but very welcome.

HARVESTING

- Begin picking when the pods are about 4 in. long. A pod is ready if it snaps easily when bent and before the tell-tale bulges of maturity appear along its length. Pick several times a week to prevent any pods maturing — you can then expect to continue cropping for 5-7 weeks. Take care not to loosen the plants when harvesting — hold the stems as you tug away the pods, or play safe and use a pair of scissors.
- Dried beans (haricots) are obtained by leaving the pods on the plant until they turn straw-coloured, then hang the plants indoors to dry. When the pods are brittle and have begun to split, shell the beans and dry them on a sheet of paper for several days. Store the haricot beans in an air-tight container.

- For an early crop sow a quick-maturing variety in early May. If you want to pick beans before the end of June then you will have to grow the plants under cloches. Put the cloches in position in early March and sow the seeds in the soil beneath them in early or mid April. Remove the cloches in late May.
- The maincrop is sown during May. Successional sowings up to the end of June will provide pods until early October.
- For a late autumn crop sow in July and cover the plants with cloches in mid September.

CALENDAR

	JAN	FEB	MAR	APR	MAY	JUN	JUL	AUG	SEP	OCT	NOV	DEC
Sowing Time												
Picking Time												

For key to symbols — see page 7

IN THE KITCHEN

To enjoy french beans at their best, pick young pods and cook them whole within an hour of harvesting. Sometimes you will find that the pods are well past this stage, and flat-podded beans are stringy once they have matured. The best plan is to shell them and treat them as flageolets — fresh green beans cooked like peas. You can even wait for a later stage, leaving the pods to mature on the plant and then shelling and drying indoors to produce haricots for winter use.

FREEZING An excellent vegetable for freezing. Wash and trim young pods and then blanch them for 3 minutes (2 minutes if you have cut the pods into chunks). Freeze in polythene bags or rigid containers. Use within 12 months.

STORAGE Keep in a polythene bag in the refrigerator — french beans will stay fresh for up to 1 week. Stored in a perforated basket in the kitchen they will keep for up to 3 or 4 days.

COOKING Whole or cut into pieces — it's a matter of taste. The usual practice is to cook small pencil-podded beans whole but to slice large flat-podded types into 1 in. slices. In either case, wash the pods and remove both tops and tails with a sharp knife. Cook in boiling salted water for 7 minutes (whole beans) or 5 minutes (sliced beans). Serve hot as a vegetable or cold as a salad. If you like haricot beans, grow a suitable variety (see below) and prepare them as described on page 16. To cook, put the beans in cold water and bring to the boil. Switch off the heat and let them stand for an hour. Drain, and then serve as a hot vegetable or in an oil-and-vinegar dressing as a salad.

VARIETIES

Most french bean varieties grow as compact bushes 12–18 in. high. There are a few, however, which are climbers and will clamber up supports to a height of 6 or 7 ft.

GREEN varieties

Flat-pod

Pencil-pod

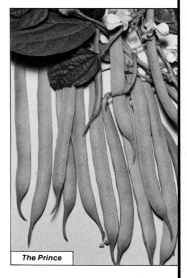

The Prince

These make up the most popular group, with scores of old and new favourites. The well-established ones are generally Flat-podded or 'English' varieties — flat, rather wide and with a tendency to become stringy as they mature. The Pencil-podded types are usually stringless.

HUNTER: The pods are long, wide, straight and stringless — this high-yielding climber is widely available.

ANNABEL: A compact variety which bears masses of thin stringless pods. It is a good choice if you want to grow french beans in pots or growing bags.

THE PRINCE: Aptly named — the most popular of all french bean varieties. It is a dwarf-growing Flat-pod which is recommended for exhibition.

MASTERPIECE: Another old favourite Flat-pod — suitable for early sowing. An excellent general-purpose bean, say the experts.

CANADIAN WONDER: A heavy cropping Flat-pod — once popular but no longer to be found in all the catalogues.

TENDERGREEN: Perhaps the most popular of all the Pencil-podded types, and justly so. Early, stringless, excellent for freezing and prolific.

LOCH NESS: A stringless Pencil-pod which will withstand colder conditions than other varieties.

CROPPER TEEPEE: The Pencil-pods are large with white seeds — a reliable heavy-cropping variety with good disease resistance.

NASSAU: A stringless Flat-pod with a good reputation for high quality flavour and easy picking. The pods reach 6 in. or more.

MASAI: This is one of the Kenyan varieties — the short 'filet' pods are very narrow and can be cooked whole.

PROS: A truly continental bean — round, narrow and stringless.

CHEVRIER VERT: The most popular haricot variety, which you will find in some but not all catalogues. You can cook them at the flageolet stage or allow them to dry as cream-coloured haricot beans.

BLUE LAKE WHITE SEEDED: The most popular climbing variety, its 5 ft stems producing a plentiful supply of white-seeded Pencil-pods. Beans can be dried as haricots.

COLOURED varieties

Yellow Waxpod

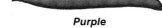

Purple

Kinghorn Wax

Coloured pods have an obvious novelty value, but they also have practical advantages. The pods can be easily seen at picking time and the Yellow Waxpods have an excellent flavour.

MONT D'OR (yellow): The 6-in. round pods have a waxy flesh and contain black seeds. Cook whole — considered by many to be the best of the Waxpods.

KINGHORN WAX (yellow): A stringless Waxpod renowned for its flavour. The flesh is creamy yellow.

PURPLE QUEEN (purple): One of the best purple Pencil-pods. Good flavour, high yields — beans turn dark green when cooked.

PURPLE-PODDED CLIMBING (purple): Grows about 5 ft high. Decorative with its pendent bunches of dark purple beans which turn green when cooked.

TROUBLES

See pages 20–22

1 in. = 2.5 cm, 1 ft = 30 cm, 1 oz = 28 gm, 1 lb = 450 gm

BEAN, RUNNER

The scarlet runner or runner bean belongs to a handful of vegetables which can be seen everywhere in summer — clambering up bamboo wigwams, climbing up plastic netting or twining around strings or stout poles. The long, flat pods are Britain's favourite home-grown beans — a wise choice when you remember that a 10 ft double row can produce 60 lb or more between August and the arrival of the first heavy frosts of winter. Of course, you will not achieve anything like this yield if you treat runner beans as the 'easy' crop described in some catalogues. You will need to prepare the ground thoroughly in winter and weekly watering will be necessary in dry weather once the pods have begun to form. Picking every other day in late summer will be essential even if you have to throw away the pods. Let a few pods reach maturity and the flower-producing mechanism switches off — annoying, but unavoidable. Runner beans are prolific providers of fresh food, but there is also a decorative aspect — a row forms a dense, attractive screen and a bean-covered wigwam in the border makes a brightly-coloured focal point when in full flower.

SEED FACTS

Actual size

Expected germination time:	7–14 days
Approximate number per ounce:	30
Amount required for a 10 ft double row:	1 oz
Expected yield from a 10 ft double row:	60 lb
Life expectancy of stored seed:	2 years
Approximate time between sowing and picking:	12–14 weeks
Ease of cultivation:	Not really easy — support, thorough soil preparation and constant picking are all essential

SEED SOWING

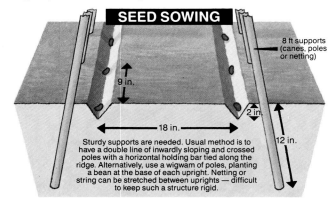

8 ft supports (canes, poles or netting)

9 in.

18 in.

2 in.

12 in.

Sturdy supports are needed. Usual method is to have a double line of inwardly sloping and crossed poles with a horizontal holding bar tied along the ridge. Alternatively, use a wigwam of poles, planting a bean at the base of each upright. Netting or string can be stretched between uprights — difficult to keep such a structure rigid.

LOOKING AFTER THE CROP

- Loosely tie the young plants to the supports, after which they will climb naturally. Protect from slugs.
- Hoe regularly — mulching will help to conserve moisture. Water regularly in dry weather once the first pods have formed. Don't bother misting to help pollination — it's an old wives' tale. Liquid feed occasionally during the cropping season.
- Remove the growing points once the plants reach the tops of the supports. At the end of the season dig in the roots and stem bases.

HARVESTING

- Pick regularly once the pods have reached a decent size (6–8 in.) but before the beans inside have started to swell. If you remove pods as soon as they reach this stage then harvesting should continue for at least 8 weeks. This calls for picking every couple of days — allowing even a small number to ripen will stop production.
- The problem is that you will probably have a glut of beans at some stage — for notes on storage see page 19.

SOIL FACTS

- Runner beans produce disappointing results in hungry, badly-drained soil. Acid conditions are also undesirable — lime, if necessary, in late winter.
- Pick a sheltered spot where the dense shade cast by the plants will not be a problem. Dig in autumn and add an abundant supply of compost or well-rotted manure. Rake in a general-purpose fertilizer about 2 weeks before sowing or planting.

- The standard method of growing runner beans is to sow the seeds outdoors when the danger of frost is past — the end of May in the south or early June in the north. Always sow a few extra seeds at the ends of the rows — use the seedlings as transplants to fill gaps.
- A second sowing in June in mild areas will ensure an October crop.
- Runner beans are often raised by planting out seedlings when the danger of frost is past. These seedlings are either shop-bought (make sure that they have been properly hardened-off) or raised at home from seeds sown under glass in late April. This planting-out method is strongly recommended for the colder areas of the country.

CALENDAR

	JAN	FEB	MAR	APR	MAY	JUN	JUL	AUG	SEP	OCT	NOV	DEC
Sowing Time (outdoors)					■	■						
Sowing Time (indoors)				■ ■	■ ■							
Picking Time								■	■	■		

IN THE KITCHEN

You will no doubt remember your annoyance when you cooked shop-bought runner beans and then found them to be inedible because of their stringiness. Never let this happen with your home-grown crop — pick them at the stage when the commercial grower would regard the pods as uneconomically small. The best method of coping with the excess is to freeze what you can't use immediately — if you haven't got a freezer then you can shell the beans after drying the pods and treat them as haricots for winter use (see page 17) or you can salt them (alternate layers of 3 lb of sliced beans with 1 lb salt).

FREEZING Wash and trim young pods and then slice them into chunks. Blanch for 2 minutes, cool, drain and then freeze in polythene bags or rigid containers. Use within 12 months.

STORAGE Keep in a polythene bag in the refrigerator — runner beans will stay fresh for up to 1 week. Stored in a perforated basket in the kitchen they will keep for up to 3 or 4 days.

COOKING The standard method of cooking runner beans is to wash them and then cut off the tops and tails. Pull off the stringy edges. Cut the pods into 2 in. diagonal chunks and boil in salted water for 5–7 minutes. Drain and serve hot — crowned with a knob of butter. The experts tell us that it is better to cook them whole and slice after cooking, to make sure that the water is kept boiling vigorously and to leave off the lid to ensure that there will be no loss of flavour, goodness nor colour.

VARIETIES

STICK runner beans

Nearly all runner beans will grow 8–10 ft high and bear pods which can reach 10–20 in. long. They are grown on tall supports and the usual flower colour is red. There is a bi-colour variety (Painted Lady) and the white and pink varieties are self-pollinating — a point to remember if you have been disappointed by lack of pod formation in previous years.

POLESTAR: Red flowers produce a heavy yield of top quality pods — the cropping season is long and some consider it the best stringless variety.

ACHIEVEMENT: Long straight pods, making it a good exhibition variety. Recommended for freezing.

ENORMA: An improved form of Prizewinner — produces the sort of pod which wins prizes at the horticultural show. The flavour is better than average.

RED KNIGHT: A red-flowering variety which is stringless, and that is unusual. Good flavour, suitable for freezing.

MERGOLES: White flowers, white seeds and stringless pods. An excellent choice for kitchen use — sets well, freezes well and crops over a long period. Your seed catalogue may offer Desiree instead — there isn't a great deal of difference.

STREAMLINE: An old favourite, dependable and still popular. A heavy cropping variety but it will be hard for the older types to hold off the appeal of the new stringless runner beans.

DESIREE: Not in the previous edition of this book but now in many catalogues. White seeds in stringless narrow pods, freezes well — a good choice.

SCARLET EMPEROR: A popular all-round performer — long, straight beans which are produced earlier than the maincrop.

KELVEDON MARVEL: An early cropper, producing its rather short pods about 14 days before the standard varieties.

SUNSET: You can't miss it — the flowers are pale pink and self-fertilizing. It produces a very early crop and is recommended for freezing.

PAINTED LADY: Well-named — the white-faced flowers have bright red lips. The pods are relatively short, but it is an attractive plant for using as a screen.

CRUSADER: Often called the 'exhibitor's runner bean' because of the outstanding length of its pods.

Enorma

GROUND runner beans

A few varieties (Kelvedon Marvel, Scarlet Emperor and Sunset) which are naturally tall-growing are sometimes sown 2 ft apart and grown as short and bushy plants by pinching out the growing point of the main stems when they are about 12 in. high. Side shoots are pinched out at weekly intervals and the stems are supported by short twigs. The pods appear earlier than on climbing plants and you are spared the work of creating tall supports, but there are disadvantages. The cropping period is short and the yield is comparatively low, the pods are often curled and their surface soiled.

DWARF runner beans

A few true dwarfs are available — the plants grow about 18 in. high and the pods are 8 in. long. They should be grown about 6 in. apart in rows 2 ft wide. A good choice where space is limited, but yields cannot compare with their climbing relatives.

HAMMOND'S DWARF SCARLET: The popular red-flowering form which is early maturing and will continue to crop for many weeks if picked regularly.

PICKWICK: One of the modern stringless varieties which are steadily replacing the Hammond's Dwarfs. Pickwick is a strong bushy plant which needs little or no support.

Pickwick

TROUBLES

See pages 20–22

1 in. = 2.5 cm, 1 ft = 30 cm, 1 oz = 28 gm, 1 lb = 450 gm

BEAN and PEA TROUBLES

Black bean aphid is the main danger to broad beans and chocolate spot is the most serious disease. The chief disorder of runner beans is the failure of the flowers to set, but french beans are rarely attacked by serious complaints if you plant them at the right time. Peas have two big problems — birds and pea moth maggots.

	Symptom	Likely Causes
Seeds & Seedlings	— missing	3 or 16
	— little or no germination	1 or 2 or 8 or **Millepede** or **Damping off** (see page 110)
	— tunnelled before sowing	1
	— tunnelled after sowing	2
Stems	— brown streaks outside	13 or 20
	— brown streaks inside	18
	— brown or purple spots	12 or 21
	— wilted, dying	8 or 18
	— mouldy	17
	— infested with aphids	4 or 5
	— brown or blackened at base	8
Leaves	— yellowed or yellow patches	6 or 8 or 15 or 18
	— silvery patches	10
	— spotted	12 or 13 or 20 or 21
	— notched	9
	— holed	**Slugs & Snails** (see page 110)
	— white, mauve or brown mould	6 or 7
	— infested with aphids	4 or 5
	— bronzed, speckled	**Red spider mite** (see page 56)
Flowers	— absent	11
	— present, but pods absent	14
Pods	— absent	14 or 16
	— distorted	4 or 6 or 10
	— torn	16
	— spotted, dry texture	6 or 13 or 20 or 21
	— spotted, wet texture	12
	— spotted, mouldy texture	7 or 17
	— silvery patches	10
Beans & Peas	— tunnelled, maggots present	19
	— brown spot in centre	15

TUNNELLED SEEDS

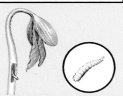

1 SEED BEETLE

Seeds of peas and beans are sometimes found to bear small, round holes. Within these tunnels are the tiny seed beetle grubs. Affected seeds either fail to germinate or produce weak seedlings.

Treatment: None.

Prevention: Buy good quality seed. Never sow seeds if they are holed.

TUNNELLED SEEDLINGS

2 BEAN SEED FLY

All bean varieties are susceptible to attack by these soil-living grubs. Damaged seeds fail to germinate; tunnelled seedlings wilt and become distorted. Early crops are worst affected.

Treatment: Destroy damaged seedlings.

Prevention: Prepare a good seed bed or plant compost-raised seedlings.

3 MICE

Mice can be serious pests, as they are capable of clearing whole rows of pea seeds and seedlings overnight. Old fashioned remedies are to dip the seed in paraffin or alum, or to put spiny branches along the rows. A mouse bait, such as Racumin, can be used if the site is known to have a mouse problem.

4 BLACK BEAN APHID

A serious pest of broad beans in spring and french beans in July and August. Large blackfly colonies stunt growth, damage flowers and distort pods.

Treatment: Spray with permethrin or heptenophos at the first signs of attack. Repeat as necessary.

Prevention: Pinch out the tops of broad beans once four trusses of pods have formed.

APHIDS ON LEAVES

5 PEA APHID

Not often a serious pest, but in a hot, damp summer large colonies can severely damage peas. Growth is stunted and flowers are damaged.

Treatment: Spray with permethrin or heptenophos at the first signs of attack. Repeat as necessary.

Prevention: No practical method available.

6 | DOWNY MILDEW

Yellowish blotches on the leaves of peas, with a pale mauve or brown mould on the underside. Attacks occur in cool, wet seasons. Infected pods are spotted and distorted.

Treatment: Spray with mancozeb at the first signs of disease. Repeat at fortnightly intervals.

Prevention: Practise crop rotation. Burn affected plants after picking the crop.

MOULDY LEAVES

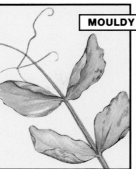

7 | POWDERY MILDEW

White powdery patches appear on both sides of the leaves of peas. Attacks occur in dry seasons and are worst in sheltered gardens. Infected pods are covered with white patches.

Treatment: Spray with carbendazim at the first signs of disease. Repeat at fortnightly intervals.

Prevention: Burn affected plants after picking the crop.

BLACKENED STEMS

8 | FOOT ROT & ROOT ROT

Leaves turn yellow and shrivel; roots and stem bases turn brown or black and soon start to rot.

Treatment: Lift and burn badly affected plants. Water soil with Cheshunt Compound to check the spread of the disease to other plants.

Prevention: Rotate crops.

NOTCHED LEAVES

¼ in. brown beetles

9 | PEA & BEAN WEEVIL

Tell-tale signs are U-shaped notches at the edges of the young leaves. Growth is retarded but older plants generally soon recover. Seedlings, however, can be killed by a severe attack.

Treatment: Spray with fenitrothion at the first signs of attack.

Prevention: Hoe around the plants in April and May.

SILVERY PODS

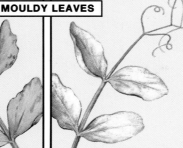

10 | PEA THRIPS

Silvery patches appear on leaves and pods. The pods are distorted and the yield is reduced. Attacks are worst in hot, dry weather. Minute black or yellow insects are just visible.

Treatment: Spray with fenitrothion or permethrin.

Prevention: Dig over the soil after removing an infected crop.

11 | NO FLOWERS

Peas and beans sometimes fail to produce flowers. This uncommon complaint can be due to a severe infestation of capsid bug (see page 84) or pea thrips which causes the flower buds to wither. But the most likely cause of a shortage of flowers is the presence of too much nitrogen in the soil. Always use a balanced fertilizer containing phosphates and potash for peas and beans.

12 | HALO BLIGHT

Small brown spots on leaves, each one being surrounded by a yellow 'halo'. Pods develop water-soaked spots. Plants are stunted and yields are reduced. Attacks are worst in a wet season.

Treatment: Lift and destroy diseased plants.

Prevention: Practise crop rotation. Never soak seed before sowing.

SPOTS ON LEAVES

French beans, Runner beans

Broad beans

13 | CHOCOLATE SPOT

Small brown spots on leaves; dark streaks along the stems. Pods may be affected and the seeds discoloured. In a bad attack the spots join together and the plant is killed.

Treatment: Lift and destroy diseased plants. Spray remaining plants with carbendazim.

Prevention: Apply Growmore fertilizer before sowing and do not grow the plants too closely together.

BEAN & PEA TROUBLES
continued

14 NO PODS

One of the major problems with runner beans is their tendency to lose their flowers without forming pods. Sparrows can be the culprits, and so can bumble bees. Cool weather at flowering time results in a lack of pollinating insects, but the failure of beans to set is always worst in a hot dry season. Keeping the roots moist by digging in compost, by mulching and watering is helpful, but recent research has shown that the practice of spraying the flowers is of little value. The best way to avoid trouble is to grow a white- or pink-flowering variety.

BROWN-CENTRED PEAS

15 MARSH SPOT

Tell-tale sign is a brown-lined cavity in the centre of each pea. The cause is a shortage of manganese in the soil. The only outward sign is a slight yellowing between the leaf veins.

Treatment: None.

Prevention: Incorporate compost into the soil before sowing. Apply a sequestered compound. Repeated spraying with foliar feed may help.

TORN PODS

16 BIRDS

Birds can be a nuisance in several ways. Pigeons devour pea seeds and seedlings, and sparrows will tear open pea pods. Sparrows will also damage runner bean flowers and so prevent pods from being produced. Scarers and cotton are not really effective — netting is by far the best answer.

ROTTEN PODS

17 GREY MOULD (Botrytis)

The pods of french beans and occasionally peas may develop a grey velvety mould in wet weather. This mould may also coat the stem surface.

Treatment: Pick and burn affected pods. Spray with carbendazim to protect remaining pods.

Prevention: Spray with carbendazim at flowering time if grey mould is a recurrent problem in your garden.

BROWN-STREAKED TISSUE

18 FUSARIUM WILT

Outward signs are stunted growth, yellowing or rolled leaves and little or no crop. If you cut open the stem of an infected plant the tell-tale signs of wilt are revealed. Reddish-brown longitudinal streaks run through the stem tissue, but no external browning occurs.

Treatment: Remove and burn affected plants.

Prevention: Grow wilt-resistant varieties.

MAGGOTY PEAS

⅓ in. greenish maggots

19 PEA MOTH

Maggoty peas are well known to all vegetable growers, especially in S. England. Pea moth maggots burrow through the pods and into the seeds, making them unusable. Early and late sown crops often escape damage.

Treatment: None.

Prevention: Spray with fenitrothion 7–10 days after the start of flowering.

20 ANTHRACNOSE

Brown sunken spots on pods. Stem cankers appear and leaves bear brown patches. At a later stage these brown spots and patches may turn pink. In a bad attack the plant may be killed.

Treatment: Lift and destroy diseased plants. Spray remaining plants with carbendazim.

Prevention: Rotate crops.

DRY SPOTS ON PODS

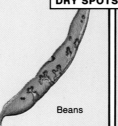

Beans

Peas

21 LEAF & POD SPOT

Brown sunken spots on pods. Peas may be discoloured. Leaves and stems bear similar brown spots and in a bad attack they may join together. Early crops suffer most, especially in a wet season.

Treatment: Lift and destroy diseased plants.

Prevention: Rotate crops.

1 in. = 2.5 cm, 1 ft = 30 cm, 1 oz = 28 gm, 1 lb = 450 gm

BEET, LEAF

Many people who like spinach find it a difficult vegetable to grow. If the soil isn't right and the weather is dry it can quickly run to seed, and so it gets crossed off next year's seed list. It is surprising that these gardeners do not turn to the leaf beets. Both types (swiss chard and spinach beet) are very easy to grow, succeeding in ordinary soils and refraining from bolting when the weather turns dry. There are other benefits. A spring sowing will enable you to pick from July right through to the following June if you cover the plants with cloches or straw during winter. Furthermore, the leaves of swiss chard are attractive enough for it to be grown in the flower border, and also versatile enough for it to be used as a dual-purpose vegetable.

SEED FACTS

Leaf beet 'seed' is really a fruit, each corky cluster containing several true seeds.

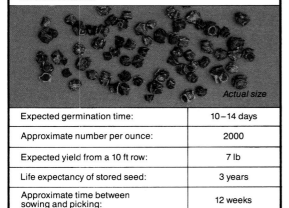

Actual size

Expected germination time:	10–14 days
Approximate number per ounce:	2000
Expected yield from a 10 ft row:	7 lb
Life expectancy of stored seed:	3 years
Approximate time between sowing and picking:	12 weeks
Ease of cultivation:	Easy

SOIL FACTS

● Rich, well-manured soil is the ideal but any reasonable soil in sun or light shade will do.
● Dig the soil in autumn and incorporate a liberal amount of compost or well-rotted manure. Rake in Growmore fertilizer 2 weeks before sowing.

SEED SOWING

Cover with soil

4 in.

15 in.

1 in.

LOOKING AFTER THE CROP

● Thin the seedlings to 1 ft apart when they are large enough to handle.
● Hoe regularly to keep the land weed-free. Bolting is most unlikely, but remove any flower-heads which may appear.
● Water at fortnightly intervals during dry spells. Mulching will help to conserve moisture.

HARVESTING

● Pull off outer leaves when they are large enough for kitchen use — do not wait until they have reached their maximum size. Harvest carefully (do not disturb the roots) and regularly, leaving the central foliage to develop for later pickings.
● Cover the plants with cloches or straw in late autumn to ensure winter and spring cropping.

IN THE KITCHEN

Both swiss chard and spinach beet are used and cooked like spinach, although both of them are really members of the beet family. The flavour, however, is stronger than the refined true spinach varieties which are available these days and so you should always pick the foliage of leaf beet while it is still quite young and fresh.

STORAGE Avoid storage if possible. If you must store it, place washed leaves in a polythene bag in the refrigerator — leaf beet will stay fresh for up to 2 days.

COOKING See page 93 for instructions. With swiss chard use the green foliage as a spinach substitute and cook the stalks as for asparagus (page 11), steaming the fleshy leafstalks for about 20 minutes. Alternatively you can chop them into sections and boil for 15 minutes.

VARIETIES

SWISS CHARD: Other names — silver chard, seakale beet. This attractive plant grows about 1½ ft high and bears distinctive foliage — the leafstalks are white and fleshy, and the white veins stand out against the crumpled, green spinach-like leaves. Varieties such as Lucullus, Fordhook Giant and White Silver 2 are occasionally listed.

RHUBARB CHARD: Other name — ruby chard. Similar in growth habit to swiss chard, but the stalks are thinner and red. A striking plant for the border, but the flavour is inferior to the white variety. The variety Feurio is claimed to be resistant to bolting.

SPINACH BEET: Other name — perpetual spinach. Similar to spinach, but the leaves are larger, darker and fleshier.

TROUBLES

Both swiss chard and spinach beet are virtually trouble-free, but slugs may attack young plants in spring. Sprinkle Slug Pellets around the plants.

CALENDAR

	JAN	FEB	MAR	APR	MAY	JUN	JUL	AUG	SEP	OCT	NOV	DEC
Sowing Time												
Picking Time												

1 in. = 2.5 cm, 1 ft = 30 cm, 1 oz = 28 gm, 1 lb = 450 gm

For key to symbols — see page 7

BEETROOT

Home-grown beetroot can be eaten all year round — pulled for use fresh from the garden from June until late autumn and then taken from store until March. The gap between March and June is bridged by pickled beets, making beetroot a year-round easy-to-grow vegetable which is justifiably popular. This vegetable is rather slow to start but growth is rapid once the seedlings are through. The secret is to avoid any check to growth and to pull the roots before they become large and woody like so many shop-bought specimens. This calls for sowing short rows at monthly intervals and watering in dry weather — in this way you can gather beets in peak condition right through the summer.

SEED FACTS

Beetroot 'seed' is really a fruit, each corky cluster containing several true seeds. Pelleted seed is available.

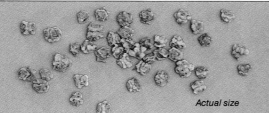

Actual size

Expected germination time:	10–14 days To hasten germination, soak 'seeds' for several hours before sowing
Approximate number per ounce:	2000
Expected yield from a 10 ft row:	10 lb (Globe varieties) 18 lb (Long varieties)
Life expectancy of stored seed:	3 years
Approximate time between sowing and lifting:	11 weeks (Globe varieties) 16 weeks (Long varieties)
Ease of cultivation:	Easy

SOIL FACTS

- For prize-winning long roots you will need deep, sandy soil but almost any reasonable land will produce good crops if it is adequately prepared.
- Pick a sunny spot and dig in autumn or early winter — add peat or well-rotted compost if the humus content is low. Apply lime if the soil is known to be acid. In spring prepare the seed bed — rake in Growmore fertilizer 2–3 weeks before sowing.

SEED SOWING

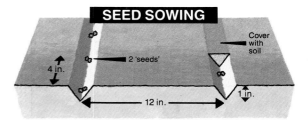

LOOKING AFTER THE CROP

- When the seedlings are about 1 in. high, thin out to leave a single plant at each station. Throw away these thinnings — do not attempt to plant them. Protection against birds may be necessary at this stage.
- The ground must be kept weed-free. Use a hoe, taking great care not to touch the roots.
- Dryness leads to woodiness and low yields — a sudden return to wet conditions can lead to splitting. To avoid these problems, water moderately at fortnightly intervals during dry spells. Mulching will conserve moisture.
- When the roots have reached golf-ball size, pull up alternate plants and use these thinnings for cooking. Leave the remainder to reach maturity.

HARVESTING

- Pull out roots of Globe varieties as required. They should not be left to grow larger than cricket balls — there should be no white rings when a root is cut in half.
- Roots grown for storage should be lifted in October. Long varieties should be carefully prised out of the soil with a fork, making sure that the prongs never touch the roots. Shake off the soil and discard all damaged specimens. Place the roots between layers of dry peat in a stout box and store in a shed. The crop will keep until March.
- After pulling beetroots for immediate use or for storage, twist off the foliage to leave a 2 in. crown of stalks. Cutting off the leaves with a knife will result in bleeding.

- For a very early crop which will be ready in late May or early June, sow a bolt-resistant variety under cloches or in a frame in early March.
- The main sowing period begins outdoors in mid April. A second sowing of Globe varieties in mid May will provide a regular supply of tender roots.
- When growing for winter storage sow in late May or June — the roots from earlier sowings may be too coarse at lifting time in October.
- For a late autumn crop sow Detroit-Little Ball in July.

CALENDAR

	JAN	FEB	MAR	APR	MAY	JUN	JUL	AUG	SEP	OCT	NOV	DEC
Sowing Time												
Lifting Time												

1 in. = 2.5 cm, 1 ft = 30 cm, 1 oz = 28 gm, 1 lb = 450 gm

For key to symbols — see page 7

IN THE KITCHEN

Beetroots are mainly used to add colour and flavour to salads. Boiled or pickled, they are sliced to accompany the lettuce, tomatoes and radishes in the typical British salad. As a hot vegetable, boiled or baked, beets are more popular in the U.S. than in England, and in Eastern Europe they provide the basis of *borsch* soup. Other uses include chutney and wine-making.

FREEZING Use small beets which are no more than 2 in. across. Wash and boil as described in this section. After skinning and cooling, cut the roots into slices or cubes and freeze in a rigid container. Use within 6 months.

STORAGE Keep in a polythene bag in the refrigerator — roots will stay fresh for up to 2 weeks.

COOKING Beets should be washed in cold water, removing neither the leaf stalks nor the thin root at the base. On no account should you peel or damage the skin — bleeding results in loss of colour and flavour. Boil for ¾–2 hours, depending on size, in salted water. After boiling remove the skin by rubbing. Serve hot as a vegetable or allow to cool for pickling in vinegar or serving fresh in a salad. The young leaves of ordinary beetroot varieties and the more mature foliage of the yellow and white types can be cooked in the same way as spinach. Try baked beets for a change. Wash carefully and arrange in a baking dish. Bake at 325°F until tender (¾–2 hours, depending on size).

VARIETIES

GLOBE varieties
Other names: Round or Ball varieties

The Globe varieties are by far the most popular group for the ordinary gardener. These beets are generally quick-maturing and are the ones chosen to provide roots for cooking in summer. There are now monogerm types available which produce a single seedling from each 'seed' — this makes thinning a much easier task but the space between 'seeds' should be reduced to 2 in.

For early sowing choose a bolt-resistant type — one which will not readily run to seed in poor growing conditions. For May or June sowing you have the whole range to choose from — the Detroit group is usually chosen to provide a maincrop for late summer use or storage.

The red-rooted varieties remain the usual choice, adding colour to salads and occasionally to tablecloths. Try a white- or yellow-fleshed variety for a change. The leaves can be cooked as 'greens' and the roots have an excellent flavour.

Red
BOLTARDY: Widely available — the usual choice for early sowing. Bolt-resistant. Smooth-skinned with deep red flesh.
DETROIT 2: With the older Detroit it is the standard Globe variety for later planting. Renowned for its flavour.
MONOPOLY: Bolt-resistant like Boltardy with the added advantage of being a monogerm variety (one seedling per 'seed').

RED ACE: A recent F₁ hybrid which is excellent for exhibition — the flesh colour is dark red. Better than most in dry weather.
DETROIT 2–LITTLE BALL: The favourite choice for late sowing. Produces 'baby' beets which are excellent for pickling and bottling.
DETROIT 2–NEW GLOBE: A good choice for the show bench. The shape is uniform, the texture is good and the flesh is free from rings.

Yellow
BURPEE'S GOLDEN: A fine variety from the U.S. which is now widely available in Britain. The skin is orange, and the yellow flesh does not bleed when cut. Many consider the flavour to be superior to red varieties — leaves can be cooked as 'greens'.

White
ALBINA VEREDUNA: The most popular white variety — sometimes sold as Snowhite. Not widely available like Burpee's Golden or the popular reds, but well worth looking for. The flavour is excellent and the leaves can be cooked as 'greens', but it does not store well.

CYLINDRICAL varieties
Other names: Tankard or Intermediate varieties

Not many types are listed in the catalogues, although these beetroots are a good choice if you are growing for winter storage. Each root provides many slices of similar size.
CYLINDRA: An oval beet with excellent keeping qualities. Deep red flesh. It is the most popular Cylindrical variety.
FURONO: An improved version of the old favourite Formanova. Full-grown roots are an ideal family size — 7 in. long and 2 in. across.

LONG varieties
Other names: Long-rooted or Tapered varieties

The Long varieties require sandy, free-draining soil outdoors and a large pan indoors, so they are not really suitable for the average household. Their popularity has declined, but they remain favourites with the keen exhibitor.
CHELTENHAM GREEN TOP: By far the most popular and highly recommended Long variety. Stores well.
CHELTENHAM MONO: A broad-shouldered Long variety like the better-known Green Top, with the advantage of one plant per 'seed'.

Monopoly

Cheltenham Green Top

1 in. = 2.5 cm, 1 ft = 30 cm, 1 oz = 28 gm, 1 lb = 450 gm

BEETROOT TROUBLES

Beetroot is an easy crop to grow, and is generally trouble-free. Black bean aphid and mangold fly are occasionally troublesome, but yields are not usually seriously affected. You may find that the leaves are discoloured — beetroot is one of the most sensitive indicators of trace element deficiency in the soil.

	Symptom	Likely Causes
Seedlings	— eaten	**Birds** or **Slugs** (see page 110)
	— toppled over	**Damping off** (see page 110)
	— blackened	3
Leaves	— holed	**Flea beetle** (see page 30)
	— blistered	1
	— rolled	5
	— spotted	6
	— infested with blackfly	**Black bean aphid** (see page 20)
	— mouldy patches	**Downy mildew** (see page 94)
	— mottled	5
Plants	— run to seed	4
Roots	— small and leathery	**Dry soil** or **Fertilizer shortage**
	— large and leathery	**Delayed harvesting**
	— blackened inside, cankered outside	2
	— eaten	**Mice** (see page 20) or **Squirrels** or **Swift moth** (see page 43) or **Cutworm** or **Millepede** (see page 110)
	— covered with purple mould	**Violet root rot** (see page 43)
	— scabby patches	**Common scab** (see page 85)
	— split	**Splitting** (see page 43)
	— forked	7

BLISTERED LEAVES

1 | MANGOLD FLY (Leaf Miner)

Small white grubs burrow inside the leaves, causing tunnels which later turn into blisters. Attacks occur from May onwards, and the effects are most serious on young plants. Badly damaged leaves turn brown and growth is retarded.

Treatment: Pick off and destroy affected leaves. Spray with malathion at the first sign of attack.

Prevention: None.

3 | BLACK LEG

Black leg is a serious disease of seedlings, causing them to turn black and shrivel. It occurs when seeds are sown too thickly in compacted soil which becomes waterlogged in wet weather. If an attack occurs, remove diseased plants and water remainder with Cheshunt Compound.

4 | BOLTING

Plants sometimes run to seed before roots have developed. Dry soil or a shortage of organic matter is the usual cause, but it will occur if you sow too early or if you wait too long before thinning the seedlings. Grow a resistant variety such as Boltardy or Monopoly if bolting has been a problem in the past.

7 | FANGING

Forked roots are usually caused by adding fresh manure shortly before sowing. Other causes are growing beetroot in stony soil or in heavy ground which has not been properly cultivated. The answer is to use land which has been manured for a previous crop or to add well-rotted compost in the autumn before sowing.

BLACKENED ROOTS

2 | HEART ROT

Leaves wilt in the summer and the tops of the roots develop brown, sunken patches. A cut root reveals blackened areas within the flesh. The cause is boron deficiency, and attacks are worst on light, over-limed land in a dry season.

Treatment: Repeated spraying with a trace element spray may help.

Prevention: If soil is known to be boron deficient, apply 1 oz borax per 20 sq. yards before planting — take care not to overdose.

ROLLED LEAVES

5 | SPECKLED YELLOWS

Yellow patches develop between the veins, and in a severe attack the whole leaf turns yellow and then brown. The tell-tale sign is the inward rolling of the leaf edges. The cause is manganese deficiency.

Treatment: Apply a sequestered compound. Repeated spraying with a trace element spray may help.

Prevention: Do not overlime the soil.

SPOTTED LEAVES

6 | LEAF SPOT

Brown spots appear on the leaves. The pale central area of each spot sometimes drops out. Leaves may be badly disfigured by these numerous small spots but the effect on the yield of roots is not serious.

Treatment: None. Pick off and destroy badly diseased leaves.

Prevention: Practise crop rotation. Apply a balanced fertilizer, such as Growmore, before sowing seed.

BRASSICAS

The single genus *Brassica* provides the cornerstone of the average vegetable plot. Botany books talk about *B. bullata*, *B. capitata*, *B. gemmifera* and so on, but to us they are cabbages, brussels sprouts, etc. Not all are leafy vegetables — both turnips and swedes are brassicas and so is kohl rabi. But for the gardener the word 'brassica' is usually reserved for the varieties grown as greens — the all-important group which flourish so well in our climate and which share the same cultural likes and dislikes. Brassicas have been a staple part of our diet for thousands of years — long before newcomers like potatoes and runner beans came to our shores. But we must forget old prejudices — in recent years there has been a steady stream of new brassica varieties offering new tastes, and during the same period our ideas about the way to cook brassicas have also changed — the days of school cabbage and boarding house brussels sprouts should now be a thing of the past!

SECRETS OF SUCCESS

- Do not grow brassicas on the same plot more often than one year in three. The main reason for this move-around is to avoid the build-up of soil pests and diseases which thrive on the cabbage family — the dreaded club root disease is the prime example.
- Dig deeply in autumn — the roots must be allowed to reach the water reserves well below the surface.
- Brassicas require firm soil — leave several months between digging and planting in order for the surface to consolidate.
- Lime if necessary — brassicas will disappoint if the soil is acid. Aim for a pH of 6.5–7.5.
- Transplant at the right stage and make sure that you plant firmly.
- Consider using protective discs (see page 28) around the base of each seedling if cabbage root fly has been a problem in the past.
- Many pests and diseases can attack brassicas — treat problems as soon as they are seen.

SOWING

Leafy brassica	Sow in a seedbed, then transplant to a permanent bed	Sow where the plants are to grow to maturity
Broccoli	All varieties	—
Brussels sprouts	All varieties	—
Cabbage	Nearly all varieties	Chinese cabbage varieties
Cauliflower	All varieties	—
Kale	Nearly all varieties	Rape kale varieties

- As shown above, nearly all leafy brassicas are planted in a seed bed and then transferred to another part of the plot where they will grow to maturity. In this way the 'permanent bed' can be utilised for another vegetable until the seedlings are ready for transplanting.
- Choose a sunny but sheltered spot for the seed bed. The soil must be fertile — if it was not manured for a previous crop then add compost when digging in autumn. Before sowing rake (do not fork) the surface and add a general-purpose fertilizer. You can incorporate a nematode-based insecticide if cabbage root fly has been a nuisance in the past. Tread to remove air pockets and to make the surface firm — rake lightly and then follow the sowing instructions.

PLANTING

- The permanent bed (the area where the plants will grow to maturity) should be deeply dug in autumn — ideally it will have grown peas or beans a few months earlier. If the soil has not been recently manured it is essential that compost is incorporated during this autumn digging.
- Do not fork over the ground in spring — simply tread down, rake lightly and remove surface debris. A firm footing for the seedlings is essential.
- The seedlings will be ready for transplanting 5–7 weeks after sowing — look up the specific brassica in this book for details. Water the row the day before the seedlings are to be lifted.
- Lift carefully, retaining as much soil as possible around the roots. Do not dig up too many at one time, and keep the roots covered so that they do not dry out. Mark out the planting row with string and make holes at the required distances with a trowel or dibber — if the soil is dry fill the holes with water and begin transplanting once they have drained.
- Look up the specific plant for details of planting depth. Make sure that the plants are properly firmed in with fingers, dibber or the back of a trowel.

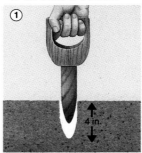
① 4 in.

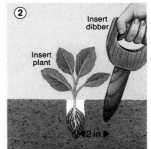
② Insert dibber | Insert plant | 2 in.

③ Press towards plant

④ Tug test: Test one plant — leaf should tear before plant is uprooted

- Water the base of each transplant as soon as planting is finished — keep the rose on the watering can to ensure that the plants will not be disturbed. If the weather is warm and dry before the transplants are established, cover them with newspaper and water the soil frequently.

1 in. = 2.5 cm, 1 ft = 30 cm, 1 oz = 28 gm, 1 lb = 450 gm

BRASSICA TROUBLES

Kale is generally a trouble-free vegetable, but the other members of the brassica family are subject to a wide range of pests and diseases. The worst of these brassica enemies are cabbage root fly, cabbage caterpillars, mealy aphid, whitefly, club root, flea beetle and pigeons. But you must not assume that an insect or fungus disease is the cause every time something goes wrong. As the following pages make clear, the most likely cause of blown brussels sprouts, heartless cabbages and button-headed cauliflowers is you — the ground was left too spongy or the seedlings were not planted firmly. You may have left acid soil unlimed or you may have planted a brassica crop in land which produced poor cabbages or cauliflowers last year. If you are new to gardening, read the appropriate page carefully before growing one of the brassicas.

	Symptom	Likely Causes
Seedlings	— eaten	11 or 13 or 16 or 27
	— toppled over	6 or Damping off (see page 110)
	— peppered with small holes	16
	— severed at ground level	27
Stems	— tunnelled, maggots present	28
	— blackened zone near soil level	6
Leaves	— swollen, distorted	18
	— narrow, strap-like	9
	— curled, blistered	20
	— whitened	17
	— diseased	1 or 5 or 7 or 8
	— coloured between green veins	22 or 23
	— holed	10 or 11 or 13 or 16 or 26
	— infested with greenfly	20
	— tiny white moths	21
	— caterpillars	10 or 26
Roots	— swollen	3 or 4
	— tunnelled, maggots present	2
	— eaten	24
Plants	— bluish leaves, wilting in sunshine	2 or 4
	— blind; plants not growing	9 or 18 or Blind transplants
	— wilting, dying	24 or 28
Brussels sprouts	— buttons open and leafy	15
Cabbage	— no hearts	2 or 12
	— split hearts	14
Cauliflower	— small heads	2 or 9 or 19 or 25
	— brown heads	25

1 DOWNY MILDEW

Yellowing of upper surface. White furry fungus growth beneath. Usually restricted to young plants; over-crowding and a moist atmosphere encourage its spread. Growth severely checked.

Treatment: Spray with mancozeb at the first sign of disease.

Prevention: Sow seeds in sterilised compost. Choose a fresh site for raising seedlings if downy mildew has been a problem in the past.

TUNNELLED ROOTS

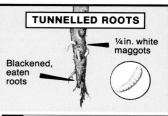

¼ in. white maggots

Blackened, eaten roots

2 CABBAGE ROOT FLY

Tell-tale signs are blue-tinged leaves which wilt in sunny weather; recent transplants are particularly susceptible. Young plants die; older ones grow slowly. Cabbages fail to heart, cauliflowers form tiny heads.

Treatment: Apply a nematode-based insecticide immediately after planting out, or put discs made out of roofing felt around the base of the stems. Alternatively place fine netting over the young plants.

3 GALL WEEVIL

Much less serious and much less common than club root. Swellings generally form close to ground level. Growth may be checked slightly, but there is rarely any serious effect on yield.

Treatment: Not worth while. Spread can be reduced by watering around plants with permethrin.

Prevention: Soil-pest killers which have been used to prevent more serious problems may give some control of gall weevil.

SWOLLEN ROOTS

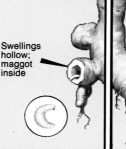

Swellings hollow; maggot inside

Swellings not hollow; no maggots

4 CLUB ROOT (Finger & Toe)

Tell-tale signs are discoloured leaves which wilt in sunny weather. A serious disease which can be disastrous in a wet season. Plants may die or grow very slowly.

Treatment: None. Lift diseased plants and burn. In the case of a severe attack do not plant brassicas on the site for several years.

Prevention: Make sure the land is adequately limed and well drained. Dip transplant roots in thiophanate-methyl before planting.

5 WHITE BLISTER (White Rust)

White spots appear on leaves. The fungus may spread in a mild, damp season to form a white felt over the leaves. Growth is stunted and plants may die. Sprouts are more susceptible than other brassicas.

Treatment: Cut off and burn diseased leaves. Thin out plants to reduce over-crowding.

Prevention: Do not grow brassicas on land affected in the previous season.

DISEASED LEAVES

6 WIRE STEM

Base of stem becomes black and shrunken. Seedlings often die; the plants which survive grow very slowly and stems break easily.

Treatment: None.

Prevention: Avoid growing seedlings in wet and cold soil or compost. Cheshunt Compound may help. Avoid over-crowding.

SHRUNKEN STEMS

7 BLACK ROT

An uncommon but serious disease. Seedlings are killed — mature plants are severely stunted, bearing yellow leaves and characteristically black veins. Lower leaves generally fall. If the stem is cut across a dark brown ring is revealed. Worst attacks occur in a warm, wet summer.

Treatment: None. Lift diseased plants and burn.

Prevention: None. Rotate crops.

8 LEAF SPOT (Ring Spot)

Brown rings up to 1 in. across appear on mature leaves. Badly infected foliage may turn yellow and fall. Most likely to occur in S.W. areas. It is encouraged by wet weather.

Treatment: Cut off and burn diseased leaves. Spray with mancozeb.

Prevention: Do not grow brassicas on land affected by leaf spot in the previous season.

9 WHIPTAIL

Leaves are thin and strap-like. Plant growth is poor, cauliflower heads may be very small or fail to develop. Caused by molybdenum deficiency due to acid soil.

Treatment: Repeated spraying with a trace element spray.

Prevention: Make sure soil is adequately limed before sowing or planting.

NARROW LEAVES

10 CABBAGE CATERPILLARS

Look for cabbage caterpillars when holes begin to appear in leaves. The cabbage moth tends to burrow into the heart. The risk period is April–October, and attacks are worst during a hot dry summer and in coastal areas.

Treatment: Spray with permethrin or fenitrothion as soon as the first attacks occur. Repeat as necessary.

Prevention: Inspect underside of leaves if you see white butterflies hovering over the plants. Remove and crush any eggs which have been laid.

LARGE HOLES IN LEAVES

SMALL CABBAGE WHITE — velvety
LARGE CABBAGE WHITE — hairy
CABBAGE MOTH — smooth

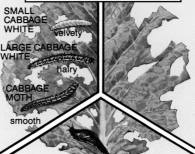

11 PIGEONS

Pigeons are a serious pest in many areas, stripping away the soft portions of the leaves until only the stalks and veins remain. Droppings make the produce tedious to prepare for cooking. Troublesome throughout the year, especially in winter.

Treatment: None.

Prevention: Bird scarers are of limited value. Use nylon netting, making sure that the plants are completely enclosed.

12 HEARTLESS CABBAGES

There are several reasons why cabbage plants fail to heart. Too little organic matter in the soil and too little compaction of the ground before planting are common reasons. So is failing to plant the seedlings firmly. Drought increases the risk; so does a shady site. Proper feeding will help, but use a balanced fertilizer, such as Growmore or a potassium-rich soluble feed, and not straight nitrogen.

13 SLUGS & SNAILS

Leaves and stems may be severely attacked during wet weather. The pests are generally not seen during the day, so look for the tell-tale slime trails. Young plants are particularly susceptible and may be killed.

Treatment: Scatter methiocarb or Slug Pellets around the plants at the first signs of attack.

Prevention: Keep surrounding area free from rubbish.

14 SPLIT HEARTS

There are two major reasons why cabbage heads suddenly split. In summer the usual cause is rain after a long period of dry weather. Foliar feeding at the first sign of trouble helps to harden the leaf tissue, but it is better to prevent trouble by watering regularly during drought. In winter the cause is a sudden sharp frost; consider lifting and storing mature heads if very cold weather is forecast.

1 in. = 2.5 cm, 1 ft = 30 cm, 1 oz = 28 gm, 1 lb = 450 gm

BRASSICA TROUBLES continued

15 BLOWN BRUSSELS SPROUTS

Brussels sprouts sometimes produce open, leafy sprouts instead of hard, round buttons. These blown sprouts should be removed promptly. The causes are similar to the factors responsible for heartless cabbages — not enough well-rotted organic matter in the soil, too little consolidation of the ground before planting and failure to plant firmly. Make sure the plants are kept well watered during dry weather and avoid planting too closely. Choose an F_1 hybrid variety.

SMALL HOLES IN LEAVES

WHITENED LEAVES

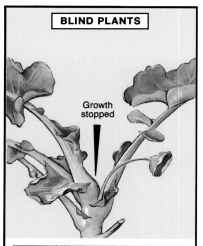

BLIND PLANTS

Growth stopped

16 FLEA BEETLE

A serious pest, especially in April and May during warm, settled weather. Young leaves bear numerous, small round holes. Growth is slowed down and seedlings may be killed. The tiny beetles jump when disturbed.

Treatment: Spray the seedlings with derris as soon as the first signs of damage are noticed. Water damaged plants if the weather is dry.

Prevention: Treating seed with an insecticidal seed dressing before sowing will prevent early attacks.

17 FROST

Frost can be extremely damaging to brassicas. If the plants are not firmly anchored in the soil then frost can reach the roots and lead to the death of the plant. Frosts can also damage the leaves of non-hardy varieties. The blanched areas are quickly attacked by fungi or bacteria and extensive rotting can occur.

Treatment: Remove and burn damaged leaves.

Prevention: Always plant firmly. Frost damage is worse on soft growth so always use a properly balanced fertilizer when preparing the soil.

18 SWEDE MIDGE

Attacks are uncommon, but the results are devastating. Leaf stalks near the growing point are swollen and distorted, and the plants become blind. Look carefully for the minute white larvae on the leaf stalks. Northern and S.W. districts are most at risk.

Treatment: Lift and burn badly affected plants. Spraying or dusting with lindane as soon as the first signs are noticed may stop it spreading to other plants.

Prevention: No practical method available.

19 BUTTON CAULIFLOWERS

Many gardeners fail to grow satisfactory cauliflowers. Buttoning often takes place, which is the production of very small heads early in the season. These button heads quickly run to seed. Unfortunately there are many causes. It may be due to an early attack by a pest such as flea beetle or the shortage of a trace element such as boron or molybdenum. Or the cause may be cultural — poor soil, insufficient consolidation of the ground before planting, loose planting, drought or failure to harden off the seedlings properly before planting.

20 MEALY APHID

Large clusters of waxy, greyish 'greenflies' occur on the underside of leaves and tips of plants from June onwards in hot, dry weather. Affected leaves curl and turn yellow. Sooty moulds develop if the attack is severe and the pests can be numerous enough to render sprouts unusable.

Treatment: Not easy to control. Spray thoroughly with permethrin or heptenophos.

Prevention: Dig up and destroy old brassica stalks.

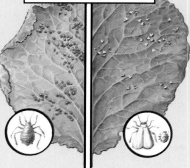

INSECTS ON LEAVES

21 CABBAGE WHITEFLY

Outbreaks have become much more widespread in the past few years. Tiny white moths and larvae feed on the underside of leaves. Affected plants are weakened and sooty moulds develop. The adults are active throughout the year and fly into the air when disturbed.

Treatment: Not easy to control. Spray with permethrin at 3 day intervals until the infestation has been cleared. Best results are obtained by spraying in the morning or evening.

Prevention: No practical method available.

22 | MAGNESIUM DEFICIENCY

Yellowing between the leaf veins begins on the older leaves, and these yellow areas may eventually turn orange, white, red or purple. Magnesium deficiency is much more common than manganese deficiency.

Treatment: Apply a trace element spray around the plants. Repeated spraying with a foliar feed may help.

Prevention: Incorporate compost into the soil during autumn digging. Use a fertilizer containing magnesium.

MOTTLING BETWEEN VEINS

23 | MANGANESE DEFICIENCY

It is not always easy to distinguish between manganese and magnesium deficiency by looking at a single leaf. Manganese deficiency symptoms, however, usually start on young as well as old leaves, and the leaf edges are often curled inwards and scorched.

Treatment: Apply a trace element spray around the plants. Repeated spraying with a foliar feed may help.

Prevention: Incorporate compost into the soil during autumn digging.

24 | CHAFER GRUBS

The visual symptoms of chafer grub attack are wilting leaves and dying plants. On lifting affected specimens damaged roots are seen and fat, curved grubs may be found in the soil. These slow-moving pests can feed throughout the year. Gardens made from newly-dug grassland are the areas most likely to suffer.

Treatment: None.

Prevention: Hand pick and destroy the grubs when autumn digging. Use a nematode-based insecticide.

ROOTS EATEN

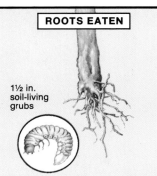

1½ in. soil-living grubs

BROWN CURDS

25 | BORON DEFICIENCY

Cauliflowers are extremely sensitive to boron deficiency in the soil. Young leaves are distorted, and the heads are small and bitter. The main symptom is the development of brown patches on the curds.

Treatment: Repeated spraying with a foliar feed may help.

Prevention: Incorporate compost into the soil during autumn digging. If soil is definitely known to be boron deficient, apply 1 oz borax per 20 sq. yards before planting — take care not to overdose.

SKIN-COVERED HOLES

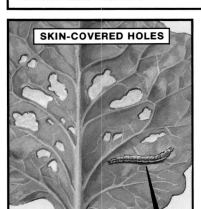

½ in. green caterpillars

SEVERED STEMS

1–2 in. soil-living caterpillars

27 | CUTWORM

These large grey or brown caterpillars live just below the surface. Young plants are attacked at night and stems are severed at ground level. Leaves and roots may also be eaten. Plants are most at risk in June and July.

Treatment: Hoe the soil around the plants regularly during the danger months. Pick up and destroy caterpillars which are brought to the surface.

Prevention: Use a nematode-based insecticide.

26 | DIAMOND-BACK MOTH

These green caterpillars can be a serious summer nuisance in coastal areas. They feed on the underside of the foliage and, unlike the cabbage caterpillars, generally leave the upper skin intact. When disturbed they drop from the plant on a silken thread. In a severe attack the leaf is completely skeletonized.

Treatment: Spray with permethrin as soon as the first attack occurs.

Prevention: None.

TUNNELLED STEMS

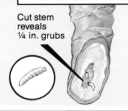

Cut stem reveals ¼ in. grubs

28 | CABBAGE STEM FLEA BEETLE

Infested plants wilt and die. Cut open the stem of one of the plants if you suspect cabbage stem flea beetle; the tell-tale sign is the presence of small, cream-coloured grubs. Attacks occur between August and October.

Treatment: Lift and burn infested plants.

Prevention: Do not grow brassicas on land affected by cabbage stem flea beetle in the previous season.

BROCCOLI

Frozen broccoli spears from the supermarket have introduced this vegetable into countless homes, but these green heads are really calabrese, whereas the garden-grown variety is usually purple sprouting broccoli. So there is some confusion which is not helped by the catalogues and textbooks which can't seem to agree on the correct names to use. Very simply, the word 'broccoli' should be restricted to the sprouting sorts which virtually all work on the cut-and-come-again principle. The name 'winter cauliflower' should be used for the heading types which form one large white head in winter or spring. The broccolis are sown in spring and planted out in summer and there are three types — calabrese for harvesting in autumn and purple or white for cutting in the following spring. These purple and white types are hardy, high-yielding and fill the gap between the sprouts and the spring cabbages.

SEED FACTS

Actual size

Expected germination time:	7–12 days
Approximate number per ounce:	8000
Expected yield per plant:	1½ lb
Life expectancy of stored seed:	4 years
Approximate time between sowing and cutting:	12 weeks (Calabrese) 44 weeks (Purple and White varieties)
Ease of cultivation:	Easier than cauliflower but still not really easy — there is transplanting to do and various troubles to watch out for

SOIL FACTS

- Broccoli, like other brassicas, can fail in loose and starved soil. Ideally the ground should be firm and rich in organic matter.
- Pick a reasonably sunny site for the place where the plants will grow to maturity. Dig in autumn — work in plenty of well-rotted manure or compost if the soil is poor. Lime, if necessary, in winter.
- In spring apply Growmore fertilizer. Consider using protective discs (see page 28) if cabbage root fly is known to be a problem. Do not fork over the surface before planting the seedlings — tread down gently, rake lightly and remove surface rubbish.

SOWING & PLANTING

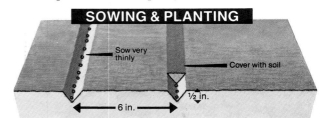

Sow very thinly
Cover with soil
½ in.
6 in.

- Thin the seedlings to prevent them from becoming weak and spindly. They should be about 3 in. apart in the rows.
- The seedlings are ready for transplanting when they are 3 in. high. Water the rows the day before moving the transplants to their permanent quarters. Plant firmly, setting the seedlings about 1 in. deeper than they were growing in the seed bed. Leave 1½ ft between purple and white sprouting broccoli, 1 ft between green sprouting broccoli. Water after planting.

LOOKING AFTER THE CROP

- Hoe regularly and provide some means of protection for the young plants against birds.
- Summer care consists of watering in dry weather and applying a mulch to conserve moisture. Occasional feeding with a liquid fertilizer will improve the crop. Broccoli is a trouble-prone crop so watch for pests. Spray with permethrin if caterpillars appear.
- With the approach of winter draw up soil around the stems and stake the plants if the site is exposed. Always firm the stems if they are loosened by wind or frost. Pigeons can be a menace at this time of the year — netting may be necessary.

HARVESTING

- The time to cut is when the flower shoots ('spears') are well formed but before the small flower buds have opened. Once in flower the spears are woody and tasteless.
- Cut or snap off the central spear first — in a few varieties this will be a cauliflower-like head. Side shoots will be produced and these should be picked regularly, but never strip a plant completely.
- The spears are generally 4–6 in. long and cropping should continue for about 6 weeks. If you let any of them flower, however, production will stop at an earlier stage.

- The date you can expect to start cutting depends on the variety and the weather. Early Purple Sprouting will be ready for its first picking in January if the winter is mild but mid spring is the peak harvesting period for the purple and white varieties.
- The green varieties will be ready for cutting in autumn — choose Express Corona or Green Comet if you are in a hurry. Cropping will extend into winter if prolonged frosts do not occur.

CALENDAR

	JAN	FEB	MAR	APR	MAY	JUN	JUL	AUG	SEP	OCT	NOV	DEC
Sowing Time				■	■							
Planting Time						■	■					
Cutting Time	■	EARLY vars.		LATE vars.				GREEN vars.				

For key to symbols — see page 7

IN THE KITCHEN

Broccoli may look like a small version of cauliflower but its flavour is usually closer to asparagus. Calabrese is the most asparagus-like and white sprouting broccoli is the closest in taste to cauliflower — it can be used as a substitute for making 'cauliflower' cheese. Don't judge broccoli from the flavour of shop-bought spears which are then boiled — to discover the *real* flavour you should steam (not boil) the spears and this should take place within hours of picking.

FREEZING An excellent vegetable for freezing. Soak in salted water for 15 minutes, then rinse and dry. Blanch for 3–4 minutes — cool and drain. Pack carefully and freeze in rigid containers.

STORAGE Keep in a polythene bag in the refrigerator — broccoli will stay fresh for up to 3 days.

COOKING The standard method is to peel off the skin if it is tough, remove any large leaves and then cook in boiling salted water for 10 minutes. Drain carefully and then serve hot with white sauce or melted butter, or cold with a vinaigrette. Steaming is preferred by the food experts — stand the spears upright in 2 in. of gently boiling water for 15 minutes. Keep the pan covered so that the heads are steamed. On the Continent you will find broccoli cooked in many interesting ways — *broccoli alla romana* (braised in white wine), *broccoli alla siciliana* (braised with anchovies, olives and red wine) and broccoli fritters (washed and dried heads dipped into batter and then deep fried until golden-brown).

VARIETIES

PURPLE SPROUTING varieties

This is the hardiest and the most popular broccoli for growing at home. It is extremely useful for heavy soils and cold areas where little else can overwinter. The heads turn green when cooked. There are three popular varieties — planting all three will give you continuous cropping from January until May.

RED ARROW: A recent introduction which is claimed to give higher yields than the popular older varieties and with a better-than-average flavour.

EARLY PURPLE SPROUTING: The most popular variety — ready for cutting in February or March. Prolific and hardy with a long cropping season— the one to choose if you plan to grow only one sort of broccoli for spring use.

LATE PURPLE SPROUTING: Like the other purples, winter-hardy and robust — plants grow about 3 ft tall. The spears will not be ready for picking until April.

PURPLE SPROUTING: Sometimes the seed packet doesn't tell you whether it is 'Early' or 'Late'. You will find that the spears appear in March and April.

WHITE SPROUTING varieties

This group produces small cauliflower-like spears. The varieties are less popular than the purple sprouting sorts but some people prefer the flavour and the white appearance of this crop. If you propose to grow white sprouting broccoli then the choice of variety is very simple — there is just 'Early' and 'Late'.

EARLY WHITE SPROUTING: The one to grow if you want to cut the crop in March and early April.

LATE WHITE SPROUTING: Extends the harvesting period for broccoli lovers — spears appear in April and early May.

CALABRESE varieties

Calabrese or green sprouting broccoli is a useful but much underrated vegetable. Unlike the purple and white sprouting types, it produces its crop of delicately-flavoured spears before the onset of winter. Some varieties produce a succession of spears stretching from early autumn until the first frosts — if you want plants which bear a single large head in August then choose Green Comet.

EXPRESS CORONA: An F_1 hybrid — one of the earliest of all the green sprouting types. About 45 days after planting out the central head is ready for cutting — side shoots then freely develop to give a succession of succulent spears.

GREEN COMET: Another F_1 hybrid and another very early cropper. Unlike Express Corona, the central head is exceptionally large — up to 7 in. across and weighing about 1 lb. There is, however, little spear production after the main head has been cut.

ITALIAN SPROUTING: This is the basic variety which has kept its place in some catalogues despite the appearance of modern F_1 hybrids. It has an excellent reputation for flavour and a long cropping season.

CORVET: An F_1 hybrid which matures in about 60 days after transplanting. It gives you the best of both worlds — the primary head is large and firm, but after its removal there is a succession of secondary spears.

ROMANESCO: Not just another variety — it has two distinctive features. Romanesco is a late cropper, its heads appearing in November, and the flavour is outstanding. The texture is very soft and the lime-green spears should be steamed and served like asparagus.

SHOGUN: An F_1 hybrid which bears large blue-green heads with many lateral shoots below them. It is tolerant of cold conditions and a wide range of soil types. Early maturing — good for freezing.

PERENNIAL variety

Perennial broccoli is a tall-growing vegetable — leave about 3 ft between the plants. In spring or early summer about 8 small and pale green heads are produced, each one looking like a small cauliflower. Grow the variety **NINE STAR PERENNIAL** — plant it against a fence and fork in a general-purpose fertilizer each spring. Apply a mulch in early summer, never let the flower buds open and you will obtain heads year after year.

TROUBLES

See pages 28–31

Early Purple Sprouting

Express Corona

BRUSSELS SPROUTS

You must face the fact that if your brussels sprouts disappoint the family at mealtime then you are to blame. Loose, open sprouts have little flavour but they are not caused by poor weather — the usual reason is loose soil or incorrect planting. Even if the sprouts are picked in peak condition — firm, fresh and tightly packed, they can be ruined by overcooking — the traditional 'landlady' sprout which has lost most of its colour and all of its crispness. Sprouts should never disappoint if you choose one of the modern F_1 hybrids and the instructions on this page and on pages 27–31 are followed. You can begin picking in September and finish in March if you grow both early and late varieties, each plant remaining productive for about eight weeks. According to the books (if not the tasting tests) sprouts are at their best when they have frost on them. The books will also tell you to plant them about 2½ ft apart — if your plot is a small one forget these instructions — plant Peer Gynt at 18 in. intervals for an early crop of small but delicious sprouts.

SEED FACTS

Actual size

Expected germination time:	7–12 days
Approximate number per ounce:	8000
Expected yield per plant:	2 lb
Life expectancy of stored seed:	4 years
Approximate time between sowing and picking:	28 weeks (Early varieties) 36 weeks (Late varieties)
Ease of cultivation:	Not difficult, but you must follow the basic cultural rules and watch out for a variety of pests

SOIL FACTS

- The main cause of failure is planting in loose, infertile soil. The ground must be *firm* and adequately supplied with humus.
- Pick a reasonably sunny spot with shelter from high winds for the place where the plants will grow to maturity. Dig in autumn — work in plenty of well-rotted manure or compost if the soil is poor. The ground must not be acid — lime, if necessary, in winter.
- In spring apply Growmore fertilizer — consider using protective discs (see page 28) if cabbage root fly is usually a problem. Do not fork over the surface before planting the seedlings — tread down gently, rake lightly and remove surface rubbish.

SOWING & PLANTING

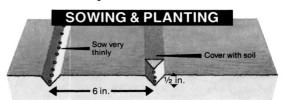

Sow very thinly

Cover with soil

6 in.

½ in.

- Thin the seedlings to about 3 in. apart in the rows to prevent them from becoming weak and spindly.
- The seedlings are ready for transplanting when they are 4–6 in. high. Water the rows the day before moving the transplants to their permanent quarters. Plant firmly, setting the seedlings with their lowest leaves just above the soil surface. Leave 2½ ft between the plants and water after planting.

LOOKING AFTER THE CROP

- Birds are a problem — protect the seedlings from sparrows and the mature crop from pigeons.
- Hoe regularly and water the young plants in dry weather. The mature crop rarely needs watering if the soil has been properly prepared. Brussels sprouts respond remarkably well to foliar feeding in early summer. Both caterpillars and aphids can be a menace — spray with permethrin.
- As autumn approaches earth-up around the stems and stake tall varieties before the high winds of winter arrive. The old practice of removing the tops of the plants to hasten maturity is no longer recommended.

HARVESTING

- Begin picking when the sprouts ('buttons') at the base of the stem have reached the size of a walnut and are still tightly closed. Snap them off with a sharp downward tug or cut them off with a sharp knife.
- Work steadily up the stem at each cropping session, removing yellowed leaves and any open ('blown') sprouts as you go. Remember to remove only a few sprouts at any one time from each individual stem.
- When all the sprouts have gone, cut off the stem tops and cook as cabbage. Dig up and dispose of the stems.

- Sow an early variety outdoors in mid March and plant out in mid May to provide sprouts during October and November. To obtain September sprouts, sow the seeds under cloches in early March and plant out in early May.
- For a later crop which will produce sprouts between December and March, sow a late variety in April and plant out in June.

CALENDAR

	JAN	FEB	MAR	APR	MAY	JUN	JUL	AUG	SEP	OCT	NOV	DEC
Sowing Time												
Planting Time												
Picking Time												

IN THE KITCHEN

Overcooked sprouts, straw-coloured and soggy, are a much-quoted example of bad British cookery. The secret of success is to pick them whilst they still feel hard and boil briskly for the minimum time required to turn them chewy but not mushy. Even this small amount of boiling is not essential — small sprouts can be shredded and served as part of a salad. Freezing is often recommended and is indeed the only way of coping with a glut, but it is not wholly satisfactory. Boil frozen sprouts for only 2−3 minutes before serving.

FREEZING Use only small, firm sprouts. Strip off the outer leaves if damaged and soak for 15 minutes in cold water. Blanch for 3 minutes, cool and then drain thoroughly. Dry the sprouts on a paper towel and pack into polythene bags, leaving no air space, before freezing.

STORAGE Keep unwashed in a polythene bag in the refrigerator — brussels sprouts will stay fresh for up to 3 days.

COOKING Boiling is the standard method of cooking sprouts. Cut off the basal stalk and strip away the outer leaves. Cut a cross at the base with a sharp knife. Wash in cold water — if there are aphids within the sprouts soak in salted water for 15 minutes. Add 1 in. of water to a large pan and bring to the boil. Add the sprouts slowly so that the water does not stop boiling — cover the pan and keep the water bubbling merrily for 7−8 minutes. Drain thoroughly, add a knob of butter (optional) and serve. Christmas Dinner calls for something a little extra — boil the sprouts for 5 minutes and then braise with cooked chestnuts in butter for a further 5 minutes. Alternatively you can braise the parboiled sprouts with onions in a small amount of stock and bacon fat.

VARIETIES

F₁ HYBRID varieties
The modern F_1 hybrids are becoming increasingly popular. This popularity is due to the compact growth habit of most of them and the large number of uniform buttons which crowd the stems. The sprouts tend to mature all at the same time, which is an advantage if you intend to freeze them, but it is often quoted as a disadvantage if you wish to pick over a protracted period. This disadvantage is overrated — the F_1 hybrids generally hold their mature buttons for many weeks without 'blowing'.

PEER GYNT: The favourite brussels sprout which you will find in all the catalogues. The medium-sized buttons appear early — September–December with November as the peak month.

OLIVER: An early variety for picking in September or October — the plants are quite short but the sprouts are large. The flavour is good and the yields are high.

CITADEL: A better choice than Peer Gynt if you want a later variety which will be reaching its peak on Christmas Day. The dark green sprouts are not large but they are highly recommended for freezing.

WIDGEON: A variety which crops at about the same time as Citadel but is claimed to have better disease resistance and a better flavour.

DOLMIC: Try this one if you have had no luck with brussels sprouts in the past — the suppliers claim that it is exceptionally tolerant of defective soil or climatic conditions. Picking starts in late October and can be expected to go on until February.

SHERIFF: This one offers something different — a heavy crop of small sprouts with none of the bitterness after cooking which is associated with this vegetable. Good resistance to powdery mildew is another advantage. A late variety for January–March picking.

RAMPART: Another late variety which holds its sprouts for a long period without blowing. Tall-growing — the sprouts are quite large and noted for their flavour.

FORTRESS: You can't do much better than Fortress if you want a late variety for picking between January and March. The dark green buttons are firm and the tall plants are unaffected by very cold weather.

TROIKA: A '3 way cross' which is cheaper than the true F_1 hybrids. Pick from December to February — it has a good reputation for disease resistance and high yields.

Peer Gynt

STANDARD varieties
The old favourites, sometimes called ordinary or open-pollinated varieties, have now been largely overshadowed by the F_1 hybrids. Their sprouts have none of the uniformity or high quality of the modern hybrids and they quite quickly blow if not picked off the stem once they have matured. Though no longer recommended by some experts they still retain one or two advantages. Here you will find the largest sprouts and perhaps the best flavours, and the pleasure of picking each sprout as it comes to perfection.

EARLY HALF TALL: An alternative choice to the F_1 hybrid Peer Gynt if you want a compact plant which will crop between September and Christmas.

BEDFORD: The market gardeners of Bedfordshire originated this variety, noted for its large sprouts on tall stems. There are Bedford-Fillbasket if you want the heaviest yields and the largest sprouts, and Bedford-Asmer Monitor if you want a compact plant for a small garden.

NOISETTE: The gourmet's sprout — small buttons with a pronounced nutty flavour. A French favourite — they say it should be braised in white wine.

RUBINE: The red sprout — serve raw in salad or boil it like any other variety. Not just a novelty — the flavour is claimed to be unexcelled by any other type.

CAMBRIDGE NO. 5: A late variety producing large sprouts. Once popular but now disappearing from the catalogues.

ROODNERF: A group of varieties — Roodnerf-Seven Hills, Roodnerf-Early Button, etc., which keep their sprouts without blowing for a longer period than other standard sprouts.

Bedford-Fillbasket

TROUBLES
See pages 28–31

CABBAGE

Features on the cultivation of the cabbage often begin with the statement that you can gather fresh heads from the garden all year round. This is quite true — by choosing the proper varieties, having enough land to spare and then sowing and transplanting at the right time you can indeed produce a non-stop supply, but this concept does not always thrill the family. On the vegetable plot a cabbage plant wastes a lot of space for just a single head and in countless homes this head is transformed into a soggy, rather evil-smelling vegetable in the kitchen. Neither fault is necessary — as noted below you can cut-and-come-again with spring and summer cabbages, and the homely cabbage can be an appetising vegetable with a number of uses when properly cooked. In many catalogues a host of varieties are offered, and nearly all of them fall neatly into one of the three major groups — spring, summer or winter cabbage. The season refers to the time of harvesting, not planting, and nobody can quite decide what to do about the cabbages such as Winnigstadt which are ready for cutting in autumn. Some textbooks put them in the winter group — most catalogues and this guide class them with the summer cabbages. For something different try the red and the chinese varieties — a new taste for an old vegetable.

TYPES

| SPRING | SUMMER | WINTER | SAVOY | RED | CHINESE |

SEED FACTS

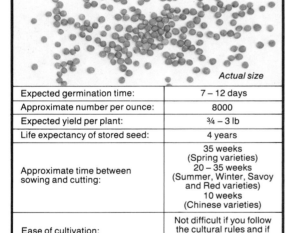

Don't sow too many at one time — just a small row every few weeks.

Actual size

Expected germination time:	7 – 12 days
Approximate number per ounce:	8000
Expected yield per plant:	¾ – 3 lb
Life expectancy of stored seed:	4 years
Approximate time between sowing and cutting:	35 weeks (Spring varieties) 20 – 35 weeks (Summer, Winter, Savoy and Red varieties) 10 weeks (Chinese varieties)
Ease of cultivation:	Not difficult if you follow the cultural rules and if club root, cabbage root fly and other pests stay away

SOIL FACTS

- Cabbage requires well-consolidated soil, so leave several months between digging and planting. Some humus must be present but this must never be freshly applied.

- Pick a reasonably sunny spot for the site where the plants are to grow — you can use an area recently vacated by a non-brassica crop (see page 27). Dig in autumn — work in some compost or manure if the soil is poor. The ground must not be acid — lime, if necessary, in winter.

- About a week before planting apply a general fertilizer for all types except spring cabbage — this group needs to be grown slowly in a sheltered spot. Consider using protective discs (see page 28) if cabbage root fly is usually a problem. Do not fork over the surface before planting — tread down gently, rake and remove surface rubbish.

SOWING & PLANTING

Sow very thinly

Cover with soil

6 in.

½ in.

- Thin the seedlings to prevent them from becoming weak and spindly. They should be about 3 in. apart in the rows.

- The seedlings are ready for transplanting when they have 5 or 6 leaves. Water the rows the day before moving the transplants to their permanent quarters. Dip roots in thiophanate-methyl if club root is feared. Plant firmly and water in thoroughly.

- Allow 1 ft between the plants if the variety is compact — leave 1½ ft either way if the variety produces large heads. With spring cabbage leave only 4 in. between plants in rows 1 ft apart — the thinnings provide spring greens in March.

- Chinese cabbage has its own rules — see page 38.

LOOKING AFTER THE CROP

- Birds are a problem — protect the seedlings from sparrows. Hoe carefully until the crop is large enough to suppress weeds.

- Water if the weather is dry. Always apply a liquid feed as the heads begin to mature.

- In autumn earth-up the stems of spring cabbage. During winter firm down any plants loosened by wind or frost.

HARVESTING

- In March thin out the spring cabbage rows and use the young plants as spring greens. Leave the remaining plants to heart up for cutting in April or May.

- Cabbages are harvested by cutting with a sharp knife close to ground level. With spring and summer cabbages cut a ½ in. deep cross into the stumps — a secondary crop of small cabbages will appear from the cut surfaces.

- In most cases cabbages are cut as required for immediate use. Both red and winter white cabbages can be harvested in November and then stored for winter use. Cut off roots and stem, remove outer leaves and then place in straw-lined boxes in a cool, dry place. The crop should keep until March.

IN THE KITCHEN

Boiling is just one of the many methods of using cabbages in the kitchen. First of all, there is raw cabbage — not as unappetising as it may sound. Shredded white or red cabbage is a useful salad ingredient, but white cabbage is more usually mixed with grated carrots, apples, etc. and tossed with mayonnaise to produce coleslaw. The standard method of serving chinese cabbage is to add a vinaigrette dressing to the shredded leaves. Then there is pickled cabbage — in vinegar for red cabbage or in brine for white cabbage *(sauerkraut)*. For most of us cabbage is a vegetable for cooking and not for eating raw or pickled, but boiling should not be regarded as the only or even the best way of cooking. There is stir frying — the recommended method for chinese cabbage and a welcome alternative for ordinary varieties. Baked cabbage stuffed with minced meat is popular in eastern Europe and cabbage leaves can be used as a substitute for vine leaves to make the Greek dish *dolmades*. Cabbage soup, cabbage casserole, braised cabbage — there are many recipes to turn to if you are tired of plain boiled cabbage.

FREEZING Use only fresh, crisp heads. Wash and coarsely shred — blanch for 1 minute. Pack into polythene bags for freezing.

STORAGE Keep wrapped in plastic cling film in the refrigerator — cabbage will stay fresh for up to 1 week — chinese cabbage for several weeks.

COOKING Boiling cabbage properly is something of an art. Wash and prepare just before cooking — shred or cut into wedges depending on your taste. Fill a large pan with 1 in. of lightly salted water and bring to the boil. Add the coarse leaves a handful at a time — the water should not stop boiling. Put the leaves of the young heart on top of the old leaves and replace the lid. Keep on medium heat for 5 minutes (shredded cabbage) or 10 minutes (cabbage wedges). Drain and then toss with butter and black pepper. Or put in a baking dish, cover with cream sauce and grated cheese, and then brown under the grill. Red cabbage needs different treatment — braise with butter, vinegar, sugar, onions and sliced apples — the *apfelrotkohl* of Germany.

VARIETIES

SPRING cabbages

April

These cabbages are planted in the autumn to provide tender spring greens (collards) in early spring and mature heads later in the season. They are generally conical in shape and smaller than the summer and winter varieties.

DURHAM EARLY: Dark green and conical. Popular, especially as a source of spring greens. An early-maturing type producing medium-sized heads.

OFFENHAM 1-MYATT'S OFFENHAM COMPACTA: A broad-leaved, dark green variety for sowing in early August and cutting in May. Grow for greens and heads.

APRIL: Highly recommended — very early, compact and reliable. The shape is conical and there are few outer leaves.

FIRST EARLY MARKET 218: The one to choose if you want a large-headed spring cabbage. The heads are conical and dark green.

PIXIE: Small and tightly packed heads make this early variety an ideal choice for close planting in beds. A replacement for the old variety Dorado.

OFFENHAM 2-FLOWER OF SPRING: No worries about the weather with this one — it is very hardy. The conical heads are large and solid.

SPRING HERO: Something different — a ball-headed spring cabbage. This F_1 hybrid is both early and hardy, producing round heads which weigh up to 2 lb each. Sow in August, not July.

	JAN	FEB	MAR	APR	MAY	JUN	JUL	AUG	SEP	OCT	NOV	DEC
Sowing Time							▓	▓				
Planting Time									▓	▓		
Cutting Time			▓	▓	▓							

SUMMER cabbages

Stonehead

These cabbages mature in summer or autumn. They are usually ball-headed, with some conical exceptions such as the ever-popular Greyhound and the F_1 hybrid Hispi. The normal pattern is to sow outdoors in April, transplant in May and cut in August or September. For June cabbages sow an early variety under cloches in early March and transplant in April.

GREYHOUND: The compact, pointed heads mature quickly, making Greyhound an excellent variety for early sowing.

HISPI: This modern variety is even earlier than the old favourite Greyhound. Same shape — dark green leaves and good flavour. Stands for a long time without splitting.

PRIMO (GOLDEN ACRE): The favourite ball-headed summer cabbage — compact and very firm.

DERBY DAY: So named because it will be ready for cutting by Derby Day from a February sowing.

STONEHEAD: An F_1 hybrid which produces heavy round heads, although the plants are compact enough to allow close planting in beds. Stands well without splitting.

MINICOLE: An F_1 hybrid which is becoming increasingly popular. The small, oval heads are produced in early autumn and will stand for up to 3 months without splitting.

WINNIGSTADT: An old favourite — the large, pointed heads are ready for cutting in September or October.

	JAN	FEB	MAR	APR	MAY	JUN	JUL	AUG	SEP	OCT	NOV	DEC
Sowing Time		▓	▓	▓								
Planting Time			▓	▓	▓							
Cutting Time							▓	▓	▓	▓		

WINTER cabbages

Celtic

These cabbages mature in winter. They are generally ball-headed or drum-headed, green or white, all suitable for immediate cooking. The white varieties are also used for coleslaw and can be stored for months — see page 36. The normal pattern is to sow in May, transplant in July and cut from November onwards.

CELTIC: The crown prince of winter cabbages — an F_1 hybrid of a savoy and winter white cabbage. Ball-headed, rock-hard, blue-green and capable of standing for months without splitting.

CHRISTMAS DRUMHEAD: The early one — dwarf, blue-green and ready from late October.

JANUARY KING: Drum-headed savoy type of cabbage — you can tell it by its red-tinged leaves. A December–January variety.

HOLLAND LATE WINTER: The old favourite white cabbage for coleslaw and storage.

TUNDRA: An excellent choice — ready in November but still suitable for cutting in March. Unrivalled for winter hardiness.

	JAN	FEB	MAR	APR	MAY	JUN	JUL	AUG	SEP	OCT	NOV	DEC
Sowing Time				▓	▓							
Planting Time						▓	▓					
Cutting Time	▓	▓	▓								▓	▓

SAVOY cabbages

Ormskirk Late

These cabbages are easily recognisable by their crisp and puckered dark green leaves. They are grown as winter cabbages but there is a wider harvesting span — there are varieties which mature in September and others which come to maturity as late as March.

BEST OF ALL: The standard choice if you want a large drum-headed type which will mature in September.

ORMSKIRK LATE: The other end of the scale — this old favourite does not reach cutting size until February or March. The heads are large and dark green.

SAVOY KING: This F_1 hybrid has been hailed by many as the best savoy of all. The foliage is light green — unusual for a savoy, and the heads are unsurpassed for size. Sow early for a September crop.

WIROSA: A good choice if you want to gather good quality heads on Christmas Day.

	JAN	FEB	MAR	APR	MAY	JUN	JUL	AUG	SEP	OCT	NOV	DEC
Sowing Time				▓	▓							
Planting Time						▓	▓					
Cutting Time	▓	▓	▓						▓	▓	▓	▓

RED cabbages

Ruby Ball

These cabbages are extremely popular in many parts of Europe, but Britain is an exception. We buy it pickled in jars and we see them on display in the supermarket, but we do not generally plant them on the vegetable plot. Grow it like a summer cabbage, cutting in early autumn for cooking or late autumn for storing over winter.

RED DRUMHEAD: The favourite variety, producing firm hearts which are dark red in colour. A compact plant suitable for the small plot.

RUBY BALL: An F_1 hybrid from America — claimed to be an improvement on earlier varieties. There are few outer leaves and the round heart is firm. Ready for cutting in late summer.

HARDORA: A late-maturing cabbage for storing, but you will have to hunt for a supplier.

	JAN	FEB	MAR	APR	MAY	JUN	JUL	AUG	SEP	OCT	NOV	DEC
Sowing Time			▓	▓								
Planting Time				▓	▓							
Cutting Time									▓	▓		

CHINESE cabbages

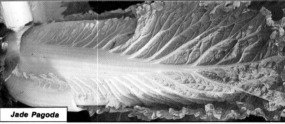
Jade Pagoda

These cabbages are the 'chinese leaves' sold by supermarkets. Tall and cylindrical, they look more like a cos lettuce than a cabbage. Cultivation is also uncabbage-like — sow at about 4 in. spacings in drills 1 ft apart, then thin to leave 1 ft between the plants. Bolting is the problem — do not transplant and remember to water regularly in dry weather. Loosely tie the heads with raffia in August.

TIP TOP: Large — each head weighs up to 2 lb, and is less likely to bolt than the older varieties. Sow in July.

KASUMI: A reliable barrel type with good bolt resistance, but the heads are not tightly packed.

PE-TSAI: One of the older types — pale green and tall, up to 2 ft high. Do not sow before July.

JADE PAGODA: A Michihili type — the heads are taller and thinner than the others described here.

	JAN	FEB	MAR	APR	MAY	JUN	JUL	AUG	SEP	OCT	NOV	DEC
Sowing Time						▓	▓					
Cutting Time									▓	▓		

TROUBLES
See pages 28–31

For key to symbols — see page 7

CAPSICUM

The varieties of capsicum which are becoming increasingly popular are the large sweet peppers. These mild-flavoured fruits are now widely used in salads and for baking, but their small and fiery relatives, the chilli peppers, remain much less popular. Capsicum is a relative of the tomato and requires similar growing conditions — it is really a greenhouse crop but can be grown outdoors in the south if you are lucky with the weather and use barn cloches during the early stages of growth. The plants grow about 3 ft tall under glass or 2 ft outdoors, and the fruits are ripe when plump and green. Leaving them on the plant until they turn red will not improve the flavour.

SEED FACTS

Expected germination time:	14–21 days
Expected yield per plant:	6–10 fruits
Life expectancy of stored seed:	5 years
Approximate time between sowing and picking:	18 weeks
Ease of cultivation:	Difficult outdoors — needs protection plus regular watering and feeding

SOIL FACTS

- For outdoor cultivation, well-drained fertile soil in a sunny, sheltered location is necessary. Add a general-purpose fertilizer before planting.
- In the greenhouse grow in 9 in. pots filled with compost or plant in growing bags — 3 per bag.

SOWING & PLANTING

- Raise seedlings under glass at 60–70°F. Sow 2 seeds in a compost-filled peat pot — remove weaker seedling. Harden off before planting outdoors.

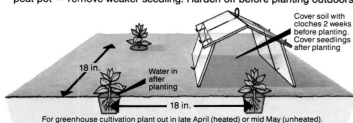

Cover soil with cloches 2 weeks before planting. Cover seedlings after planting

18 in. Water in after planting 18 in.

For greenhouse cultivation plant out in late April (heated) or mid May (unheated).

CALENDAR

	JAN	FEB	MAR	APR	MAY	JUN	JUL	AUG	SEP	OCT	NOV	DEC
Sowing & Planting (Outdoor crop)			▪			✿						
Sowing & Planting (Greenhouse crop)		▪▪	▪	✿	✿							
Picking Time								▬	▬	▬		

1 in. = 2.5 cm, 1 ft = 30 cm, 1 oz = 28 gm, 1 lb = 450 gm

LOOKING AFTER THE CROP

- It is necessary to repot in several stages until the plants are ready to be moved to their permanent site.
- Mist plants regularly to keep down red spider mite and encourage fruit set. Some form of support is necessary — attach stems to stakes or horizontal wires. Pinching out the growing tip is not recommended.
- Water regularly but do not keep the compost in bags or pots sodden. Add a potassium-rich feed with each watering once the fruits have begun to swell.

HARVESTING

- Pick the first fruits when they are green, swollen and glossy. Cut as required — a mature green pepper will turn red in about 3 weeks under glass.

IN THE KITCHEN

Sweet peppers have many uses in the kitchen. Narrow rings provide a crunchy ingredient for summer salads or they can be served as a hot vegetable after frying. Chunks can be grilled as part of a *kebab* or added to casseroles or stews — green and red peppers are essential ingredients for *ratatouille* (French vegetable stew). Or the whole fruit may be used — fill it with minced meat, diced chicken, etc. and then bake.

STORAGE Keep in a sealed rigid container in the refrigerator — capsicums will stay fresh for up to 2 weeks.

COOKING Wash and dry the peppers, then slice off the stalk and small 'lid'. Remove the seeds with a spoon and the inner pith with a small knife. Slice, cube or leave whole depending on the recipe. If it is to be cooked, blanch in boiling water for 5 minutes before stuffing or adding to a casserole.

VARIETIES

REDSKIN: A dwarf variety for growing in pots, bags or beds in a sheltered spot. The pointed fruit turn bright red when mature.

NEW ACE: A good all-purpose pepper — early, high yielding and more tolerant of cool conditions than most varieties.

GYPSY: An F_1 hybrid which is regarded as an improvement on the older variety Canape. 'Early maturing' and 'very heavy crops' according to the catalogues.

CALIFORNIA WONDER: The block-shaped red and green fruits have a mild flavour — a reliable open-pollinated variety.

TROUBLES

RED SPIDER MITE

Sweet peppers are susceptible to red spider mite — keep careful watch for pale mottling and bronzing of the leaves. Tiny mites can be found on the underside. Spray thoroughly with malathion or derris.

APHID

Greenfly can be a nuisance on both the outdoor and greenhouse crop. The answer is to spray with permethrin or heptenophos.

BLOSSOM END ROT

Brown patches appear at the bottom of the fruit — a frequent problem where growing bags are used. Incorrect watering is the usual cause.

For key to symbols — see page 7

CARROT

It seems that the British eat more carrots than any other nation in Europe, but it was the Dutch who first brought this vegetable to our shores during the reign of Elizabeth I. If you want to impress the family or win a prize at the local horticultural show, the secret of growing exceptionally long and straight-sided carrots is to make a deep hole, shaped like a giant ice cream cone, with a crowbar. Fill this hole with potting compost and sow three seeds of St Valery at the top. Thin the seedlings to leave the strongest and spray regularly with a foliar feed. Of course this is no way to grow carrots for the kitchen — these days we want shorter ones which are easier and quicker to grow. Varieties continue to change and so do our ideas about cultivation. The modern recommendation is to grow a carrot bed with the plants close enough to eliminate the need for hoeing. Sow very thinly to reduce or eliminate the need for thinning — a labour-free crop to grow nowadays but the menace of the dreaded carrot fly (see page 42) is always there . . .

SEED FACTS

Mix seed with sand or fine peat to prevent sowing too thickly. Better still, sow pelletted seeds 1 in. apart.

Actual size

Expected germination time:	17 days
Approximate number per ounce:	20,000
Expected yield from a 10 ft row:	8 lb (Early) 10 lb (Maincrop)
Life expectancy of stored seed:	4 years
Approximate time between sowing and lifting:	12 weeks (Early) 16 weeks (Maincrop)
Ease of cultivation:	Not difficult if soil is good and carrot fly keeps away

SOIL FACTS

- Carrots are hard to please. The soil must be deep, fertile and rather sandy if you want to produce fine long specimens. If your soil is rather heavy or stony, grow short-rooted varieties. Where land has been manured during the past year, don't grow carrots at all.
- Pick a sunny spot — dig in autumn, adding peat if necessary but not manure nor compost. Prepare the seed bed 1–2 weeks before sowing — rake a general-purpose fertilizer into the surface.

SEED SOWING

Sow very thinly — Cover with soil — 6 in. — ½ in.

LOOKING AFTER THE CROP

- Thin out the seedlings when they are large enough to handle. The plants should be about 2–3 in. apart. Take care when thinning or the root-ruining carrot fly will be attracted to your garden by the smell of the bruised foliage. Water if the soil is dry and thin in the evening. Firm the soil around the remaining plants and burn or bury the thinnings.
- Pull out or hand hoe any weeds between the seedlings, but once well-established the use of a hoe is not recommended. The dense foliage cover provided by the closely-packed plants should keep down annual weeds — others should be removed by hand.
- Water during periods of drought in order to keep the ground damp — a downpour on dry soil may cause root splitting.

HARVESTING

- Pull up small carrots as required from June onwards. Ease out with a fork if the soil is hard.
- October is the time to lift maincrop carrots for storage. Use a fork to lift the roots and then remove the surface dirt. Damaged roots should be used in the kitchen or thrown away — only sound carrots should be stored. Cut off the leaves to about ½ in. above the crowns and place the roots between layers of sand or dry peat in a stout box. Do not let the carrots touch — store in a dry shed and inspect occasionally so that any rotten roots can be disposed of before infecting their neighbours. The crop will keep until March.

- For a very early crop which will be ready in June, sow a short-rooted variety under cloches or in a cold frame in early March.
- For an early crop which will be ready in July, sow a short-rooted variety in a sheltered spot in late March or April.
- For maincrop carrots sow intermediate- or long-rooted varieties between mid April and early June for lifting in September and October.
- For a tender crop in November and December, sow a short-rooted variety in August and cover with cloches from October.

CALENDAR

	JAN	FEB	MAR	APR	MAY	JUN	JUL	AUG	SEP	OCT	NOV	DEC
Sowing Time												
Lifting Time												

IN THE KITCHEN

Some of the vegetables in this book may be new to you, but everybody knows the carrot. Few vegetables can match its versatility — cut into sticks as snacks, shredded for salads, sliced for stews and casseroles or boiled whole as a hot vegetable. Even so, there are uses which are not commonplace — pickling, stir frying, jam-making, wine-making and even as the basic ingredient of carrot cake — a delicious U.S. dessert. For eating raw, remember to lift carrots when they are still quite small — this is the time of maximum sweetness.

FREEZING Lift carrots for freezing when they are finger-sized. Trim the ends and wash, then blanch for 5 minutes. Cool and rub off skins if necessary. Freeze in polythene bags.

STORAGE Keep as cool as possible. Store them in a polythene bag in the refrigerator — carrots will stay fresh for up to 2 weeks.

COOKING Top and tail the carrots with a knife and remove any damaged or diseased parts. Don't peel unless the carrots are old — small roots should merely be scrubbed with a brush. Cook young carrots whole — larger ones should be sliced diagonally. Boiling is the usual method of cooking, and the common fault is to drown them. Use just enough lightly salted water to cover the carrots and then boil for 10 – 20 minutes, depending on size and age. Drain and serve with a knob of butter and chopped parsley. Steaming takes longer (½ – 1 hour), but retains more of the flavour. Stir frying is perhaps the tastiest method — lightly fry thin slices with chopped onions. Growing carrots at home means you can have supplies fresh from the garden or taken out of store for 9 months of the year, but there is the annoying problem of some of the roots being riddled with maggot holes. If not too badly damaged, use for grating as a salad ingredient or for boiling and then mashing as a hot vegetable.

VARIETIES

SHORT-ROOTED varieties

Golf ball round or finger long, these short-rooted carrots mature quickly. They are the first to be sown, and the early crop is either used immediately or frozen. The favourites are Amsterdam Forcing and Early Nantes, but there are now many others. Small, perhaps, but top of the league for flavour. Sow every 2–3 weeks between early spring and July to provide a steady supply of succulent roots.

AMSTERDAM FORCING: Reputed to be the earliest of all for growing in the open or under cloches — cylindrical with a blunt (stump) end. There is little core and it is an excellent carrot for freezing.

EARLY NANTES 2: The roots are longer and more tapered than Amsterdam Forcing, but it is similar in many ways — early, tender and good for freezing.

EARLY FRENCH FRAME: A round carrot — an excellent choice for shallow soils. Can reach 2 in. across but is best harvested before reaching such a mature stage. The variety Rondo belongs to this group.

EARLY SCARLET HORN: A good carrot of the Nantes type which is recommended for sowing under cloches in early March.

SYTAN: This Nantes-type carrot is claimed to have some carrot fly resistance — the intermediate-rooted Fly Away claims even more.

KUNDULUS: A good carrot for bad soils, say the catalogues. The short cylindrical roots are almost ball-like — a wise choice for the small plot.

Amsterdam Forcing

INTERMEDIATE-ROOTED varieties

These medium-sized carrots are the best all-rounders for the average garden. They are generally sown later than the short varieties, the young roots being pulled for immediate use and the remainder left to mature as maincrop carrots for winter storage.

CHANTENAY RED CORED: The popular choice, which seems to appear on everybody's list of recommended varieties of medium-sized carrots. Thick and stump-rooted, the flesh is deep orange and the skin very smooth. There are many good selections, such as Royal Chantenay.

BERLICUM BERJO: An improvement on the old variety Berlicum — the cylindrical roots are stump-ended and it has a good reputation for keeping well, high yields and attractive colour.

AUTUMN KING: The roots are unusually large for carrots in this group, but they are distinctly stump-rooted with none of the finely-pointed taper of the long-rooted varieties. Autumn King has several virtues — it is extremely hardy and will stay in the soil over winter, and carrot fly find it less attractive than some other varieties. There are several excellent strains, including Vita Longa.

JAMES SCARLET INTERMEDIATE: An old favourite with a good reputation for all-round performance. It is half-long, broad and tapered.

FLAKKEE: Like Autumn King, this Dutch variety has roots which are too long to warrant the label 'intermediate'. But they are blunt-ended and so cannot be classed with the long-rooted varieties.

MOKUM: An F_1 hybrid which produces cylindrical roots up to 9 in. long. It matures very rapidly, and can be sown from March until July.

NANTES TIP TOP: The aristocrat of the Nantes group — a popular choice for showing. The 6 in. roots are uniformly cylindrical and core-free.

LONG-ROOTED varieties

These are the long, tapered giants of the show bench. They are usually grown in specially prepared soil and are not really suitable for general garden use unless your ground is deep, rich and light.

NEW RED INTERMEDIATE: Despite its name, one of the longest of all carrots. It has good keeping qualities.

ST VALERY: This is the one which the exhibitors so often choose. The roots are long, uniform and finely tapered.

New Red Intermediate

1 in. = 2.5 cm, 1 ft = 30 cm, 1 oz = 28 gm, 1 lb = 450 gm

CARROT and PARSNIP TROUBLES

Carrots are not considered easy to grow successfully — if your soil is heavy and sticky then long, straight roots are virtually an impossibility. The answer is to choose a short-rooted variety in such a situation, but this won't help you against carrot fly. In some areas pest attacks reach such proportions that the growing of this vegetable is hardly worthwhile. No variety is resistant, and no single control method can be relied upon to be completely successful. The answer is to use a combination of control measures — see the section below. Parsnips are less susceptible to pests — canker is the major disease and growing a resistant variety is the answer.

	Symptom	Likely Causes
Seedlings	— failed to appear	Sowing too deeply
	— toppled over	Damping off (see page 110)
Leaves	— mottled yellow, later red	9
	— reddish, later yellow	1
	— badly distorted	10
	— collapsed, leaf stalks black	7
	— tunnelled, blistered	Celery fly (see page 49)
	— covered with blackfly	Black bean aphid (see page 20)
Plants	— toppled over, brown affected area	Basal stem rot (see page 56)
Roots in the garden	— split	12
	— forked	8
	— hollowed out	13
	— green-topped	2
	— small	5
	— covered with purple mould	6
	— covered with white mould	7
	— scurfy black patches	4
	— black patches, decay inside	11
	— tunnelled	1 or Wireworm (see page 110)
	— eaten	Cutworm (see page 110) or Millepede (see page 110) or Slugs & Snails (see page 110)
Roots in store	— covered with purple mould	6
	— covered with white mould	7
	— sunken black areas	3
	— soft, evil-smelling	Soft rot (see page 85)

TUNNELLED ROOTS

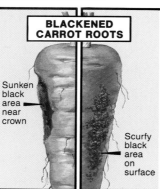

¼ in. creamy maggots

1 CARROT FLY

Tell-tale signs are reddish leaves which wilt in sunny weather. At a later stage the leaves turn yellow. This pest is the major disorder of carrots and also attacks parsnips. Seedlings are killed; mature roots are riddled and liable to rot. Attacks are worst in dry soils.

Treatment: None.

Prevention: Grow carrots well away from tall plants. Sow thinly and destroy all thinnings. Apply pirimiphos-methyl to the soil before sowing or cover the seedlings with fine netting in spring. If carrot fly is known to be a problem in your area, lift early varieties no later than August and delay the sowing of maincrop carrots until June — lift maincrops as soon as they are large enough.

2 GREEN TOP

The tops of carrot roots are sometimes found to be green when the crop is harvested. Unlike potatoes green carrots are not harmful but they are unsightly. Green top is caused by sunlight on the exposed crowns, and it is easily prevented by earthing-up to cover the tops of the roots during the growing season.

3 BLACK ROT

A storage disease of carrots, which renders the root useless. The large black lesions are easily seen in store, but there are no symptoms on the growing crop.

Treatment: Burn diseased roots immediately.

Prevention: Store roots properly. Do not use the land for carrots next year.

BLACKENED CARROT ROOTS

Sunken black area near crown

Scurfy black area on surface

4 CLAYBURN

This carrot disorder is neither common nor serious, and is always associated with pockets of clay in a loamy soil. Harmful salts contained in the clay cause the damage, but the culinary value is not affected.

Treatment: None.

Prevention: Dig out clay from soil used for growing carrots if you are growing for exhibition.

5 SMALL ROOTS

Aphids and virus will stunt growth and reduce yield, but even in the absence of pests and diseases many gardeners produce disappointingly small carrots. Poor soil conditions are usually to blame — you must dig the soil deeply and break up clays by adding well-rotted compost or manure at least one or two seasons before growing carrots. If the plants are slow growing, spray with a foliar feed at regular intervals or water with a liquid feed. Carrots respond well to this in-season feeding.

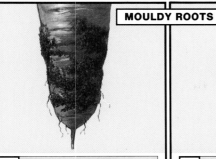

MOULDY ROOTS

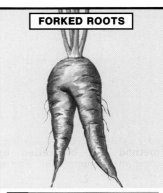

FORKED ROOTS

6 | VIOLET ROOT ROT

An occasional disease of carrots and parsnips. The only above-ground symptom is a slight yellowing of the foliage, but harvested roots show a felt-like mass of purplish threads covering the lower parts.

Treatment: None. Destroy all diseased roots.

Prevention: Never store any roots which are affected by violet root rot or the whole crop will be lost. Do not grow root crops or asparagus on land affected in the previous season.

7 | SCLEROTINIA ROT

The major disease of carrots in store. White woolly mould covers and soon destroys the roots. Occasionally it attacks the growing crop — lower leaf stalks and crown turn black.

Treatment: None. If attacks are seen in the garden, water healthy plants with Cheshunt Compound after removing diseased plants. Remove rotten roots immediately.

Prevention: Keep weeds under control. Store only sound roots in a dry, airy place. Do not grow carrots, parsnips or celery on land affected by sclerotinia rot in the past 2 seasons.

8 | FANGING

Fanging is usually caused by adding manure or compost to the soil shortly before seed sowing. Other causes are growing carrots in stony soil or in heavy ground which has not been properly dug.

Treatment: None.

Prevention: Use land which has been manured for a previous crop. Don't make the bed too firm.

DISCOLOURED LEAVES

DISTORTED LEAVES

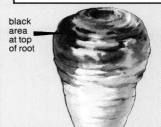

BLACKENED PARSNIP ROOTS

black area at top of root

9 | MOTLEY DWARF VIRUS

Central leaves show a distinct yellow mottling, outer leaves have a reddish tinge. This virus is spread by the carrot-willow aphid. Growth is greatly reduced and the yield is small if the plants are attacked at the seedling stage.

Treatment: None.

Prevention: Keep young carrots free from aphids by spraying with permethrin, heptenophos or pirimicarb.

10 | CARROT-WILLOW APHID

Greenfly attacks can be serious in a warm, dry summer. The leaves are distorted, discoloured and stunted. Plants are weakened, but even more serious is the transmission of motley dwarf virus by this pest.

Treatment: Spray at the first sign of attack with permethrin, heptenophos or pirimicarb.

Prevention: No practical method available.

11 | PARSNIP CANKER

A serious disease of parsnips, which can be caused by several factors — soil acidity, presence of fresh organic matter in the soil, root damage and irregular rainfall. The blackened areas on the roots crack and the parsnips rot.

Treatment: None.

Prevention: Lime soil. Don't sow too early. Do not grow a susceptible variety on the same site next year — choose a resistant variety such as Avonresister or White Gem.

12 | SPLITTING

Much more serious than the fanging of carrots, because these roots will not store. The cause is heavy rain or copious watering after a prolonged dry spell.

Treatment: None. Use split roots immediately.

Prevention: Water regularly in times of drought. Apply a mulch of peat or compost around the crop in dry weather.

SPLIT ROOTS

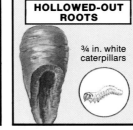

HOLLOWED-OUT ROOTS

¾ in. white caterpillars

13 | SWIFT MOTH

These soil-living caterpillars, which move backwards when disturbed, hollow out the roots of carrots and parsnips.

Treatment: None. Burn affected roots. Destroy caterpillars.

Prevention: Controlled by permethrin, heptenophos or pirimicarb used for carrot fly prevention.

CAULIFLOWER

'Cauliflower,' wrote Mark Twain, 'is nothing but cabbage with a college education.' He was, of course, referring to its more refined flavour, but for the gardener there is an equally important difference — cauliflower is more difficult to grow. It needs rich and deep soil, and during the growing season there must not be any check to growth. Failure to provide these requirements will often result in the production of tiny 'button' heads and a lot of wasted effort. So proper soil preparation, careful planting and regular watering are essential, and so is the choice of suitable varieties. Types are available which will produce heads at almost any time of the year, but avoid the Roscoff varieties which are harvested between December and April — they are only reliable in Devon and Cornwall. Grow mammoths such as Autumn Giant to impress the neighbours or at the other end of the scale plant the summer variety Predominant 6 in. apart to produce mini-cauliflowers for the freezer.

SEED FACTS

Actual size

Expected germination time:	7–12 days
Approximate number per ounce:	8000
Expected yield per plant:	1–2 lb
Life expectancy of stored seed:	4 years
Approximate time between sowing and cutting:	18–24 weeks (Summer and Autumn varieties) 40–50 weeks (Winter varieties)
Ease of cultivation:	Tricky — needs good soil, careful transplanting, regular watering . . . and protection against its enemies

SOIL FACTS

- Cauliflower needs well-consolidated soil, so the basic requirement is to leave several months between digging and planting.
- Pick a reasonably sunny site for the place where the plants will grow to maturity. Avoid a frost pocket for winter varieties. Dig in autumn — work in plenty of well-rotted manure or compost. Lime, if necessary, in winter.
- In spring apply Growmore fertilizer — consider using protective discs (see page 28) if cabbage root fly is known to be a problem. Do not fork over the surface before planting the seedlings — tread down gently, rake lightly and remove surface rubbish.

SOWING & PLANTING

Sow very thinly

Cover with soil

6 in.

½ in.

- Thin the seedlings to prevent them from becoming weak and spindly. They should be about 3 in. apart in the rows.
- The seedlings are ready for transplanting when they have 5 or 6 leaves. Water the rows the day before moving and lift the seedlings carefully with as much soil as possible around the roots. Dip roots in thiophanate-methyl if club root is feared. Plant firmly, setting the seedlings at the same level as in the seed bed. Leave 2 ft between summer and autumn varieties, 2½ ft between winter varieties.

LOOKING AFTER THE CROP

- Hoe regularly and provide some means of protection for the young plants against birds.
- Cauliflowers must never be kept short of water, especially in the early stages, or very small heads will quickly form. Feed occasionally as this crop is a hungry one.
- With summer varieties bend a few leaves over the developing curd to protect it from the sun.
- Protect the winter crop from frost and snow by breaking a few leaves over the curd.

HARVESTING

- Begin cutting some of the cauliflowers while they are still fairly small rather than waiting for them all to mature and produce a glut. You have waited too long once the florets start to separate.
- Cut in the morning when the heads still have dew on them, but if frosty weather wait until midday. If you wish to keep the heads for up to 3 weeks before use, lift the plants, shake the earth off the roots and hang upside down in a cool shed. Mist the curds occasionally.

- **Summer varieties:** In late March or early April transplant seedlings which have been raised under glass from a January sowing to provide a June-July crop. Or sow outdoors in early April and transplant in June for cropping in August–September.
- **Autumn varieties:** Sow outdoors between mid April and mid May and transplant in late June.
- **Winter varieties:** Sow outdoors in May and transplant in late July.

CALENDAR

	JAN	FEB	MAR	APR	MAY	JUN	JUL	AUG	SEP	OCT	NOV	DEC
Sowing Time												
Planting Time												
Cutting Time			WINTER vars.			SUMMER vars.			AUTUMN vars.			

IN THE KITCHEN

There are two popular ways of serving cauliflower. It is either boiled and served with or without a white sauce or it is covered with a cheese sauce after boiling and baked in the oven to provide the old stand-by — cauliflower cheese. It is a pity not to be more adventurous with this fine vegetable — serve the sprigs raw with mayonnaise as the French do or dip them in batter and fry until golden-brown. In this way you can have your cauliflower cold as *crudités* or hot as cauliflower fritters, and you can also find recipes for soups, soufflés and pickles.

FREEZING Divide into sprigs — only use firm, tight heads. Blanch for 3 minutes in water to which lemon juice has been added. Cool and drain — pack carefully and freeze in polythene bags.

STORAGE Keep wrapped in plastic cling film in the refrigerator — cauliflower will stay fresh for up to 1 week.

COOKING Compact heads can be boiled whole but it is more usual to divide them up into sprigs. Leave the small basal leaves attached — cut a cross with a sharp knife at the bottom of each stalk. Most cauliflower is overcooked — it should be slightly crisp, not soggy. Correct cooking calls for adding a little lemon juice to 1 in. of water in a pan and then bringing it to the boil. Remove from the heat and add the sprigs carefully so that the stalks and not the florets are in the water. Replace the lid and boil for about 10 minutes. Drain thoroughly before serving with a white or parsley sauce. Alternatively dress with melted butter and black pepper.

VARIETIES

SUMMER varieties

These cauliflowers mature during the summer months from seed sown in a cold frame in September, in a greenhouse or on the windowsill in January or outdoors in April. They are compact plants — you can choose an early variety, such as Snowball, which will produce heads in June or July, or you can grow a later-maturing type like All the Year Round which will be ready for cutting in August from an outdoor sowing.

ALL THE YEAR ROUND: An old favourite. The curds are large and you can crop all summer and early autumn by sowing early under glass and then outdoors in April or May.

SNOWBALL: The usual choice if you want an early variety. The tight heads are not large — for well-rounded 2 lb cauliflowers of the Snowball type choose the F₁ hybrid Snow Crown.

DOK-ELGON: All the Year Round has had its day, according to many experts. This is the one to grow for kitchen or exhibition if you want a late summer cauliflower.

BAMBI: There are several mini-cauliflowers which can be sown directly in the plot and are later thinned to leave them at 6 in. x 6 in. spacings. Bambi is one — others include Cargill and Predominant.

DOMINANT: A mid-season variety which matures in July. Good for freezing — its heads are large and its constitution is robust.

ALPHA: An early one with a high reputation for resisting premature heading when things go wrong. There are several strains — you may find it listed as Climax, Polaris or Paloma.

Snowball

AUTUMN varieties

These cauliflowers mature during the autumn months and are of two quite different types. There are the large and vigorous varieties such as Autumn Giant and Flora Blanca, and there are the more compact Australian varieties such as Barrier Reef and Canberra.

AUTUMN GIANT: Once Autumn Giant and its various strains dominated this group — now the newer types are taking over. Still worth choosing if you want large heads in early winter. Veitch's Self Protecting is the usual selection but there are others.

FLORA BLANCA: Another name for the old favourite Autumn Glory. Grow this one for the autumn show — giant, pure white heads are ready for cutting in September and October.

CANBERRA: A popular Australian variety which matures in November. The curds are well protected by the broad leaves.

BARRIER REEF: Another Australian variety with the usual characteristics — compact growth and good curd cover by the leaves. It is ready for cutting from late October onwards.

Walcheren Winter

Purple Cape

WINTER varieties

'Winter cauliflower' is the technically incorrect name for the group of varieties listed below. The standard types mature in spring, not winter, and they are really heading broccoli. Although less delicately-flavoured than true cauliflowers the popular varieties of winter cauliflower are easier to grow.

ENGLISH WINTER: This was once the basic hardy variety, producing large heads between March and June. The numerous strains include St George (April), Leamington (April) and Late June (June).

WALCHEREN WINTER: This Dutch variety has taken over from English Winter. It is equally hardy and the heads are of higher quality. There are several strains — Armado April (April), Markanta (May) and Maystar (May) are examples.

ST AGNES: A typical Roscoff variety, maturing as early as December. Sounds attractive — cauliflower for Christmas Dinner, but all the Roscoffs are frost-sensitive. Suitable only for the south west.

VILNA: This addition to the range appears in numerous catalogues — it is fully hardy and the rather loose heads are ready for cutting at the end of May.

PURPLE CAPE: Something different — a hardy winter cauliflower which produces purple heads in March. Cook the young leaves as well as the curd.

TROUBLES

See pages 28–31

CELERIAC

Celeriac or turnip-rooted celery is popular on the Continent but has never found favour in Britain. All the major seed suppliers offer their own variety, but there isn't much difference between them. In each case a knobbly, swollen stem-base is produced, about 4−5 in. across, with a distinct celery flavour. The catalogues will tempt you with its ease compared to the ever-popular celery — no earthing-up, no bolting, little danger from pests or diseases and good storage properties. But it really isn't a vegetable for everyone — you will have to raise your own seedlings as very few garden centres offer them, and you must provide rich, moisture-retentive soil and plenty of water in dry weather.

SEED FACTS

Actual size

Expected germination time:	12−18 days
Expected yield from a 10 ft row:	7 lb
Life expectancy of stored seed:	5 years
Approximate time between sowing and lifting:	30−35 weeks
Ease of cultivation:	Rather difficult — good soil preparation, regular watering and deleafing all necessary

SOIL FACTS

- Fertile, moisture-retentive soil is essential. Pick a reasonably sunny spot and dig in autumn. Incorporate as much manure or compost as you can.
- About a week before planting apply a general-purpose fertilizer.

SOWING & PLANTING

- Raise seedlings under glass in early spring. Plant 2 seeds in a compost-filled peat pot — remove weaker seedling. Harden off before planting outdoors.

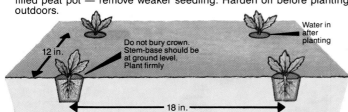

12 in.

Do not bury crown. Stem-base should be at ground level. Plant firmly

Water in after planting

18 in.

LOOKING AFTER THE CROP

- Hoe regularly and feed occasionally — a mulch in early summer will help to conserve moisture.
- Remove side shoots — from midsummer onwards remove the lower leaves so as to expose the crown.
- In late September draw soil around the swollen stem-bases.

HARVESTING

- Aim for maximum size — neither flavour nor texture deteriorate with age. Lifting begins in October — in most areas you can cover the roots with straw or peat and then lift as required until early spring.
- If your soil is heavy and the site exposed, it is better to lift the crop in November. Twist off the tops, cut off the roots and store in boxes filled with damp peat. Keep in a cool shed.

IN THE KITCHEN

If you are fond of celery then you will certainly like celeriac. Grate it coarsely or cut it into strips to add zest to a winter salad — the French mix it with mustard mayonnaise to produce *céleri-rave à la rémoulade*. Use the leaves to garnish salads or add flavour to soups or serve the 'root' hot as a winter vegetable. A versatile vegetable indeed!

FREEZING Cut into cubes and blanch for 3 minutes. Dry and open freeze — then store in polythene bags.

COOKING Celeriac is a difficult vegetable to clean — scrub thoroughly. Slice thickly and peel like a turnip, then cube. Boil for ½ hour in lightly salted water to which lemon juice has been added. Drain and serve with melted butter or a white sauce.

VARIETIES

MARBLE BALL: A well-known variety — medium-sized, globular and strongly flavoured. Stores well over winter.

IRAM: Medium-sized like Marble Ball, but remains white when cooked.

TELLUS: Another variety which remains white after boiling. Quick-growing with a smoother skin than most varieties.

BALDER: Medium-sized roots with a strong celery flavour — reliable and easy to grow.

GIANT PRAGUE: This round turnip-shaped variety appears in more catalogues than any other celeriac.

SNOW WHITE: A 'nutty' flavour, according to the suppliers. Large and white when cooked.

TROUBLES

SLUGS

These pests find young plants attractive — use Slug Pellets if necessary.

CARROT FLY

Not often a serious pest, but if carrot fly has plagued your garden in previous seasons then see control measures on page 42.

CELERY FLY

Attacks are much less frequent than on celery, and all that is usually necessary is to pick off the occasional blistered leaflet. If the problem is more serious, see control measures on page 49.

CALENDAR

	JAN	FEB	MAR	APR	MAY	JUN	JUL	AUG	SEP	OCT	NOV	DEC
Sowing Time			■ ■									
Planting Time					🌱 🌱							
Lifting Time										▓	▓	

CELERY

Newcomers to vegetable growing soon learn that growing traditional celery involves a lot of effort. Trenches must be prepared and the stems must be earthed-up at intervals until only the green leafy tips are showing. This latter process of earthing-up is often called blanching, but that is something of a misnomer. The main purpose is not to whiten the stems — it is to lengthen and reduce the stringiness of the stalks and to improve the flavour. Nowadays we have self-blanching varieties and so both trenching and earthing-up are no longer necessary. These varieties are less crisp and less flavoursome, and cannot be left in the ground once the frosts arrive, but they do make celery growing easier. Easier, but not easy. Humus-rich soil is still necessary and so are regular watering and feeding.

SEED FACTS

Actual size

Expected germination time:	12–18 days
Approximate number per ounce:	70,000
Expected yield from a 10 ft row:	12 lb
Life expectancy of stored seed:	5 years
Approximate time between sowing and lifting (Trench varieties):	40 weeks
Approximate time between sowing and lifting (Self-blanching varieties):	25 weeks
Ease of cultivation:	Difficult — especially the Trench varieties

SOIL FACTS

- All varieties require a sunny site and well-prepared soil. For self-blanching types dig a bed in April — incorporate a generous dressing of manure or compost.
- For trench varieties prepare a 'celery trench' in April as shown — allow to settle until planting time.
- Just before planting rake a general-purpose fertilizer into the surface inch of the bed or trench.

SOWING & PLANTING

- Sow seeds under glass and harden off the seedlings before planting outdoors. Seedlings are ready for transplanting when there are 5 or 6 leaves.

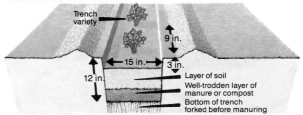

- Self-blanching varieties are planted 9 in. apart in a square block (not in rows) so that the crowded plants will shade each other. Trench varieties are set out at 9 in. intervals — fill the trench with water after planting.

LOOKING AFTER THE CROP

- Celery is a thirsty and hungry crop — water copiously in dry weather and liquid feed with a soluble fertilizer during the summer months.
- Blanch trench varieties in early August when they are about 1 ft high. Remove any side shoots, surround the stalks with newspaper or corrugated cardboard and tie loosely, after which the trench should be filled in with soil. In late August mound moist soil against the stems and in mid September complete earthing-up to give a steep-sided mound with only the foliage tops showing. Do not let soil fall into the celery hearts. In frosty weather cover the tops with straw.
- With self-blanching celery tuck straw between the plants forming the outside line of the bed.

HARVESTING

- Lift self-blanching varieties as required — finish harvesting before the frosts arrive. Remove the outer plant first, using a trowel so that neighbouring plants will not be damaged.
- Lift trenching varieties according to type — white types up to Christmas and the coloured ones in January. There is no need to wait for a sharp frost — there is little scientific evidence that frost improves quality. Start at one end of the earthed-up row — replace soil to protect remaining plants.

- Buy celery seedlings for planting in late May–mid June. Or raise your own by sowing seed under heated glass between mid March and early April — make sure that the seedlings do not receive any check to growth and ensure that the plants are properly hardened off before planting.
- Self-blanching varieties will be ready for lifting between August and October. The trench varieties are grown for winter use from October onwards.

CALENDAR

	JAN	FEB	MAR	APR	MAY	JUN	JUL	AUG	SEP	OCT	NOV	DEC
Sowing Time			▨	▨								
Planting Time					🌱	🌱						
Lifting Time												

1 in. = 2.5 cm, 1 ft = 30 cm, 1 oz = 28 gm, 1 lb = 450 gm

For key to symbols — see page 7

IN THE KITCHEN

For most people celery is a vegetable to be eaten raw rather than cooked. Sticks served whole for eating with cheese or chopped for inclusion in green salads, or diced and mixed with apple, shrimps and mayonnaise as an *hors d'oeuvre*. Celery sticks filled with cream cheese or pâté are a party favourite. The proper preparation of celery for eating raw shows the versatility of this vegetable — cut off the roots and remove the outer stalks for cooking. Trim off the leaves and use for flavouring soup or as a garnish. Now separate the sticks and scrub thoroughly — do not leave them standing upright for hours in water before eating or they will lose their crispness. For celery curls, immerse thin strips in ice-cold water for 2 hours.

FREEZING Cut scrubbed sticks into 1 in. lengths and blanch for 3 minutes — cool and drain. Pack into polythene bags and freeze. Frozen celery is no use in salads as the crispness is lost, but it is perfectly satisfactory for cooked dishes.

STORAGE Keep in a polythene bag in the refrigerator — celery will stay fresh for up to 3 days.

COOKING There are many ways of cooking celery, but boiling is not one of them. Outer stalks should be cut into sections or slices and used in stews, soups or stir fried. The leaves can be chopped and added to meat dishes as a substitute for parsley or you can deep fry them as a crisp accompaniment for fish. The best way to cook celery hearts is to braise them in the Continental way. Simmer in boiling water for 10 minutes and then braise for about 45 minutes over low heat, the drained celery hearts being arranged over a bed of carrots and onions in meat or chicken stock in an ovenproof dish. Thicken the liquid and continue to braise for a few more minutes.

VARIETIES

White   *Pink*   *Red*

TRENCH varieties

These varieties are not easy to grow, as trenching and subsequent earthing-up are time-consuming jobs. Choose from this group if you are an exhibitor or if you have rich, deep soil and like a challenge. Otherwise grow self-blanching celery. The white trench varieties have the best flavour but are the least hardy. Grow a pink or red celery if you want a New Year crop.

GIANT WHITE: The traditional white-stalked celery, tall and crisp and full of flavour, but demands good growing conditions. Various strains are sold by seed suppliers — you may find Solid White, Hopkin's Fenlander or Brydon Prize White in the catalogue. Prizetaker is a popular choice for the show bench.

DWARF WHITE: A short-growing variety which needs less careful blanching than Giant White.

GIANT PINK: A hardy variety for use in January or February. The crisp stalks form a solid heart and the pale pink sticks blanch easily. It may be listed as Unrivalled Pink — the strain Clayworth Prize Pink has a good reputation.

GIANT RED: Hardy and strong growing — the outer stalks are purplish-green, turning shell pink when blanched.

WHITE PASCAL: A large pure white variety with firm hearts for cutting from late autumn to December, but you will have to search for a supplier.

Giant White

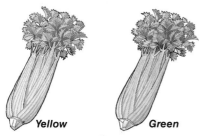

Yellow   *Green*

SELF-BLANCHING varieties

These varieties have taken some of the hard work out of celery growing. They require neither trenching nor earthing-up, and they mature before the end of summer. They are milder-flavoured and less stringy than trench varieties, and they are not winter hardy.

GOLDEN SELF-BLANCHING: The basic yellow variety — low-growing and early maturing with a fair but not outstanding flavour. Ready for cropping, like the other yellows, from August.

LATHOM SELF-BLANCHING: A better choice than Golden Self-Blanching if you want a yellow celery. It is less likely to bolt and the flavour is better. The hearts are tender and stringless, but all self-blanching varieties should be eaten on the day of harvesting whenever possible.

CELEBRITY: A new variety, claimed to be an advance on Lathom Self-Blanching. All the good properties are there, but the sticks are longer.

AMERICAN GREEN: The basic green variety — solid hearts, pale green stalks, crisp but stringless. Ready for cropping from October. The popular strain is Greensnap — there are others, such as Utah.

American Green

CELERY TROUBLES

Celery is not an easy crop to grow successfully, and its culture is made even more difficult by four serious problems which can plague this crop. Three of these problems are easily noticed whenever they occur — celery fly, celery leaf spot and slugs. The fourth problem is shortage of water, and here the effects are less obvious but no less devastating. Prolonged dryness at the roots will invariably lead to the production of plants with inedible hearts.

	Symptom	Likely Causes
Seedlings	— toppled over	**Damping off** (see page 110) or **Basal stem rot** (see page 56)
Leaves	— tunnelled, blistered	1
	— covered with brown spots	2
	— yellow, withered	**Boron deficiency** (see page 109)
	— yellow, not withered	**Cucumber mosaic virus** (see page 54)
Stalks	— tough, bitter	1
	— pithy, not crisp	**Dry soil**
	— split vertically	5
	— split horizontally	**Boron deficiency** (see page 109)
	— mouldy at base	**Sclerotinia rot** (see page 43)
	— eaten above ground level	6
	— eaten at ground level	**Cutworm** (see page 110)
Hearts	— missing, flower stalk only	3
	— rotten	4
Roots	— eaten	**Carrot fly** (see page 42)

BLISTERED LEAVES

1 CELERY FLY (Leaf Miner)

White ¼ in. maggots tunnel within the leaves causing blisters to develop. Attacks occur from May onwards, and the effects are most serious on young plants. Whole leaves may shrivel and die, and the stalks are stunted and bitter.

Treatment: Pinch out and destroy affected leaflets. Spray with malathion at the first sign of attack.

Prevention: Never plant seedlings with blistered leaves.

3 BOLTING

Bolting is a serious problem, which unfortunately is common in dry seasons. At lifting time the heart is found to contain just one inedible flower stalk instead of the expected cluster of edible stalks. There are several possible causes, the most likely being dry soil conditions around the roots. Never let plants go thirsty during drought. Bolting can also be caused by planting out seedlings which have grown too large or have been checked by cold or dryness.

6 SLUGS & SNAILS

Slugs will feed on many types of vegetables in the garden when the conditions are damp, but celery seems to have a special attraction. The stalks may be attacked at any stage of growth — slugs are often most troublesome after earthing-up. Reduce the danger by scattering Slug Pellets thinly around the plants and by removing weeds and surface rubbish.

2 CELERY LEAF SPOT (Blight)

Brown spots appear first on the outer leaflets and then spread to all of the foliage. In a wet season the whole plant may be destroyed if the disease is not checked.

Treatment: Spray with carbendazim at the first sign of disease. Repeat as necessary.

Prevention: Buy seed described as 'thiram treated' or 'hot water treated'. Never plant seedlings with spotted leaves.

SPOTTED LEAVES

ROTTEN HEARTS

4 CELERY HEART ROT

This disorder is noticed at lifting time. On cutting the plant open, the heart is found to be a slimy brown mass. The bacteria which cause the rot enter the stalks through wounds caused by slugs, frost or careless cultivation.

Treatment: None. Destroy diseased plants.

Prevention: Grow celery on well-drained land. Keep slugs under control and take care when earthing-up. Bacteria build up in the soil after an attack so do not grow celery on land affected in the previous season.

SPLIT STALKS

5 SPLITTING

Celery stalks are sometimes spoilt by vertical splitting. This disorder is usually caused by dry soil around the roots, but it can be due to an excess of nitrogen in the soil.

Treatment: None.

Prevention: Water thoroughly in dry weather, especially during the early stages of growth. Feed the plants regularly with a liquid fertilizer which contains more potash than nitrogen.

CHICORY

All the chicories can be used to make a crisp winter salad, but they are not to everyone's taste. The admirers find them refreshing and tart — the haters find them bitter. There are two basic types to choose from. The forcing chicories are the more popular, producing plump leafy heads ('chicons') from roots kept in the dark during the winter months. The usual colour is white, but you can force a red variety to produce the white and maroon leaves served as *radicchio* in Continental salads. The other chicories are the non-forcing ones which do not require blanching — they produce large lettuce-like heads which are ready for harvesting in autumn.

SEED FACTS

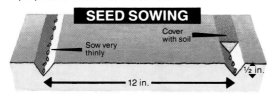

Actual size

Expected germination time:	7–14 days
Approximate number per ounce:	20,000
Expected yield from a 10 ft row:	6 lb
Life expectancy of stored seed:	5 years
Approximate time between sowing and cutting:	18–30 weeks
Ease of cultivation:	Non-forcing varieties are easy — Forcing varieties call for more work

SOIL FACTS

- Chicory is not fussy about soil type, but it does need a sunny site.
- Dig the soil in autumn or winter and incorporate compost if the soil is short of humus. Prepare the seed bed a few days before sowing — rake a general-purpose fertilizer into the surface.

SEED SOWING

Sow very thinly

Cover with soil

12 in.

½ in.

LOOKING AFTER THE CROP

- Hoe to keep down weeds — water when the weather is dry. Thin the seedlings to 6 in. (forcing varieties) or 12 in. (non-forcing varieties) apart.
- Forcing varieties: Lift parsnip-like roots in November. Discard ones which are fanged or less than 1 in. across at the crown. Cut back leaves to 1 in. above the crown — cut back roots to a length of 6 in. Pack them horizontally in a box of sand in a cool shed — keep until required. Force a few at a time between November and March. Plant 5 in a 9 in. pot — surround each root with moist peat or compost, leaving the crown exposed. Cover the pot with an empty larger one — block up drainage holes to prevent the entry of light. Keep at 50–60°F to promote chicon formation.

HARVESTING

- Forcing varieties: The chicons are ready when they are about 6 in. high — this will take 3–4 weeks from the start of forcing. Cut just above the level of the crown. Water the compost and replace the cover — smaller, secondary chicons will then be produced.
- Non-forcing varieties: Cut heads in late autumn — use immediately or store in a cool shed for later use. Provide some frost protection over plants if they are not to be cut until the winter.

IN THE KITCHEN

Crisp and raw — that's the best way to serve chicory. Shop-bought chicons are bitter because they have been exposed to daylight — home-grown ones kept in the dark until preparation time are much less bitter. A few tips — discard outer layer of leaves, do not leave chicory soaking in water and add tomatoes or a sweet dressing to the salad if you are not a chicory fan.

STORAGE Keep in a black polythene bag in the refrigerator. Non-forcing chicory will stay fresh for up to 1 month, but chicons should not be stored for longer than necessary.

COOKING Add chicons to boiling, salted water — allow to simmer for 10–15 minutes. Drain and serve with cheese sauce or braise for 20 minutes in butter, nutmeg, pepper and lemon juice.

VARIETIES

WITLOOF: The traditional forcing variety, sometimes called Belgian or Brussels Chicory. Good and reliable, but really needs forcing under an 8 in. peat or soil layer to keep chicons tightly folded.

NORMATO: A modern forcing variety which doesn't need a soil layer when forcing.

SUGAR LOAF: Pain de Sucre in some catalogues — the traditional non-forcing variety.

CRYSTAL HEAD: One of the modern non-forcing varieties — others include Snowflake and Winter Fare. These new ones are hardier than Sugar Loaf.

PALLA ROSSA: Treat as a forcing or non-forcing variety. Red-leaved, non-hardy.

CALENDAR

		JAN	FEB	MAR	APR	MAY	JUN	JUL	AUG	SEP	OCT	NOV	DEC
Sowing Time	FORCING vars.					▓	▓						
	NON-FORCING vars.				▓	▓	▓	▓					
Cutting Time	FORCING vars.	▓	▓	▓								▓	▓
	NON-FORCING vars.									▓	▓	▓	

TROUBLES

SOIL PESTS

Cutworms and swift moth caterpillars can be troublesome, so consider using a nematode-based insecticide before sowing seed if soil pests have been a problem in the past. Slugs will ruin leaves in mild, damp weather — apply Slug Pellets if damage is seen.

CUCUMBER, GREENHOUSE

A well-grown specimen of a greenhouse ('frame') cucumber, straight and cylindrical, smooth-skinned and glistening, may reach 18 in. or more in length. A thing of beauty, especially on the show bench, but also a thing which is difficult to grow. Cucumbers under glass need warmth and care plus regular watering and feeding, tying and stopping, protecting from pests and diseases, and so on. Ideally the humidity should be higher than that provided for tomatoes, but many people grow the two vegetables together under glass quite successfully. The temptation these days is to grow cucumbers outdoors as there is so much less work involved and varieties have improved. But if you want to pick fruits in May or June for early summer salads then growing under glass is the only answer.

SEED FACTS

Expected germination time:	3 – 5 days
Expected yield per plant:	25 cucumbers
Life expectancy of stored seed:	6 years
Approximate time between sowing and cutting:	12 weeks
Ease of cultivation:	Difficult — growing cucumbers under glass is time-consuming and costly

Actual size

SOIL FACTS

● Usually only a few plants are grown — do not plant in border soil. Use J.I. Compost No. 3 in 10 in. pots or buy growing bags.

SOWING & PLANTING

● Raise seedlings under glass — warmth (70–80°F) is essential. Place a single seed edgeways ½ in. deep in seed compost in a 3 in. peat pot. Sowing should take place in late February or early March for planting in a heated greenhouse or late April for an unheated greenhouse or frame. Keep compost moist — feed if necessary.

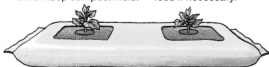

● Plant out in late March (heated greenhouse) or late May (unheated greenhouse) — 1 per pot, 2 per growing bag. Water in after planting.

CALENDAR

	JAN	FEB	MAR	APR	MAY	JUN	JUL	AUG	SEP	OCT	NOV	DEC
Sowing & Planting Time		■■	🌱🌱	🌱■	🌱							
Cutting Time												

LOOKING AFTER THE CROP

● The temperature after germination must be maintained at a minimum of 60°F (Ordinary varieties) or 70°F (All-Female varieties).

● Keep the compost thoroughly moist but never waterlogged — little and often is the rule. Keep the air as moist and well ventilated as the other plants in the house will allow. Spray the floor (not the plants) to maintain high humidity.

● Train the stem up a vertical wire or cane. Pinch out the growing point when this leader reaches the roof. The tip of each side shoot is pinched out at 2 leaves beyond a female flower. Female flowers have a miniature cucumber behind them — male flowers have just a thin stalk. Pinch out tips of flowerless side shoots when 2 ft long.

● Remove all male flowers from Ordinary varieties — fertilized fruit is bitter.

● Feed every 2 weeks with a tomato fertilizer once the first fruits have started to swell.

HARVESTING

● Cut (do not pull) when the fruit has reached a reasonable size and the sides are parallel. Cropping will cease if you allow cucumbers to mature and turn yellow on the plant.

VARIETIES

ORDINARY varieties

These are the cucumbers for the exhibitor. They are the traditional cucumbers of the summer salad — long, straight, smooth and dark green.

TELEGRAPH: An old variety, named when the telegraph was a new invention. Despite its age, Telegraph is still popular.

BUTCHER'S DISEASE RESISTING: Another old favourite which is not as smooth-skinned as Telegraph but is reputed to be a heavier cropper.

CONQUEROR: An excellent choice for a cold greenhouse or frame — the fruits are long, smooth and high in flavour.

ALL-FEMALE varieties

These modern F₁ hybrids have several advantages. As they bear only female flowers the tiresome job of removing male flowers is unnecessary. They are also much more resistant to disease and rather more prolific. There are two drawbacks — the fruits tend to be shorter than the Ordinary varieties and a higher temperature is required. If your house is unheated, choose an Ordinary variety.

PEPINEX: The first of the females, formerly known as Femina. A good example of the group — high yields, lack of bitterness and no gummosis.

TOPSY: Tops for flavour, according to the experts. Yields, however, are not very good and the seeds are not widely available.

PETITA: The fruits are only about 8 in. long but a large number are borne. Stands less than ideal conditions better than most All-Females, but often produces some male flowers.

BIRGIT: A widely-used commercial variety which has become popular in recent years. Crops are heavy and the quality is very good.

EUPHYA: A variety noted for its high resistance to powdery mildew. Another one is Tyria.

FEMSPOT: Early with good disease resistance, but it needs a minimum temperature of 60°F.

TROUBLES

See pages 54–56

CUCUMBER, OUTDOOR

Until fairly recently the outdoor or ridge cucumber was the poor country cousin of the much more elegant greenhouse cucumber with its long and straight-sided fruits. The outdoor types were short and dumpy fruits covered with bumps and warts, but things have changed. There are now outdoor varieties which bear smooth-skinned cucumbers nearly 1 ft long, varieties which are unrivalled for flavour and juiciness, varieties from which the indigestibility has been eradicated. The outdoor cucumber has come of age and there is no longer any need to grow this vegetable under glass in order to obtain reasonably smooth and reasonably long fruits. The name 'ridge cucumber' comes from the old habit of growing them on raised beds or ridges — these days they are usually grown on the flat. The plants are climbers like their greenhouse cousins — outdoors the vines are left to scramble along the ground or are supported by netting, posts, poles, etc.

SEED FACTS

Soak seeds overnight before sowing.

Actual size

Expected germination time:	6 – 9 days
Expected yield per plant:	10 cucumbers
Life expectancy of stored seed:	6 years
Approximate time between sowing and cutting:	12 – 14 weeks
Ease of cultivation:	Not easy — soil has to be prepared and regular watering and feeding are needed

SOIL FACTS

- A sunny spot protected from strong winds is essential — outdoor cucumbers are neither hardy nor long-suffering.
- The soil must be well drained and rich in humus. Most households will need only a few plants, so prepare planting pockets as shown above about 2 weeks before seed sowing or planting.

SOWING & PLANTING

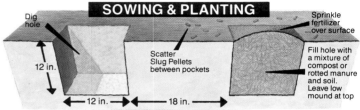

Dig hole

Scatter Slug Pellets between pockets

Sprinkle fertilizer over surface

Fill hole with a mixture of compost or rotted manure and soil. Leave low mound at top

12 in.

12 in. 18 in.

- Sow 3 seeds 1 in. deep and a few inches apart at the centre of each pocket. Cover with a large jar or cloche to hasten germination. When the first true leaves have appeared thin out to leave the strongest seedling.
- Alternatively you can raise the seedlings indoors, but this method is less satisfactory. Place a single seed edgeways ½ in. deep in seed compost in a 3 in. pot. Keep at 70–80°F until germinated — gradually harden off seedlings before planting in pockets outdoors. Disturb the roots as little as possible when planting out — water in thoroughly.

LOOKING AFTER THE CROP

- Pinch out the growing tip when the plants have developed 6 or 7 leaves. Side shoots will then develop, and these can be left to trail over the ground or be trained up stout netting. Any shoots not bearing flowers should be pinched out at the 7th leaf.
- Keep the soil moist. Water *around* the plants, not over them. Mist lightly in dry weather.
- Place black polythene over the soil in summer before fruit formation. This will raise soil temperature, conserve moisture, keep down weeds and protect the fruit from rot.
- Once the first fruits have started to swell, feed with liquid tomato fertilizer.
- Fertilization is essential — never remove the male flowers.

HARVESTING

- Don't try to grow record-breaking fruits. They should be cut before they reach maximum size, as this will encourage further fruiting. Most types will be 6–8 in. long, gherkins 4 in. long and apple cucumbers the size of a duck's egg.
- Use a sharp knife — don't tug the fruits from the stem. The harvesting period is quite short, as the plants will be killed by the first frosts. Despite this, good soil, proper care and continuous picking will result in the production of many fruit until the end of September.

- Sow outdoors in late May or early June. In the Midlands and northern areas cover the seedlings with cloches if you can for a few weeks. Cropping should start in early August.
- For an earlier crop sow seeds under glass in late April. Plant out the seedlings in early June when the danger of frost has passed.

CALENDAR

	JAN	FEB	MAR	APR	MAY	JUN	JUL	AUG	SEP	OCT	NOV	DEC
Sowing Time (outdoors)					▉							
Sowing Time (indoors)				🪴	🌱							
Cutting Time								▉	▉			

IN THE KITCHEN

Cucumber is generally served raw so that its crisp, refreshing flavour can be enjoyed to the full. Thin slices (there is no need to peel them) are a basic ingredient of the green and mixed salad, and every Greek restaurant offers the cucumber-enriched yoghurt dish known as *sadziki*. Cucumber sandwiches evoke memories of pre-war summers — the expression 'cool as a cucumber' was in everyday use more than a century ago. Hollowed-out cucumber chunks filled with cream cheese can be served as a party snack and carrot juice, lemon juice and cucumber mixed in a blender makes an excellent summer drink.

FREEZING Not a good idea for cucumbers as the crispness is lost.

STORAGE Keep wrapped in plastic cling film in the refrigerator — cucumbers will stay fresh for up to 1 week.

COOKING Cucumber is not just a salad vegetable — cut firm fruits into slices, dip in egg and breadcrumbs and fry like courgettes. Or you can treat them like miniature marrows and stuff them — boil hollowed-out halves for 5 minutes and then fill with chopped meat, onions, breadcrumbs, etc. Bake until brown.

PICKLING Pickled gherkins are a delicious accompaniment to meat dishes, from the lordly roast to the humble hamburger. Wash the fruits and rub with a cloth to dry and remove any prickles. Place in a dish and cover with salt for 24 hours. Rinse thoroughly and pack into glass jars. Cover the gherkins with warm malt vinegar and add ½ teaspoonful of dill seed. Cover each jar with an air-tight lid — the pickles will be ready in about 2 months.

VARIETIES

STANDARD RIDGE varieties

The traditional varieties are thick and medium-sized, with a rough knobbly surface. In recent years a number of F₁ hybrids have appeared offering a better shape, improved hardiness, less disease and extra length.

MARKETMORE: An improved form of King of the Ridge. Dark green with straight fruits up to 8 in. long — good disease resistance.

BUSH CROP: A compact F₁ variety for beds or containers — resistant to virus.

BURPEE HYBRID: Vigorous and prolific — an excellent choice. The 9 in. cucumbers have a smooth, dark green skin and the plant is noted for its reliability.

MARION: Look for this F₁ hybrid if virus has been a problem in the past.

LONG GREEN RIDGE: An improved form of the old favourite Bedfordshire Prize — a heavy cropping variety.

BUSH CHAMPION: You are more likely to find this F₁ hybrid in the catalogues than the similar Bush Crop. It does well in growing bags, matures quickly and is virus resistant.

Burpee Hybrid

ALL-FEMALE varieties

An interesting development — these cucumbers do not require fertilization and so the mass of seeds which characterise outdoor cucumbers is not present.

PASKA: An F₁ hybrid with glossy dark green fruit which grow to 10 in. long. Resistant to powdery mildew.

JAZZER: The fruits are seedless and the plants have good disease resistance. The cucumbers are up to 9 in. long.

JAPANESE varieties

Included here are the longest and smoothest-skinned of all outdoor cucumbers. The long-fruited varieties should be trained up a stout frame of netting or poles.

YAMATO: Smooth-skinned thin fruits which grow about 1 ft long.

KYOTO: Another variety which produces long, straight and smooth cucumbers to rival the ones on the supermarket shelf.

BURPLESS TASTY GREEN: This is the one to pick, according to most experts. The fruits are not giants like most other Japanese varieties — cut them when they are about 9 in. long and enjoy the crisp, juicy flesh from which both bitterness and indigestibility have been eradicated.

TOKYO SLICER: Shorter than Yamato and Kyoto, but what this smooth and dark-skinned cucumber lacks in length it makes up for in productivity.

GHERKIN varieties

These varieties produce small, warty fruits which are used for pickling.

VENLO PICKLING: The most widely recommended gherkin but not necessarily the best. Each seed house seems to have its own favourite variety and some of these, such as Bestal, Hokus and Conda, are claimed to be earlier and more prolific than Venlo Pickling.

APPLE varieties

This group is extremely unusual — small, round and yellow. The flavour and juiciness are outstanding.

CRYSTAL APPLE: The only variety you are likely to find listed — prolific and easy to grow.

Burpless Tasty Green

1 in. = 2.5 cm, 1 ft = 30 cm, 1 oz = 28 gm, 1 lb = 450 gm

CUCURBIT TROUBLES
CUCUMBER · MARROW · COURGETTE · SQUASH · PUMPKIN

Greenhouse cucumbers are a delicate crop, and a host of bacterial and fungal infections can attack them. Most of these troubles arise through incorrect soil preparation or careless management of the growing plants, so study page 51 if you are a beginner. Outdoor cucumbers and marrows are much simpler to grow and are generally trouble-free, although slugs, grey mould, powdery mildew and cucumber mosaic virus can cause serious losses.

	Symptom	Likely Causes
Seedlings	— eaten	10 or **Woodlice** (see page 110) or **Flea beetle** (see page 30)
	— toppled over	**Damping off** (see page 110)
Stems	— gnawed at base	**Millepede** (see page 110)
	— brown shrivelled patches	18
	— mouldy patches	6 or 16 or 22
	— soft brown rot at base	19
Leaves	— holed	10 or **Woodlice** (see page 110)
	— wilted	1 or 4 or 5 or 18 or 19 or 20
	— yellow, moving up plant	20
	— mottled yellow and green	1
	— covered with silky webbing	21
	— covered with spots	16 or 17
	— covered with mould	6 or 22
	— infested with greenfly	**Aphid** (see page 110)
	— tiny moths, sticky surface	**Greenhouse whitefly** (see page 103)
	— papery patches	23
	— brown patches, yellow halo	18
Roots	— blackened, rotten	5
	— covered with galls	4
Fruit	— no flowers	**Lack of humidity**
	— no fruit	2
	— covered with mould	6 or 12
	— sunken spots	7 or 9
	— tip rotten, oozing gum	13
	— eaten	10 or 11
	— young fruits withered	14
	— bitter	15
	— poor yield	3
	— misshapen, warty	8

MOTTLED LEAVES

1 CUCUMBER MOSAIC VIRUS

Cucumber mosaic virus is a common and extremely serious disease. Marrows are even more susceptible than cucumbers. The leaves are mottled with yellow and dark green patches. The leaf surface becomes puckered and distorted. Plants are severely stunted and may collapse in a bad attack.

Treatment: None. Destroy all infected plant material; wash hands and tools thoroughly before touching other plants.

Prevention: This disease is spread by greenfly, so spray immediately with permethrin if these pests are seen.

2 NO FRUIT

A common complaint of marrows and courgettes is the failure of fruit to set. The usual cause is poor pollination and it is wise to give nature a helping hand. This calls for fertilizing 2 or 3 female flowers (tiny marrow behind petals) by dusting a male flower (thin stalk behind petals) into the mouth of each one. This job should be done in the morning, preferably on a dry day. Make sure the soil is kept moist.

3 POOR YIELD

Greenhouse cucumbers sometimes lose their vigour shortly after the first fruits have been picked. To keep the plants cropping it is necessary to follow a few simple rules. Remove the first fruits when they are quite small. Encourage root activity by adding a mulch around the stems. Feed every 2 weeks with a tomato fertilizer. Cut the fruits when they have reached a reasonable size; if the fruits mature then flower production will cease.

4 EELWORM

Both indoor and outdoor crops may be attacked by root knot eelworm. Gall-like growths develop on the roots. Leaves are discoloured.

Treatment: None. Lift and destroy badly wilted plants.

Prevention: Do not grow cucumbers in infested soil for at least 6 years.

ROOT TROUBLES

5 ROOT ROT

Several fungal diseases can affect the root system; black root rot is the worst. The tap root turns black and the plant wilts.

Treatment: None. Lift and destroy collapsed plants.

Prevention: Grow plants in compost. Avoid cold growing conditions under glass and do not overwater.

FRUIT TROUBLES

6 GREY MOULD (Botrytis)

A grey furry mould appears on rotting fruit. Botrytis can cause serious losses outdoors in a wet season and under glass if the humidity is high. Stems are frequently infected, the point of entry being a damaged or dead area.

Treatment: Remove and burn infected fruit and leaves. Spray with carbendazim at the first signs of disease.

Prevention: Avoid overwatering. Spray plants with carbendazim if grey mould is a regular problem.

7 GUMMOSIS

A serious disease of greenhouse cucumbers grown under wet and cool conditions. Infected fruits develop sunken spots through which oozes an amber-like gum. A dark mould develops on the surface of this gum.

Treatment: Destroy all diseased fruit. Raise the temperature and reduce the humidity.

Prevention: Keep the greenhouse or frame warm and ensure adequate ventilation.

8 CUCUMBER MOSAIC VIRUS

Misshapen small fruits bearing distinctive dark green warts. The surface is either white or yellow with patches or spots of green. The severity of the symptoms increases with the temperature of the greenhouse.

Treatment: None. Healthy plants should not be handled after infected fruit have been cut. However, there is no health risk if virus-affected cucumbers or marrows are eaten.

Prevention: See page 54.

9 ANTHRACNOSE

Pale green sunken spots and patches appear near the blossom end of the fruits. The affected areas turn pink as mould develops over the surface, and eventually they become black and powdery. As the disease spreads the affected fruits turn yellow and die.

Treatment: None. Destroy infected fruit and dust plants weekly with sulphur.

Prevention: Grow cucumbers in sterilised soil or compost. Make sure that the greenhouse is adequately ventilated.

10 SLUGS & SNAILS

As marrows increase in size they become susceptible to attack by slugs and snails. The outer layers are scraped away and the soft flesh is then eaten.

Treatment: Scatter methiocarb or Slug Pellets around the plants at the first signs of attack.

Prevention: Keep area free from rubbish. Place polythene or a tile beneath each growing fruit.

11 MICE

Mice occasionally gnaw the flesh of ripening pumpkins, marrows and squashes, but they are a more serious pest at a much earlier stage — they find the seeds irresistible.

Treatment: None.

Prevention: There is no point in taking precautionary measures unless you have had damage in the past. Cover the sown area with spiny twigs or put down a bait such as Racumin.

12 SCLEROTINIA ROT

Dark rotten areas on greenhouse cucumbers develop white cottony mould. In this mould large black cyst-like bodies are formed.

Treatment: None. Pick and destroy infected fruit immediately.

Prevention: Avoid splashing the fruit during watering and prevent them from coming into contact with soil.

13 BLACK ROT

Rotting of the ends of cucumbers, and the oozing of gum in the shrivelled diseased area, indicates attack by the fungus which causes stem rot (page 56).

Treatment: None. Pick and destroy infected fruit immediately. Stop spraying the floor temporarily.

Prevention: Grow cucumbers in sterilized soil or compost.

14 WITHERING OF YOUNG FRUIT

Cucumbers and marrows stop growing when they are only a few inches long and withering spreads back from the tip. Unfortunately there are many possible causes, such as draughts, heavy pruning and the use of fresh farmyard manure. The most likely reason is faulty root action due to poor drainage, overwatering or poor soil preparation. The secret is to maintain steady growth by careful watering. If withering of young fruit does take place, remove the damaged fruit and spray with a foliar feed. For the next week withhold water and ventilate the greenhouse, but keep the floor damp as usual.

15 BITTERNESS

If the fruit is normal in appearance then one of the growing conditions is at fault. A sudden drop in temperature or soil moisture and a sudden increase in sunshine or pruning are all common causes. The second type of bitterness is associated with misshapen club-like fruits grown under glass. Here the cause is pollination; remember that male flowers must be removed. This tedious job can be avoided by growing an All-Female variety such as Pepinex. Bitter cucumbers are generally unusable, but you can try the old practice of cutting the fruit a couple of inches from the blossom end and rubbing the cut surfaces together.

CUCURBIT TROUBLES continued

SPOTS ON LEAVES

SHRIVELLED BLOTCHES

16 ANTHRACNOSE (Leaf Spot)

Small pale spots rapidly enlarge and turn brown. Each spot has a yellowish margin. In a bad attack the spots fuse and the leaf withers. Large areas of pink mould develop on the stems and leaf stalks — these areas later turn black.

Treatment: Remove and burn spotted leaves. Dust weekly with sulphur. Lift and burn badly diseased plants.

Prevention: Grow cucumbers in sterilised soil or compost. Make sure the greenhouse is adequately ventilated.

17 BLOTCH

Less common than anthracnose, and the spots are usually smaller and paler. Leaves decay rapidly in a severe attack. Unlike anthracnose, the disease does not affect the stems, and pink mould does not develop.

Treatment: Remove and burn spotted leaves. Dust weekly with sulphur. Lift and burn badly diseased plants.

Prevention: Grow cucumbers in sterilised soil or compost — choose an All-Female variety.

18 STEM ROT

Leaf blotches have a distinct yellow halo. Affected area turns brown and shrivelled. Stems are attacked (gummy stem blight) and may be killed. Fruit are also affected (black rot, see page 55).

Treatment: Remove and burn all diseased plant material. Stop damping down temporarily.

Prevention: Grow cucumbers in sterilised soil or compost.

COLLAPSED STEMS

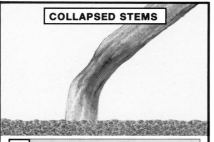

YELLOWING LEAVES

SILKY WEBBING

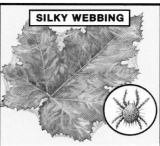

19 BASAL STEM ROT

This bacterial disease has several common names, including soft rot, cucumber foot rot and canker. The brown slimy rot attacks the base of the stems of greenhouse crops. The leaves wilt and the plant may collapse.

Treatment: If the plant is not too badly damaged dust sulphur over the brown area and then apply a moist peat mulch around the stem to cover the diseased zone. Lift and destroy affected plants if attack is severe.

Prevention: Avoid overwatering and keep water away from the base of the stem.

20 VERTICILLIUM WILT

Lower leaves turn yellow and the discoloration moves upwards. Finally all leaves become dry and wilted. Tell-tale signs are brown streaks inside the stem tissue (see page 103). Young plants in cold, wet conditions, are most susceptible.

Treatment: Keep air moist and warm. Shade the greenhouse and do not overwater.

Prevention: Grow cucumbers in sterilised soil or compost.

21 RED SPIDER MITE

Fine silky webbing occurs over the leaves and stems. The foliage appears speckled and bleached, and the tiny mites can be found on the underside. Growth is retarded and the shoots are thin and weak. The mites are green in summer and red in winter.

Treatment: Spray with derris or malathion at the first signs of attack.

Prevention: Maintain a damp atmosphere in the greenhouse.

22 POWDERY MILDEW

Leaves and stems are covered with white powdery patches. This disease occurs outdoors in a warm dry summer and under glass. It is encouraged by dry soil combined with a moist atmosphere.

Treatment: Spray with carbendazim at the first signs of disease.

Prevention: Keep the soil moist at all times and ventilate adequately under glass.

WHITE POWDERY MOULD

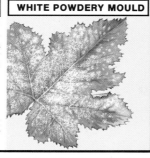

PAPERY PATCHES

23 SUN SCALD

Pale brown, papery patches sometimes occur on the margins of the leaves and shrinkage of the dry areas takes place. Exposure to bright sunlight is the cause.

Treatment: None.

Prevention: Paint glass with Coolglass. Damp down adequately, but not at midday as water droplets can act as magnifying lenses.

ENDIVE

A popular feature of the Continental but not the English salad. The French housewife buys endive as *chicorée frisée* — to make it even more confusing our plump-headed chicory (page 50) is called *endive* on the other side of the Channel! Endive has a much more distinctive taste than lettuce and has the blessing of being available between January and March from the garden. By sowing at monthly intervals you can have heads for six months or more during the year, but you will always have to blanch them before cutting in order to remove much of the bitterness. The curly-leaved varieties are sown in spring and summer for their finely divided frizzy leaves in summer and autumn. The broad-leaved sorts have lettuce-like leaves and the plants are hardier — cloche-covered heads will survive the winter.

SEED FACTS

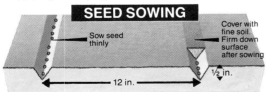

Actual size

Expected germination time:	3–7 days
Approximate number per ounce:	20,000
Expected yield from a 10 ft row:	10–15 heads
Life expectancy of stored seed:	5 years
Approximate time between sowing and cutting:	15–20 weeks
Ease of cultivation:	Not easy — good soil, regular watering and blanching required

SOIL FACTS

- Good soil is needed — endive is not happy in sticky clay. Pick a sunny spot for summer- and autumn-sown crops — a semi-shady site is suitable for spring-sown endive.
- Dig in autumn — incorporate manure or compost if the soil is short of humus. About a week before planting apply a general-purpose fertilizer.

SEED SOWING

Sow seed thinly

Cover with fine soil. Firm down surface after sowing

½ in.

12 in.

- Sow curly-leaved varieties in March–August or broad-leaved varieties in July–September for late autumn and winter use.

LOOKING AFTER THE CROP

- Thin the seedlings as soon as the first true leaves appear. Continue thinning at intervals until the plants are 9 in. (curly-leaved varieties) or 12 in. apart (broad-leaved varieties).
- Hoe regularly and feed occasionally with a liquid fertilizer. It is essential to water thoroughly in dry weather — plants will run to seed if you fail to do so.
- Begin the blanching operation about 12 weeks after sowing. Choose a few plants, as required, and make sure the leaves are dry. Loosely tie up the leaves with raffia and cover with a plastic flower pot. Block the drainage holes to exclude light. The heads will be ready in 3 weeks (summer) or 5 weeks (winter).

HARVESTING

- Sever the head with a sharp knife when the leaves have turned creamy white.

IN THE KITCHEN

Both curly-leaved and broad-leaved endive make an excellent addition to a mixed salad, providing both crispness and a touch of bitterness. Prepare by removing any damaged or green leaves and wash thoroughly. Dry the blanched leaves before serving — toss with a vinegar-based dressing.

FREEZING Not suitable.

STORAGE Endive should be used immediately. If this is not possible, store in a black polythene bag in the refrigerator for up to 3 days.

COOKING Endive can be cooked like spinach but it is much better to prepare braised endive. Wash the head thoroughly, shake off excess water and dry. Fry a chopped onion in a little butter and add to a casserole. Place endive on top and add enough stock to prevent sticking. Replace lid and bake in a moderate oven for 20 minutes.

VARIETIES

BROAD-LEAVED varieties

BATAVIAN GREEN: The most popular broad-leaved endive. Sometimes listed in the catalogues as No.5 2.

EMINENCE: This variety has a packed heart of yellow leaves — you will have to search for a supplier.

CURLY-LEAVED varieties

GREEN CURLED: The basic type of curly-leaved endive. Sometimes listed as Moss Curled.

SALLY: Noted for its tight hearts of curly leaves. An easy variety with the advantage of being self-blanching in the centre.

TROUBLES

SLUGS

These pests can be a problem at blanching time. Use Slug Pellets if necessary.

APHID

Greenflies find endive less attractive than lettuce but are sometimes troublesome. Spray with permethrin or heptenophos if they are numerous.

BOLTING

Endive sown in spring for early summer occasionally runs to seed in hot and dry weather. Avoid trouble by keeping the soil moist.

CALENDAR

	JAN	FEB	MAR	APR	MAY	JUN	JUL	AUG	SEP	OCT	NOV	DEC
Sowing Time												
Cutting Time												

1 in. = 2.5 cm, 1 ft = 30 cm, 1 oz = 28 gm, 1 lb = 450 gm

For key to symbols — see page 7

KALE

You will find this useful source of winter and spring greens listed in all the catalogues as kale or borecole, but you will not find it in all gardens. In fact only a small minority of gardeners in the southern counties bother with it, and this Cinderella status seems surprising when you consider its advantages. The hardiness of kale is unexcelled by any other vegetable — there is none of the heartache of seeing all one's hard work destroyed by a sharp and prolonged frost. Unlike other brassicas it will tolerate poor soil conditions and it is rarely troubled by those dreaded enemies of the cabbage family — pigeons, club root and cabbage root fly. Despite all these good points it is generally rejected, and the reason is the bitter taste of the end product. Some of the old varieties were more suited to feeding cattle than the family and the average gardener picks the leaves and shoots when they are far too large. Choose a good variety and pick the greenstuff when it is young and tender — cook it properly and you will soon lose your prejudice against this underrated vegetable.

SEED FACTS

Actual size

Expected germination time:	7–12 days
Approximate number per ounce:	8000
Expected yield per plant:	2 lb
Life expectancy of stored seed:	4 years
Approximate time between sowing and cutting:	30–35 weeks
Ease of cultivation:	Easy — but there is the chore of transplanting

SOIL FACTS

● Kale is much more accommodating than the other brassicas, such as cabbage, cauliflower and brussels sprouts. It will grow in nearly all soils provided that the drainage is satisfactory.

● Pick a reasonably sunny spot for the site where the plants are to grow. As the seedlings are not transplanted until June or July, it is usual to use land which has recently been vacated by peas, early potatoes or other early summer crops. Do not dig — merely consolidate the ground, remove any weeds and rake in a little fertilizer. Lime if the land is acid. The ground should not be loose nor spongy at planting time — that is the only rule.

SOWING & PLANTING

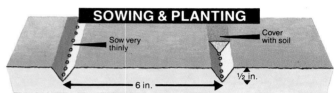

Sow very thinly | Cover with soil | 6 in. | ½ in.

● Thin the seedlings to prevent them from becoming weak and spindly. They should be about 3 in. apart in the rows.

● The seedlings are ready for transplanting when they are 4–6 in. high. Water the rows the day before moving the transplants to their permanent quarters. Plant firmly, setting the seedlings with their lowest leaves just above the soil surface. Leave 18 in. between them — water after planting.

● Rape kale varieties are sown where they will grow to maturity. Make the seed drills 18 in. apart and thin in stages to leave 18 in. between the plants.

LOOKING AFTER THE CROP

● Hoe regularly and tread firmly around the stems to prevent them from rocking in the wind. Water the young plants in dry weather.

● Pick off yellowing leaves. As autumn approaches earth up around the stems to protect the roots from frost and wind rock. Stake tall varieties if growing on an exposed site.

● In winter the plants may look a sorry sight — don't worry, in early spring there will be a crop of fresh side shoots. Feed with a liquid fertilizer in March to encourage their development.

HARVESTING

● There is more skill involved in harvesting kale than growing it. With curly kale start at the crown of the plant from November onwards, removing a few young leaves each time you pick. Use a sharp knife or a sharp downward tug. Do not gather mature or yellowing leaves for kitchen use.

● This stripping of the crown will stimulate the development of succulent side shoots. These are gathered between February and May from all varieties, breaking them off or using a sharp knife for their removal. They should be 4–5 in. long and young — mature shoots are bitter when cooked.

● If you want greens before Christmas, sow a variety of Curly-leaved kale in April. For later cropping sow Leaf & Spear or Plain-leaved kale in May. The correct time for transplanting is governed by the height of the seedlings rather than the date.

● Thin in stages to leave 18 in. between the plants.

● Rape kale is sown in late June. For later management of the crop see Sowing & Planting above.

CALENDAR

	JAN	FEB	MAR	APR	MAY	JUN	JUL	AUG	SEP	OCT	NOV	DEC
Sowing Time												
Planting Time												
Cutting Time												

IN THE KITCHEN

The taste of mature kale leaves which have been overcooked can discourage you from ever trying this vegetable again. However, it need not be bitter — the secret is to gather only young greenstuff after it has been subjected to frost and then to cook it quickly in a small amount of water, as described below. Young shoots are even more acceptable, but kale can never be turned into a delicately-flavoured vegetable. But it is rich in iron and Vitamin C, and the strong flavour can be turned to advantage. Chop the leaves and toss in a vinegar dressing to give zest to a winter salad, or boil and serve with melted butter or white sauce.

FREEZING Use tender shoots. Blanch for 1 minute — cool and drain thoroughly. Chop and then pack into polythene bags for freezing.

STORAGE Keep in a polythene bag in the refrigerator — squeeze out as much air as possible before sealing. Kale will stay fresh for up to 3 days.

COOKING Boiling is the usual method of preparation. Discard old, yellowed and damaged leaves and remove the midribs from the remainder with a sharp knife. Wash thoroughly and then add to 1 in. of boiling water — cover and keep on medium heat for about 8 minutes. The favourite accompaniments are poached eggs, bacon, pork and fatty meat. Kale can be used in other ways — in soups, stews or as a creamed vegetable. Perhaps the best way to serve the leaves and shoots is to boil or braise them with onions, parsley, spices and bacon or a ham bone — the dish known as Southern kale in the U.S.

VARIETIES

CURLY-LEAVED varieties
These 'Scotch' kales dominate the seed catalogues and are much more popular than the other types. Each leaf has an extremely frilled and curled edge, giving a parsley-like appearance.

DWARF GREEN CURLED: The usual choice for the small plot — the 1½–2 ft plants do not require staking and the leaf flavour is as good as any.

TALL GREEN CURLED: The grown-up version of Dwarf Green Curled — sometimes listed as Tall Scotch Curled. Suitable for freezing, as are all the Curly-leaved varieties listed here.

FRIBOR: An F$_1$ dwarf hybrid with dark green leaves, growing only 9 in. high. An excellent choice where space is limited.

WESTLAND AUTUMN: Another dwarf which will provide leaves from November to February. No kale has frillier leaves.

SPURT: A variety which seems to cross the boundaries between the various types. It has curly leaves but it can be grown without transplanting. Pick within 2 months of sowing.

DARKIBOR: Like Fribor a modern dark green F$_1$ hybrid, but this one is much taller.

Fribor

PLAIN-LEAVED varieties
These tall kales tend to be coarser than the Curly-leaved varieties, but they are extremely hardy and prolific, and they are easier to keep pest-free. Eat the young shoots in early spring — not the autumn leaves.

THOUSAND-HEADED KALE: Quite widely sold by seed houses, which sing the praises of the side shoots for picking and cooking from February onwards. You would do better with Pentland Brig.

COTTAGERS: The plants are quite tall — 3½ ft high with leaves which turn bright purple in winter. Once again it is the early spring shoots which are eaten.

RAPE KALE varieties
These kales provide young tender shoots between March and May, and are not grown like other varieties. They are sown where they will mature, as they detest transplanting.

HUNGRY GAP: A late cropper, like all Rape kales. Robust and reliable, producing shoots which are suitable for freezing.

ASPARAGUS KALE: The Rape kale variety to grow where space is limited. You will find this variety in the textbooks, but you will have to search to find a supplier.

LEAF & SPEAR variety
There is just one variety — a cross between a Curly-leaved kale and a Plain-leaved one. Its arrival was heralded as a new era for the lowly kale — if you can grow only one variety, pick this one.

PENTLAND BRIG: Plants grow about 2 ft tall, and their kitchen use differs from other kales. Pick young leaves from the crown beginning in November — they are fringed but less so than a Curly-leaved kale. In early spring harvest the leafy side shoots and later gather the immature flower-heads ('spears') which should be cooked like broccoli. A versatile vegetable, indeed!

Pentland Brig

TROUBLES

Brassica troubles are described on pages 28-31. Kale is remarkably resistant to most major problems such as cabbage root fly and club root, but mealy aphid, whitefly and cabbage caterpillar can be a nuisance. Spray with an insecticide at the first sign of attack.

1 in. = 2.5 cm, 1 ft = 30 cm, 1 oz = 28 gm, 1 lb = 450 gm

KOHL RABI

Not for the first time in this book we find a vegetable which is popular in some parts of Europe but has found little favour in Britain. This is perhaps surprising as kohl rabi is a root-forming brassica which does much better in hot and dry weather than the much more popular turnip. The edible swollen part of kohl rabi is not really a root at all — it is the stem base ('globe') and so is able to succeed in shallow soils where turnips and swedes would fail. It is low growing, reaching about 1 ft high. It also matures quickly, progressing from sowing to harvesting in a couple of months. Textbooks try to describe the taste of the globe but the phrases are not much use — 'a cross between turnip and cabbage' for the boiled vegetable, 'nutty with a slight celery taste' for the grated raw globe. This vegetable can be both tasty and tender, but only if you grow it quickly and lift when the globes are undersized.

SEED FACTS

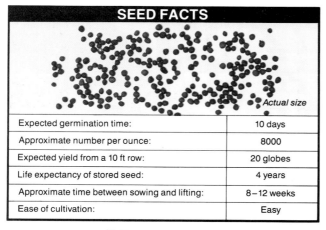

Actual size

Expected germination time:	10 days
Approximate number per ounce:	8000
Expected yield from a 10 ft row:	20 globes
Life expectancy of stored seed:	4 years
Approximate time between sowing and lifting:	8–12 weeks
Ease of cultivation:	Easy

SOIL FACTS

- The ideal situation is a sunny spot on light land. Dig in autumn — work in compost if the soil is poor. Lime, if necessary, in winter.
- In spring apply Growmore — consider using protective discs (page 28) if cabbage root fly is known to be a problem. Prepare the bed about a week later, treading down and raking the surface.

SEED SOWING

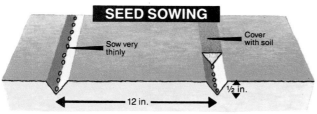

Sow very thinly

Cover with soil

½ in.

12 in.

- Sow green varieties between March and June. For a late autumn or winter crop sow a purple variety in July or August.

LOOKING AFTER THE CROP

- Thin the seedlings as soon as the first true leaves appear. Continue thinning at intervals until the plants are 6 in. apart. Provide protection against birds.
- Hoe regularly and feed occasionally if growth is slow. Soak the ground during periods of drought.

HARVESTING

- Pull the swollen stem bases ('globes') when they are midway in size between a golf ball and a tennis ball. Do not lift and store — they deteriorate once out of the ground. Leave the plants growing in the garden and pull as required until December.

IN THE KITCHEN

Kohl rabi is a versatile vegetable which few British housewives have discovered. The young globes can be grated to provide a nutty-flavoured ingredient for summer and winter salads, but it is more usual to cook before serving. Young leaves are boiled like spinach, the globes are boiled, braised or used as an ingredient for soups or stews.

FREEZING Trim, scrub, cut in strips and blanch for 2 minutes before freezing.

STORAGE Keep in a polythene bag in the refrigerator — kohl rabi will stay fresh for up to 2 weeks.

COOKING The young globes should be trimmed and scrubbed — do not peel. Boil whole or sliced for 20–30 minutes — drain and peel, then serve with melted butter or white sauce. Alternatively, the boiled globes can be mashed with butter or sour cream.

VARIETIES

GREEN VIENNA: Green-skinned, white-fleshed — an early maturing variety which is chosen for spring and summer sowing. Sometimes listed in the catalogues as White Vienna.

LANRO: Pale-skinned, white-fleshed — an F$_1$ hybrid which is noted for the quality of its texture and flavour.

PURPLE VIENNA: The globes are purple-skinned but the flesh remains white. Choose this variety for late sowing and winter harvest.

ROWEL: An F$_1$ hybrid which claims to be definitely superior to the old Viennas. The flesh is sweeter and it does not become woody if allowed to grow larger than a tennis ball.

TROUBLES

Brassica troubles are described on pages 28–31. Many of these problems are occasionally seen, but they are not likely to be serious. The crop matures quickly and so it is not affected by diseases which develop slowly nor pests which are at their peak when kohl rabi is absent from the garden. Birds and aphids can be troublesome.

CALENDAR

	JAN	FEB	MAR	APR	MAY	JUN	JUL	AUG	SEP	OCT	NOV	DEC
Sowing Time												
Lifting Time												

For key to symbols — see page 7

LEEK

The leek may be the national emblem of Wales but its horticultural heart lies in the north-eastern counties of England. Here is the home of the pot leek — grown by enthusiasts with loving care and secret potions for competition each year. The aim is to beat the 9½ lb record, but at home your aim should be to produce ½−1 lb specimens for the kitchen — smaller but tastier than the Northumbrian giants. Leeks are the easiest member of the onion family to grow — they will withstand the hardest winter, are generally untroubled by pests and diseases, and do not demand the same level of high fertility as the onion. But some textbooks exaggerate their ease by claiming that they are amongst the simplest of vegetables to grow. Not true. They need transplanting, careful earthing-up and occupy the land for a long time. Still, an excellent crop for every plot — the harvesting season lasts for six months or more and the strong white roots break up clay soil better than any spade. In the kitchen the thick white 'stem' (more correctly the shank of rolled leaves) has numerous uses.

SEED FACTS

Actual size

Expected germination time:	14 – 18 days
Approximate number per ounce:	10,000
Expected yield from a 10 ft row:	10 lb
Life expectancy of stored seed:	3 years
Approximate time between sowing and lifting (Early varieties):	30 weeks
Approximate time between sowing and lifting (Late varieties):	45 weeks
Ease of cultivation:	Not difficult, but occupies the land for a long time

SOIL FACTS

- Leeks are less demanding than onions and will grow in any reasonable soil provided it is neither highly compacted nor badly drained.
- The crop will be disappointing if the land is starved of nutrients and humus. Thorough digging in winter is required — add compost or well-rotted manure if this was not done for the previous crop.
- Choose a sunny spot for where the plants will grow. Leave the soil rough after winter digging and level the surface in the spring by raking and treading. Incorporate a general fertilizer into the surface about 1 week before planting.

SOWING & PLANTING

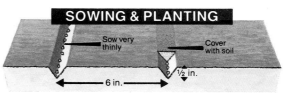

Sow very thinly

Cover with soil

½ in.

6 in.

- Thin the seedlings so that they are 1½ in. apart in the rows.
- The young leeks are ready for transplanting when they are about 8 in. high and as thick as a pencil. Water the bed the day before lifting if the weather is dry. Trim off the root ends and leaf tips, then set out in rows 12 in. apart, leaving 6 in. between the transplants.
- Make a 6 in. deep hole with a dibber, drop in the leek transplant and then gently fill the hole with water to settle the roots. Do not fill the hole with soil.

LOOKING AFTER THE CROP

- Hoe carefully to keep down weeds and make sure that the plants are not short of water during dry weather. Do not deliberately fill the holes with soil.
- Blanch to increase the length of white stem. Gently draw *dry* soil around the stems when the plants are well developed. Do this in stages, increasing the height a little at a time. On no account allow soil to fall between the leaves or grittiness will be the unpleasant result at dinner time. Finish earthing-up in late October.
- Feeding will increase the thickness of the stems. Late feeding, however, should be avoided for plants which will overwinter in the garden — late August is the time to stop.

HARVESTING

- For culinary purposes do not aim to produce giants — there is a reduction in flavour as size increases.
- Begin lifting when the leeks are still quite small — in this way you will ensure a long harvesting period. Never try to wrench the plant out of the soil — lift it gently with a fork.
- Leeks can remain in the ground during the winter months until they are required for use.

- For exhibiting in the autumn sow seed under glass in late January or February and plant outdoors during April.
- For ordinary kitchen use sow seed outdoors in spring when the soil is workable and warm enough to permit germination — for all but warm and sheltered areas this means mid March or later. Transplant the seedlings in June.
- For an April crop you can sow seed of a Late variety in June and transplant in July.

CALENDAR

	JAN	FEB	MAR	APR	MAY	JUN	JUL	AUG	SEP	OCT	NOV	DEC
Sowing Time			▓	▓								
Planting Time						▓	▓					
Sowing Time (under glass)	▓	▓		▽								
Lifting Time	▓	▓	▓	▓				▓	▓	▓	▓	▓

IN THE KITCHEN

Leeks are a favourite ingredient for the traditional soups of many countries — England's leek & potato soup, Scotland's cock-a-leekie (leek and chicken broth) and cold vichyssoise, a French import from the U.S. In the southern counties of England the use of leeks is often restricted to soups and stews — many families have rejected this vegetable after suffering sliminess and grittiness, the twin distasteful features of badly prepared boiled leeks. Both can easily be avoided, and there are many other ways of using them apart from boiling. There is no need to cook at all — slice young leeks and mix with shredded cabbage and a dressing for a winter salad.

FREEZING Remove green tops. Wash stems thoroughly, cut into small chunks and blanch for 3 minutes. Cool, drain and dry the pieces on a paper towel, then pack into polythene bags before freezing.

STORAGE Keep in a polythene bag in the refrigerator — leeks will stay fresh for up to 5 days.

COOKING Grittiness is the first problem to avoid. The best way to remove dirt is to cut off the top of the leaves and some of the coarse outer foliage — do not remove all the green tissue. Slit part way down the stem with a knife and stand in a bowl of water, green end down, for about an hour. Finally wash under a cold tap, prising leaves apart if necessary. Sliminess is the next problem — avoid it by boiling in a small amount of water for no more than 10 minutes and then draining thoroughly. Now return the leeks to the pan and heat gently for about 5 minutes to drive off the excess water. Serve with a white sauce or melted butter. There are better ways of using leeks — braise with carrots and celery in beef stock or cut into rings and stir-fry in a little butter. Leek dumplings and leek flan are age-old methods of using this versatile vegetable.

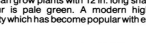

VARIETIES

EARLY varieties

SEP | OCT | NOV

These varieties are popular with exhibitors as they can be sown under glass at the beginning of the year and they will reach their maximum size in time for the autumn show. Alternatively they can be sown outdoors to provide long-stemmed leeks for the kitchen before the end of the year.

LYON 2-PRIZETAKER: A great favourite for the show bench over the years — long, thick stems with dark green leaves to catch the judge's eye. Good for the kitchen — mild flavoured.

SPLENDID: This popular strain of Gennevilliers matures in early autumn and can be harvested up to November. Shanks are about 6 in. long.

WALTON MAMMOTH: One of the Autumn Mammoth strains, highly recommended for exhibition and kitchen use. Renowned for its ability to stand up to severe winter weather.

KING RICHARD: You will find this early leek in many catalogues with the promise that with care you can grow plants with 12 in. long shanks. Leaf colour is pale green. A modern high quality variety which has become popular with exhibitors.

MID-SEASON varieties

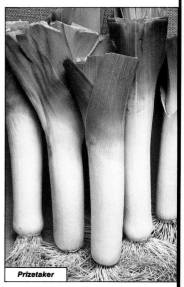

Prizetaker

DEC | JAN | FEB

These varieties mature during the winter months and one of them has long been the number one choice for the home gardener. They are of course all winter hardy, but vary considerably in length of stem.

MUSSELBURGH: This Scottish variety remains Britain's favourite home-grown leek — it is very hardy, reliable and fine flavoured. The stems are thick but not tall.

SNOWSTAR: Similar to Musselburgh in general appearance — a modern variety which the suppliers claim is more likely to win a prize at the local show.

ARGENTA: Just what you would expect from a standard mid-season variety — 5 in. of white stem, crisp flesh and a mild flavour. Matures in November or December and stands up to winter frosts.

GOLIATH: Yet another Autumn Mammoth strain like Argenta. The catalogue descriptions may make them sound quite different, but in practise they are very similar.

LATE varieties

FEB | MAR | APR

These varieties are perhaps the most useful of all for kitchen use, maturing between late January and early April when other vegetables are scarce.

GIANT WINTER-CATALINA: The variety Giant Winter has produced a number of impressive strains, and Catalina is one of the best. Heavy and thick stems are produced which can be left in the ground for a considerable time.

WINTERREUZEN: Another Giant Winter strain, sometimes listed as Giant Winter 3. The shanks are quite long and it is slow to bolt.

YATES EMPIRE: Looks like Musselburgh with thick, pure white stems but it will stand in the ground quite happily until mid April.

WINTER CROP: This variety has the reputation for being the hardiest of all — it is the one usually recommended for exposed northern sites.

Musselburgh

TROUBLES

Generally trouble-free — see pages 74–75

LETTUCE

It may seem strange that three pages should be devoted to this popular and apparently straightforward vegetable. On the average plot its cultivation is simple — a row or two in spring and again in early summer, thinning when the seedlings are obviously overcrowded and cutting when the heads are mature. Unfortunately, treating our favourite salad crop so casually often leads to disappointment. Pests and diseases take their toll, and the survivors all mature at the same time — the gap between peak condition and starting to run to seed is only a week. Buy a packet of mixed seed containing varieties which mature at different times in order to avoid a sudden glut, or preferably sow seed in very short rows at fortnightly intervals to ensure a regular succession. Another cause of disappointment is bolting before maturity — the usual cause is transplanting at the wrong time or in the wrong way but there are other causes. Finally, even with well-formed heads there is a risk of the leaves being tough and leathery — the usual reason is failure to grow the crop quickly enough. You must ensure adequate humus and moisture in the soil. So lettuces are not quite so easy as some books claim, but if you pick the right varieties, follow the instructions and invest in a few cloches you can enjoy them fresh from the garden nearly all year round.

TYPES

COS

CABBAGE: BUTTERHEAD

CABBAGE: CRISPHEAD

LOOSE-LEAF

SEED FACTS

Germination is erratic in hot weather.

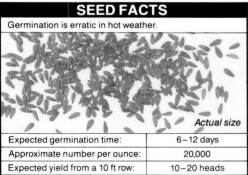

Actual size

Expected germination time:	6–12 days
Approximate number per ounce:	20,000
Expected yield from a 10 ft row:	10–20 heads
Life expectancy of stored seed:	3 years
Approximate time between sowing and cutting:	8–14 weeks (Cabbage and Cos varieties) 6–8 weeks (Loose-leaf varieties)
Ease of cultivation:	Not difficult if you sow properly and water regularly. Spring lettuce is not easy

SEED SOWING

● To grow lettuce for transplanting, sow 2 seeds in a small peat pot. Remove weaker seedling after germination — harden off before transplanting.

LOOKING AFTER THE CROP

● Thin the seedlings as soon as the first true leaves appear — avoid overcrowding at all costs. Water the day before thinning. Continue thinning at intervals until the plants are 12 in. apart (9 in. Tom Thumb and Little Gem, 6 in. Salad Bowl).

● You can try transplanting thinnings in spring or you can plant shop-bought seedlings — do not bury the lower leaves. Lettuces hate to be moved — sow seed whenever you can where the crop is to grow and mature.

● Put down Slug Pellets and protect seedlings from birds. Hoe regularly. Keep unprotected plants watered, but the soil under glass should be kept on the dry side. Ventilate glass-grown lettuce whenever possible.

● Always water in the morning or midday — watering in the evening will increase the chance of disease.

● Greenfly can render the crop unusable — spray with an insecticide. If grey mould strikes, treat with carbendazim.

SOIL FACTS

● Three basic needs have to be satisfied to obtain good lettuces. The soil must contain adequate organic matter, it must not be acid and it must be kept moist throughout the life of the crop.

● For summer lettuce choose a sunny or lightly shaded site. Dig the soil and incorporate compost in autumn or early winter. Shortly before sowing time rake the surface to produce a fine tilth and apply a general fertilizer. Apply pirimiphos-methyl if soil pests have been a problem in the past.

● Spring lettuce can be grown in a sunny spot outdoors in mild areas without glass protection, but it will not succeed in poorly drained or exposed sites.

HARVESTING

● Lettuce is ready for cutting as soon as a firm heart has formed. Test by pressing the top of the plant gently with the back of the hand — squeezing the heart will damage the tissues.

● If left after this stage the heart will begin to grow upwards, a sign that it is getting ready to bolt. You must then cut immediately for kitchen use or throw it away.

● It is traditional to cut in the morning when the heads have dew on them. Pull up the whole plant and cut off the root and lower leaves. Put the unwanted material on the compost heap.

IN THE KITCHEN

Preparing lettuce for a salad is, of course, a straightforward job but there are still a few rules to follow. Wash both sides of each leaf to remove grit and insects — every housewife knows that, but thorough drying is sometimes neglected. Shake vigorously in a salad basket or pat the leaves gently with a dry cloth — failure to do so will result in poor adhesion by the salad dressing. Keep the small leaves whole — tear the larger ones into pieces. The inner heart should be left unwashed if it is free from insects, dirt and slug holes — cut into wedges or in half rather than separating each tiny leaf. Before making the salad place the washed and dried lettuce leaves in the refrigerator for 30 minutes to crisp and chill them. Now you can arrange your usual mixture of cucumber, radishes, tomatoes, etc. or you can coat a wedge of a crisphead lettuce with the dressing of your choice and enjoy lettuce the American way.

FREEZING Not suitable.

STORAGE Keep unwashed in a polythene bag in the refrigerator — lettuce will stay fresh for up to 3 days (butterhead) or 5 days (cos or crisphead).

COOKING Lettuce is rarely regarded as a vegetable for cooking, but there are many ways of using the almost invariable glut in summer or the leaves of heads which have started to run to seed. *Pois à la française* which you enjoy in France is a combination of peas, lettuce and small onions braised in stock and a little butter. Stir-fried lettuce which is served in Oriental restaurants is prepared by cooking the leaves in hot vegetable oil for about 2 minutes. Braised lettuce, stuffed lettuce, lettuce soup . . . you will find many ideas in recipe books which are well worth trying.

CALENDAR

		JAN	FEB	MAR	APR	MAY	JUN	JUL	AUG	SEP	OCT	NOV	DEC
For a Summer/Autumn Crop: Sow outdoors in late March–late July for cutting in June–October. For an earlier crop (mid May–early June) sow under glass in early February and plant out in early March under cloches.	Sowing Time		■	✹									
	Cutting Time						▓	▓	▓	▓	▓		
For an Early Winter Crop: Sow a mildew-resistant variety such as Avondefiance or Avoncrisp outdoors in early August. Cover with cloches in late September — close ends with panes of glass. The crop will be ready for cutting in November or December.	Sowing Time								▓				
	Cutting Time											▓	▓
For a Midwinter Crop: Heated glass (minimum 45°F in winter) is necessary. Sow seed under glass in September or October — plant out as soon as the seedlings are large enough to handle. The lettuce will be ready for cutting in January–early March. Grow a forcing variety such as Kloek or Dandie.	Sowing Time								▦ ▦ ▦	✹ ✹ ✹			
	Cutting Time	▓	▓	▓									
For a Spring Crop: If you live in a mild part of the country, sow a winter-hardy variety such as Winter Density outdoors in late August–early September. Thin to 3 in. apart in October — complete thinning to 12 in. spacing in early spring. The crop will be ready in May. For less favoured areas sow in mid October under cloches — harvest in April. Use a winter-hardy or a forcing variety.	Sowing Time								▓	▓	✦		
	Cutting Time				▓	▓							

For key to symbols — see page 7

VARIETIES

Paris White

COS varieties

The cos or romaine lettuce is easy to recognise by its upright growth habit and oblong head. The leaves are crisp and the flavour is good. They are generally a little more difficult to grow than the cabbage types and take longer to mature.

LOBJOIT'S GREEN: One of the old favourites — a large, self-folding variety. Deep green and very crisp.

PARIS WHITE: Like Lobjoit's Green, this variety is popular, large, self-folding and crisp. The heart, however, is pale green.

LITTLE GEM: A quick-maturing cos lettuce which is somewhat cabbage-like in appearance. Sow early for a May or June crop — tie the heads loosely with wool. Many experts consider it to be the sweetest lettuce. The heads are small and compact.

BUBBLES: A cos lettuce of the Little Gem type — useful where space is limited. Its unique feature is the highly crinkled ('bubbled') surface of the leaves.

WINTER DENSITY: This variety challenges Little Gem for the sweetest lettuce title, but its growing season is different. Sow in August or September for an April crop.

THE LEAF LETTUCE TECHNIQUE
This technique is designed to provide the maximum crop in the shortest time — try it if space is limited. Use a cos variety and sow seeds at 1 in. intervals in rows 4 in. apart. Begin in April and make fortnightly sowings until the end of May. Do not thin — this technique produces a block of tightly packed lettuces. Make the first cut 4–6 weeks after sowing — leave the stumps in the ground to produce a second crop about 6 weeks later.

1 in. = 2.5 cm, 1 ft = 30 cm, 1 oz = 28 gm, 1 lb = 450 gm

BUTTERHEAD varieties

All The Year Round

The butterheads are still the most popular lettuce group. They are quick-maturing and will generally tolerate poorer conditions than the other types. The leaves are soft and smooth-edged — most are summer varieties but a few are hardy lettuces which are used to produce a spring crop and several others are forcing varieties for growing under glass.

ALL THE YEAR ROUND: Very popular because it is suitable for spring, summer and autumn sowing. Medium-sized, pale green and slow to bolt in dry weather.

TOM THUMB: The favourite for small plots, producing heads which are tennis ball size. Quick-maturing, fine-flavoured — grow it as a summer crop.

AVONDEFIANCE: The variety to choose if you plan to sow outdoors between June and August. The dark green heads are mildew-resistant. Slow to bolt and resistant to root aphid — no wonder it is so popular with commercial growers for late sowing.

CONTINUITY: The summer lettuce with the red-tinged leaves. Long-standing and compact — a good choice for sandy soils.

DOLLY: A variety which appeals to people who want to grow a large summer lettuce which is resistant to mosaic and slow to bolt.

BUTTERCRUNCH: The central heart of creamy leaves is hard and compact — crunchy enough to make some books list it with the crispheads. An American variety — try it for a different flavour.

HILDE: A popular choice for sowing under glass and planting out early to produce a May crop.

SUZAN: Another variety which can be sown under glass in February or outdoors in spring to produce a summer crop. Hearts are large and pale green.

WINTER CROP: One of the frost-hardy varieties which are suitable for sowing outdoors in August or September to produce a crop in spring.

IMPERIAL WINTER: Another frost-hardy lettuce for sowing in late summer and cutting in May. Very similar or perhaps identical to Winter Crop.

ARCTIC KING: Winter-hardy — the one to choose if you want a more compact spring lettuce than Imperial Winter.

KWIEK: A popular forcing lettuce for growing under glass to produce an early winter crop.

PREMIER: A forcing variety for growing under glass. Sow in October for cropping in April. The pale green hearts are large.

MAY QUEEN: Another under glass lettuce, recommended for early sowing under cloches. The leaves are red-tinged. May be listed as May King.

KLOEK: A winter lettuce for cropping in January–March. A heated greenhouse is necessary — sow seed in September or October for large, solid hearts in midwinter when lettuce is scarce.

MUSETTE: This dark green lettuce is grown for a summer/autumn crop — good resistance to disease.

CRISPHEAD varieties

Iceberg

The crispheads produce large hearts of curled and crisp leaves. In general they are more resistant to bolting than the butterheads, and their popularity is increasing in Britain. They have always been the popular group in the U.S. where the Iceberg type dominates the scene — crispheads with a solid heart and few outer leaves.

WEBB'S WONDERFUL: The No.1 crisphead lettuce in Britain — all the catalogues list this large-hearted frilly lettuce which succeeds even in hot summers.

WINDERMERE: Another excellent frilly crisphead for summer cropping — sow outdoors in March–July or under glass in February. Can be grown in a cold frame as a spring lettuce — preferred by some experts to Webb's Wonderful.

AVONCRISP: Pick this one if you are bothered about lettuce troubles or if you are sowing for an autumn crop. It is mildew-resistant, shrugs off root aphid and is not likely to bolt.

GREAT LAKES: A large, spreading crisphead. It's the original summer crisphead lettuce which came to us from America.

ICEBERG: You can buy the seed of this super-crisp white-hearted lettuce which has become so popular on the supermarket shelves. Sow in spring or early summer.

LAKELAND: An Iceberg-type of crisphead which has been bred to be more reliable in Britain than the original Iceberg variety.

MARMER: This variety was the first crisphead for growing under glass. Iceberg-type — sow in October in an unheated greenhouse and cut in April.

LOOSE-LEAF varieties

Salad Bowl

These varieties do not produce a heart. The leaves are curled and are picked like spinach — a few at a time without cutting the whole plant. Sow seed in April or May.

SALAD BOWL: The basic variety — an endive-like plant which produces intricately cut and curled leaves. Pick the leaves regularly and the plant will stay productive for many weeks. A reddish-brown variety (Red Salad Bowl) is available.

LOLLO ROSSA: The crisp leaves of this non-hearting lettuce are intricately frilled. These curled edges are tinged with red — a decorative as well as a tasty variety.

LETTUCE TROUBLES

Outdoor lettuce is an easy crop to grow, but it is not easy to grow well. You must guard against soil pests, slugs and birds; in cool, damp weather the twin major diseases (downy mildew and grey mould) can be destructive. Above all you must try to prevent any check to growth. Crops grown under glass are vulnerable to an even wider range of plant troubles, but few of them are serious in a well-grown crop.

	Symptom	Likely Causes
Seedlings	— poor or slow germination	**Seeds kept too warm**
	— eaten	**5** or **10** or **Birds** (see page 110) or **Mice** (see page 20) or **Millepede** or **Leatherjacket** (see page 22)
	— toppled over	**9** or **Damping off** (see page 110)
	— severed	**10**
Leaves	— holed	**4** or **5**
	— mouldy or powdery patches	**1** or **9**
	— brown-edged	**1** or **9** or **13**
	— large yellowish patches	**1**
	— brown spots	**4**
	— mottled	**12**
	— infested with greenfly	**8**
Plants	— run to seed	**2**
	— no hearts	**3**
	— wilted	**6** or **7** or **9** or **10** or **11**
	— rotten at base	**9**
	— base covered with grey mould	**9**
	— base covered with fluffy white mould	**Sclerotinia rot** (see page 43)
Roots	— eaten	**10** or **Millepede** or **Leatherjacket** (see page 110)
	— tunnelled	**11**
	— infested with greenfly	**6**
	— covered with white patches	**6**
	— covered with gall-like swellings	**7**

WHITE MOULDY LEAVES

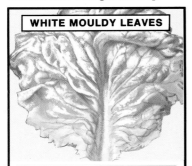

1 DOWNY MILDEW

Large yellowish patches appear between the veins of older leaves. Whitish mouldy areas develop on the underside. Later, diseased patches turn brown and die. This serious disease is worst in cool, wet conditions.

Treatment: Remove affected leaves as soon as they are seen and spray the plants with mancozeb.

Prevention: Practise crop rotation. Avoid overcrowding. Under glass make sure that the plants are adequately ventilated and not overwatered.

2 BOLTING

Lettuces produce thick flowering stems if left in the soil after hearts have formed. Sometimes the plants run to seed before they are ready for harvesting — this condition is known as 'bolting'. The cause is a check to growth at some stage of the plant's life. Careless or delayed transplanting is perhaps the commonest cause, but both overcrowding and dryness at the root are frequently responsible. Lift and place on the compost heap; cover with soil so as not to attract aphids.

3 NO HEARTS

A wide variety of factors can prevent lettuces from forming hearts. The most likely reason is shortage of organic matter — you must enrich the land with compost or manure if you want to be sure of a well-hearted crop. Other possible causes are growing the plants in a shady site, aphid attack, overcrowding and drought.

4 RING SPOT

Not common, but occasionally damaging to winter varieties. Small brown spots appear on the outer leaves, giving a rusty appearance. The centres of the spots may fall out. Rusty streaks appear on the midribs.

Treatment: Destroy badly infected plants. Spray remaining plants with a copper fungicide.

Prevention: Practise crop rotation outdoors. Ensure good ventilation under glass.

HOLED LEAVES

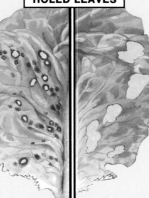

5 SLUGS & SNAILS

Both slugs and snails are a menace to lettuces at all stages of growth. Seedlings are particularly susceptible and may be killed. Leaves and stems are severely attacked in wet weather. The pests are generally not seen during the day, so look for tell-tale slime trails.

Treatment: Scatter Slug Pellets or methiocarb around the plants at the first signs of attack.

Prevention: Keep surrounding area free from rubbish.

DAMAGED ROOTS

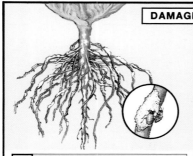

6 ROOT APHID

Greyish-coloured 'greenfly' attack the roots, which become covered with white powdery patches. Growth is stunted, and the leaves may turn yellow and wilt. Attacks are worst in late summer.

Treatment: Pull up and destroy decaying plants. Water around remaining plants with spray-strength malathion.

Prevention: Keep plants watered in dry weather. Grow resistant varieties (Salad Bowl or Avoncrisp) if attacks recur.

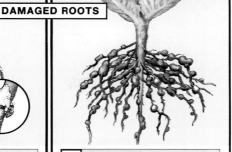

7 EELWORM

Root knot eelworm occasionally attacks lettuce plants, causing stunted growth and pale-coloured leaves. Plants wilt and die if the attack is severe. Look for the tell-tale signs on lifted plants — gall-like swellings on the roots.

Treatment: None. Dig up and destroy infested plants.

Prevention: Do not grow lettuce in affected soil for at least 6 years.

GREENFLY ON LEAVES

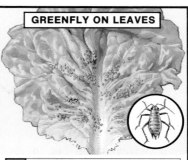

8 APHID

Greenflies can be serious pests in two ways. They spread mosaic, a virus disease, and they also cover the plants in sticky honeydew which can make them unusable. Attacks are worst in a dry spring, when leaves may be badly puckered and distorted.

Treatment: Spray at the first signs of attack. Use heptenophos, or apply permethrin if plants are ready for cutting.

Prevention: None.

ROTTEN STEMS

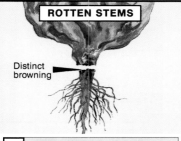

Distinct browning

9 GREY MOULD (Botrytis)

Plants are infected through dead or damaged areas, and the fungus produces a reddish-brown rot when it reaches the stem. Plants wilt and may break off at soil level. Infected tissue produces abundant masses of grey mould. This disease is encouraged by low temperature and high humidity.

Treatment: Destroy diseased plants immediately. Spray remainder thoroughly with carbendazim.

Prevention: Handle seedlings carefully. Plant so that the leaf bases are not buried.

SEVERED STEMS

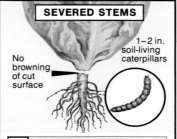

No browning of cut surface

1–2 in. soil-living caterpillars

10 CUTWORM

These large green, grey or brown caterpillars are a major threat to young lettuces. The plants are attacked at night and stems may be completely severed at ground level. With older plants the roots are gnawed which causes the lettuces to wilt. June and July are the main danger months.

Treatment: Hoe the soil around the plants. Destroy caterpillars which are brought to the surface.

Prevention: Use a nematode-based insecticide before planting.

TUNNELLED ROOTS

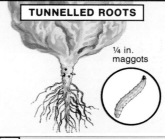

¼ in. maggots

11 LETTUCE ROOT MAGGOT

An occasional pest of lettuce grown under glass. They tunnel into the roots and eat the central tissue. Above ground the leaves wilt and growth is stunted. The main host of this pest is the chrysanthemum, where it is known as chrysanthemum stool miner.

Treatment: Dig out and destroy affected plants. Water around remaining plants with spray-strength lindane.

Prevention: Do not plant lettuce on land used for chrysanthemums in the previous season.

12 MOSAIC VIRUS

Yellow or pale green mottling appears on the leaves and growth is stunted. The veins appear almost transparent. It is spread by aphids.

Treatment: None. Lift and burn infected plants.

Prevention: Spray young plants with heptenophos or permethrin.

MOTTLED LEAVES

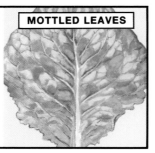

BROWN-EDGED LEAVES

13 TIPBURN

Tipburn (or 'greasiness') is a common cause of the scorching of leaf edges. It is usually due to sudden water loss by the leaves. This can happen in a warm spell in early spring or at the start of a summer heat wave.

Treatment: None.

Prevention: None.

1 in. = 2.5 cm, 1 ft = 30 cm, 1 oz = 28 gm, 1 lb = 450 gm

MARROW,
COURGETTE, SQUASH, PUMPKIN

Marrows, courgettes, squashes and pumpkins all belong to the gourd section of the cucumber family — fleshy-fruited vegetables which can be grown outdoors. There are no exact definitions for each type and the dividing lines are blurred. Until recently the vegetable marrow — large, oblong and striped, was the dominant member. Overgrown when picked and insipid when cooked, they are still widely used as a boiled vegetable or an edible casing for minced beef or other stuffing. Where space is limited, grow a bush rather than a trailing variety. Courgettes have begun to take over, and these are nothing more than marrows cut at the immature stage — the flesh is firmer and the taste superior.

SEED FACTS

Soak seed overnight before sowing.

Actual size

Expected germination time:	5–8 days
Expected yield per plant (Marrows):	4 marrows
Expected yield per plant (Courgettes):	16 courgettes
Life expectancy of stored seed:	6 years
Approximate time between sowing and cutting:	10–14 weeks
Ease of cultivation:	Not difficult if you remember to prepare the soil properly and water regularly

SOIL FACTS

- A sunny spot protected from strong winds is essential — marrows, squashes, etc. are neither hardy nor long suffering.
- The soil must be well drained and rich in humus. Most households will need only a few plants, so prepare a few planting pockets as shown on the right rather than sowing long rows.

SOWING & PLANTING

Dig hole

Scatter Slug Pellets between pockets

Sprinkle fertilizer over surface

12 in.

12 in.

48 in. (trailing varieties)

24 in. (bush varieties)

Fill hole with a mixture of compost or rotted manure and soil. Leave low mound at top

- Sow 3 seeds 1 in. deep and a few inches apart at the centre of each pocket. Cover with a large jar or cloche to hasten germination. When the first true leaves have appeared thin out to leave the strongest seedling.
- Alternatively you can raise the seedlings indoors, but this method is often less satisfactory. Place a single seed edgeways ½ in. deep in seed compost in a 3 in. peat pot. Keep at a minimum of 65°F until germinated — gradually harden off seedlings before planting in pockets outdoors.

LOOKING AFTER THE CROP

- Pinch out the tips of the main shoots of trailing varieties when they reach 2 ft long. Renew Slug Pellets at the first signs of damage.
- Keep the soil moist — water copiously *around* the plants, not over them. Syringe lightly in dry weather.
- Place black polythene or a mulch around the plants in summer before fruit formation.
- If the weather is cold or it is early in the season, fertilize female flowers (tiny marrow behind petals) with a male flower (thin stalk behind petals). Remove a mature male flower on a dry day, fold back petals and push gently into a female flower.
- Once the fruits start to swell feed every 14 days with a tomato fertilizer. Limit pumpkins to 2 fruits per plant. Keep marrows on a piece of tile or glass to prevent rotting and slug attack.

HARVESTING

- Remove the fruits for immediate use when they are still quite small — courgettes 4 in., marrows 8–10 in. long. Push your thumbnail into the surface near the stalk — if it goes in quite easily then the marrow is at the right stage for summer picking. Continual cropping is essential to prolong fruiting. Take care — cut marrows where they lie, then lift them away.
- For pumpkins, winter squashes and marrows for winter storage, allow the fruits to mature on the plants and remove before frosts. Store in a cool room indoors — they should keep until Christmas.

- Sow outdoors in late May or early June. In the Midlands and northern areas cover the seedlings with cloches if you can for a few weeks. The first courgettes will be ready in July.
- For an earlier crop sow seeds under glass in late April. Plant out the seedlings in early June when the danger of frost has passed.

CALENDAR

	JAN	FEB	MAR	APR	MAY	JUN	JUL	AUG	SEP	OCT	NOV	DEC
Sowing Time (outdoors)						▮						
Sowing Time (indoors)				▮	🌱							
Cutting Time												

1 in. = 2.5 cm, 1 ft = 30 cm, 1 oz = 28 gm, 1 lb = 450 gm

For key to symbols — see page 7

IN THE KITCHEN

Courgettes are now the most popular of the edible gourds — crisp and tasty, plentiful in the shops and bountiful in the garden from just a few plants. They need neither peeling nor seeding — merely wash and trim for serving raw or cooked. For serving in salads, blanch the whole fruits for about 2 minutes in boiling water to remove bitterness — dry, slice and serve. Mature marrows require peeling before boiling and then coring by cutting the fruit lengthways and scooping out the seeds and tough fibres. Boiling produces a watery, tasteless dish — baking or braising is better. The summer squashes are also bland but the winter squashes are different — the firm, orange fibrous flesh is still one of our undiscovered tastes.

FREEZING Courgettes (not marrows) are suitable for freezing. Cut into ½ in. slices, blanch for 2 minutes, cool, drain and pat dry. Pack into polythene bags and freeze.

STORAGE Keep courgettes in a polythene bag in the refrigerator — the fruits will stay fresh for up to 1 week.

COOKING Boil courgettes (5 – 8 minutes in very little water) if you are anti-frying, but they taste better if sliced and lightly fried. Best of all are courgette fritters — rub slices with salt to draw out water, dab dry, dip in flour or batter and then fry until golden brown. Mature marrows are excellent for wine or jam making or pickle and chutney production but boiling (10 minutes in very little water) produces an insipid vegetable. Baked stuffed marrow is better — so is braising with tomatoes and herbs. Winter squash is prepared by cutting in half through the hard rind, brushing the flesh with melted butter and then baking for 45 minutes.

VARIETIES

MARROW varieties

These varieties include all the traditional vegetable marrow shapes which are used for summer cooking and winter storage.

LONG GREEN TRAILING: Large and cylindrical with pale stripes. This is the one to grow to impress the neighbours or win prizes at the show.

LONG WHITE TRAILING: Another very large marrow, pale-skinned with excellent storage properties.

GREEN BUSH: Perhaps the best all-rounder — you can cut the small fruits as courgettes and let a few mature in late summer to produce striped green marrows.

EARLY GEM: One of the F₁ hybrid marrows which are now available. Early Gem, Zebra Cross, Emerald Cross and Tiger Cross are claimed to be earlier and more prolific than standard varieties.

COURGETTE varieties

These varieties are compact bush marrows which are grown exclusively for their immature fruits. They produce many small fruits over a long period … provided you keep cutting them.

ZUCCHINI: The most popular courgette variety — dark green fruits are produced in profusion. Serve raw in salad or cooked as a hot vegetable.

GOLDEN ZUCCHINI: Once this variety was the standard yellow courgette. The creamy flesh has a good flavour.

GOLD RUSH: This yellow variety has replaced Golden Zucchini in some of the major catalogues because it is earlier cropping.

SUPREMO: One of the newer F₁ hybrid green courgettes — others are Diamond and Onyx.

Green Bush

 Summer squash   **Winter squash**

SQUASH varieties

The summer squashes are non-standard shaped marrows with soft skins and pale, soft flesh. The winter squashes have a hard rind and fibrous, orange flesh.

CUSTARD SQUASH (Summer): This is the Patty Pan Squash of America — scalloped-edged, flat fruits which should be fried or boiled like courgettes. Both white and yellow varieties are available.

TENDER AND TRUE: The bush produces ball-shaped squashes which are mottled green. A compact and early-maturing variety.

VEGETABLE SPAGHETTI (Winter): An excellent novelty — boil for 25 minutes and cut in half. Remove seeds and then scrape out spaghetti-like strands with a fork. Home-grown spaghetti!

TABLE ACE (Winter): The winter squashes are not popular, but you will find several if you search through the catalogues — Table Ace, Hubbard Squash, Butternut, Crown Prince and Sweet Dumpling. The problem is that our season is a little too short and often too cool to ensure perfection. Still well worth the effort in southern districts.

Gold Rush

PUMPKIN varieties

These varieties include the pumpkin-shaped edible gourds — thick-skinned, very large and grown to maturity on the plant.

HUNDREDWEIGHT: Until recently this was the variety grown to produce enormous fruits which lived up to the promise of the name. This pumpkin is sometimes listed as Mammoth.

ATLANTIC GIANT: This world-beater arrived from America to make Hundredweight seem like a lightweight. You cannot hope to match the 500 lb record set over there.

TROUBLES
See pages 54–56

Vegetable Spaghetti

MUS ROOM

There is something especially exciting about the sight of the first flush of mushrooms breaking through the surface — we should feel the same way about germinating lettuce seeds . . . but we don't. There are two reasons — with mushrooms we know that it will take no more than a week or two for the tiny white pinheads to turn into button mushrooms ready for picking. Secondly, we also know that mushrooms are notoriously unpredictable — an outdoor planting is indeed a gamble, using home-made compost reduces but does not remove the risk and only the use of ready-spawned containers provides anything like the predictability associated with other vegetables.

MUSHROOMS OUTDOORS

- You may or may not be successful in raising mushrooms in a corner of your lawn. It will certainly have to be in a shady spot and the ground below will have to be enriched with well-rotted manure. Even if you are successful, there are the drawbacks of being unable to cut the grass when cropping starts and weeds cannot be treated by chemical means.
- If the above points act as a challenge rather than a deterrent, pick a damp day in spring or autumn and use golf-ball sized blocks of spawn, setting them about 2 in. below the surface at 12 in. spacings.

MUSHROOMS INDOORS

Anywhere indoors will do provided that the container or bed is shaded from direct sunlight and the temperature is in the 55–65°F range. Large fluctuations in temperature will slow down production — both cold and hot conditions will stop it. You will need specially-prepared compost which is hard to make at home, although you may be lucky enough to find a local supplier. This will have to be planted with mushroom spawn and properly tended to ensure success — a much easier course is to buy a ready-spawned container of compost from a garden centre or mail order nursery.

START FROM SCRATCH METHOD

- Start with stable manure or straw plus an activator. You will need a large heap, about 5 ft × 5 ft × 5 ft, to be reasonably sure of success and it must be well watered at the start. Leave covered until the temperature reaches at least 140°F — then turn every week until the heap is dark brown, crumbly and sweet-smelling.
- Fill boxes or buckets 9–12 in. deep — firm down with your fingers. When the temperature has fallen to 75°F the surface is ready for spawning.
- Two types of spawn are available — fungus-impregnated manure (block spawn) or impregnated rye (grain spawn). Block spawn is the easier one to use — push golf-ball sized pieces about 1 in. below the surface at 12 in. spacings.
- After a couple of weeks the spawn will have started to 'run' — white threads will be seen on the surface. At this stage add a 2 in. layer of moist casing mixture (2 parts peat, 1 part chalk).

EASY METHOD

- Buy a bucket or bag of ready-spawned compost. Avoid any pack which has obviously been in store for a long time and make sure that you start the pack into growth within 3 weeks of purchase.

LOOKING AFTER THE CROP

- A temperature of 55–65°F is necessary to promote the active development of the white fungal threads (mycelium) below the surface and the appearance of the edible fruiting bodies above. The casing should be kept moist but not wet by careful syringing with water.

HARVESTING

- The first flush will be ready for picking as button mushrooms 4–6 weeks after casing — these buttons will open into flats in about 7 days. Once the first flush has been harvested there will be a pause of about 2 weeks before the next flush appears. Cropping normally continues for about 8 weeks.
- Do not harvest mushrooms by cutting the stalks. Twist the mushroom upwards, disturbing the compost as little as possible. Cut away broken stalks and fill holes with casing mixture.
- After the final flush has been picked, use the spent manure in the garden — do not try to re-spawn for a second crop.

IN THE KITCHEN

Growing mushrooms at home is always fun because you can never really be sure what the result will be, but there is also a practical benefit — the flavour is so much better when they are eaten within hours of picking. Harvesting often takes place at the button stage when the membrane below the gills is unbroken. At this stage they are ideal for eating raw — plain or more usually in an oil and vinegar dressing. Open ('flat') mushrooms with their gills exposed are larger and have a much better flavour, but they can add a blackish colour to some dishes. Now for the golden rules. Never wash mushrooms — water will spoil the flavour. If the surface is soiled, wipe with a damp cloth. Never peel unless it is really necessary.

STORAGE There is no really satisfactory method — the flavour declines rapidly after picking. If you *have* to store them, keep in a paper bag in the refrigerator for up to 3 days.

COOKING The tastiest methods of preparation are frying (in an uncovered pan with butter and a little lemon juice for 3–5 minutes) and grilling (brushed with oil and seasoned before placing under the grill for 2–3 minutes on each side). Poach for 3–5 minutes if you are on a low-fat diet. Apart from their role as essential partners in mixed grills, hearty breakfasts and savoury omelettes, mushrooms are a basic ingredient of many classical recipes from Lancashire hotpot and *coq au vin* to *sole bonne femme* and *gebackener schwammerl*.

TROUBLES

PESTS
Several pests can cause serious problems for commercial growers, but only mushroom fly is likely to trouble the amateur. The maggots of this insect bore into the caps — spray with permethrin if small flies are seen.

DISEASES
Your small box or bucket is unlikely to be troubled.

ONION & SHALLOT from Sets

The onion sets you buy are immature bulbs which have been specially grown for planting. There are several advantages in using sets rather than seed. They are quick maturing, succeed in northern areas where seed-sown crops may disappoint and they are not attacked by onion fly nor mildew. Less skill and less soil fertility are required, but against these advantages must be set the extra cost and the extra risk of running to seed ('bolting'). Modern varieties are much less prone to bolting — another safeguard is to buy sets which are no larger than ¾ in. across. The shallots you buy are already full-sized — when planted in early spring they quickly start to grow and eventually produce a cluster of 8 to 12 similar-sized bulbs in summer.

SET FACTS

'Heat-treated' **Onion sets**: flower embryo has been killed to prevent bolting.	'Virus-free' **Shallots**: stock is free from virus yellows.
 ¹/₃ actual size	¹/₃ actual size
Expected sprouting time:	11–14 days
Approximate number per lb (Onion sets):	80
Approximate number per lb (Shallots):	30
Expected yield from a 10ft row:	7 lb
Approximate time between planting and lifting:	20 weeks (Onion sets) 18 weeks (Shallots)
Ease of cultivation:	Easy

SOIL FACTS

- All onions require good soil and free drainage, but sets need neither the fine texture nor the high organic content demanded by seed-sown onions.
- Dig in early winter and incorporate compost if available. Lime if necessary. Firm the surface before planting and rake in a general fertilizer such as Growmore.

PLANTING

Push gently into *soft* earth

4 in.

9 in.

Tip just showing. Firm soil around sets

- If planting is delayed, open package and spread out sets in a cool well-lit place to prevent premature sprouting.
- Plant onion sets 4 in. apart in mid March–mid April. Shallots require wider (6 in. apart) and earlier (mid February–mid March) planting.

CALENDAR

	JAN	FEB	MAR	APR	MAY	JUN	JUL	AUG	SEP	OCT	NOV	DEC
Planting Time		▓	▓	▓								
Lifting Time							▓	▓				

LOOKING AFTER THE CROP

- Protect from birds with black thread or netting if they are a nuisance in your area.
- Keep weed-free by hoeing and hand pulling. Push back any sets which have been lifted by frost or birds. Once the sets are established and shoots have appeared then treat as for seed-sown onions (see page 72).

HARVESTING

- **Shallots:** In July the leaves will turn yellow. Lift the bulb clusters and separate them, allowing each shallot to dry thoroughly. Remove dirt and brittle stems, and store in net bags or nylon tights in a cool, dry place. They will keep for about 8 months.
- **Onions:** See page 72.

IN THE KITCHEN

See page 73

VARIETIES

ONION varieties

STUTTGARTER GIANT: Until recently this was the variety you were most likely to be offered. The bulbs are flattened, not round, and the flavour is mild. It has good keeping qualities and is slow to bolt.

STURON: Many experts will tell you that this variety is a better choice than the old favourites. The straw-coloured bulbs are round and extremely large. Bolt resistance is excellent.

AILSA CRAIG: An old favourite — round, large and straw-coloured with white, mild-flavoured flesh.

RIJNSBURGER: Large, pale yellow and round. There are other large, round onions but this one (also listed as Giant Fen Globe) has outstanding keeping qualities. Stays fresh in store until May, according to the catalogues.

SHALLOT varieties

These small bulbs are milder in flavour than onions and are harvested in July or August. Use for cooking, garnishing or pickling — keep a few in a cool, well-lit place for planting next spring.

DUTCH YELLOW: One of the basic varieties — depending on the catalogue you will be offered Giant Yellow, Long Keeping Yellow, etc. It has now been superseded by Golden Gourmet — a better variety.

HATIVE DE NIORT: The usual choice by exhibitors — the bulbs are perfectly shaped with deep brown skins.

TROUBLES

See pages 74–75

ONION from Seed

Vegetable growing at home is not without its grumbles. The yield of pea pods is sometimes disappointing for the amount of work expended whereas broad beans present the opposite problem — a sudden glut which often goes to waste. Onions, however, present neither of these problems — few vegetables have more uses in the kitchen and so there is a constant demand. Nowadays we can obtain onions fresh from the garden or out of store almost all year round from just a couple of carefully-timed sowings. But we are creatures of habit — both peas and broad beans are two of our top-selling vegetable seeds and onions are not. If onions are not on your list read this section carefully — the new Japanese varieties have filled the June–July gap of the old days, and the new close-spacing recommendation increases the yield.

SEED FACTS

Fungicide-treated and pelleted seeds are available. Germination and seedling growth are slow in spring and also erratic in hot weather.

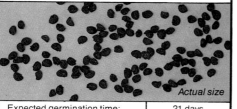

Actual size

Expected germination time:	21 days
Approximate number per ounce:	8000
Expected yield from a 10 ft row:	8 lb
Life expectancy of stored seed:	1–2 years
Approximate time between sowing and lifting:	46 weeks (August-sown varieties) 22 weeks (Spring-sown varieties)
Ease of cultivation:	Easy — if a suitable seed bed is prepared

SOIL FACTS

- Many exhibitors grow their show onions in a permanent bed in order to build up fertility, but in the kitchen plot it is a much better idea to change the site annually.
- Choose an open, sunny site with good drainage. Dig thoroughly in autumn, incorporating a liberal quantity of manure or compost. Liming will be necessary if the soil is acid.
- Before sowing or planting it is necessary to prepare a traditional 'onion bed'. Apply a general fertilizer and rake the surface when the soil is reasonably dry. Tread over the area and then rake again to produce a fine, even tilth.

SOWING & PLANTING

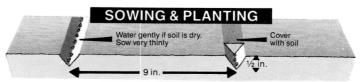

Water gently if soil is dry. Sow very thinly. Cover with soil. 9 in. ½ in.

- Thin the spring-sown crop in 2 stages — first to 1–2 in. when the seedlings have straightened up and then to 4 in. apart. Lift the seedlings carefully — the soil should be moist and all thinnings removed to deter onion fly.
- Seedlings raised under glass should be transplanted 4 in. apart, leaving 9 in. between the rows. The roots must fall vertically in the planting hole and the bulb base should be about ½ in. below the surface. Plant firmly.
- Salad onions should be planted in rows which are only 4 in. apart — thin the seedlings, if necessary, to 1 in. spacings.
- Seeds of Japanese varieties should be sown at 1 in. intervals in rows spaced 9 in. apart. Thin seedlings to 4 in. intervals in spring.

LOOKING AFTER THE CROP

- Hoe carefully or weed by hand — dense weed growth will seriously affect yield. Water if the weather is dry (not otherwise) and feed occasionally. Feed an autumn-sown crop with a liquid fertilizer in March.
- Break off any flower stems which appear. Mulching is useful for cutting down the need for water and for suppressing weeds. Stop watering once the onions have swollen and pull back the covering earth or mulch to expose the bulb surface to the sun.

HARVESTING

- The salad varieties should be pulled when the bulbs are ½–1 in. across. The harvesting season is March–October.
- When the bulb is mature the foliage turns yellow and topples over. Leave them for about 2 weeks and then carefully lift with a fork on a dry day.
- The onions which are not for immediate use must be dried. Spread out the bulbs on sacking or in trays — outdoors if the weather is warm and sunny or indoors if the weather is rainy.
- Drying will take 7–21 days, depending on the size of the bulbs and the air temperature. Inspect the bulbs carefully — all soft, spotted and thick-necked onions should be set aside for kitchen use or freezing. The rest can be stored — the exceptions are the Japanese varieties which are not suitable for storage.
- Store in trays, net bags, tights or tie to a length of cord as onion ropes. Choose a cool and well-lit place; they will keep until late spring.

- For an August or September crop sow as soon as the land is workable in the spring (late February–early April depending on the location of your garden).
- Sow in mid August for an earlier crop — Japanese varieties mature in late June — standard varieties such as Reliance and Ailsa Craig are less hardy, less reliable and later cropping (late July onwards), but they can be stored.
- In cold areas and for exhibition bulbs sow under glass in January, harden off in March and transplant outdoors in April.
- Salad onions should be sown in March–July for a June–October crop. Sow in August for onions in March–May.

CALENDAR

	JAN	FEB	MAR	APR	MAY	JUN	JUL	AUG	SEP	OCT	NOV	DEC
Sowing Time (outdoors)												
Sowing Time (indoors)												
Lifting Time												

For key to symbols — see page 7

IN THE KITCHEN

The culinary uses are so varied and the basic ways of employing onions are so well known that there would be no point in trying to list them. The Ploughman's Lunch of bread, cheese, onions and ale has sustained British workers for countless generations. At the other end of the scale French classic dishes served *à la bonne femme* or with *Bercy* sauce have relied on shallots for their subtle flavour. The onion is thought to be our oldest vegetable, but there are still some basic facts which are not universally known. First of all, the proper way to chop an onion. Cut in half lengthways and place the cut side downwards on a board. Make about five cuts, first downwards and then horizontally towards but not through the base. Finally chop downwards across the length of the onion and throw away the tough basal section — you will be left with a neat pile of cubes. If watery eyes are a problem keep hands and onions under water . . . or buy an autochopper if all else fails. Onion rings are a popular ingredient for salads, but home-grown ones are often a great deal hotter than the mild-flavoured Spanish onions bought in shops. To increase mildness simply pour boiling water over the rings, dab dry with a paper towel and serve.

FREEZING Cut into slices and blanch for 1 minute — leave button onions whole. Cool, drain and dry. Pack into polythene bags and freeze — use within 12 months.

STORAGE Salad onions can be kept in the refrigerator for up to 1 week. Do not store bulbs in this way — keep in a cool place until required.

COOKING Onions outrank even tomatoes as the great accompanists in the kitchen. For soups, stews, flans, casseroles, sauces and so on, braised chopped onions are often a basic ingredient. Remember to fry *slowly* — the onions should simmer in order to soften before browning takes place. As a hot vegetable serve boiled, baked, stir-fried, or glazed. Best of all, perhaps, are fried onion rings — dip in milk and then flour before frying until golden brown.

VARIETIES

BULB varieties

The standard varieties are grown for their large bulbs which can be stored throughout the winter months. Some have a flattened shape, others are globular. Skin colours vary from almost pure white to bright red and flavours range from mild to strong. Most of them are only suitable for spring sowing but some can be sown in August for a late July crop. The Japanese varieties make late summer sowing a much more reliable routine but their midsummer crop cannot be stored.

AILSA CRAIG: Look no further, according to some experts. A great favourite — very large, globe-shaped, excellent for exhibiting but its keeping qualities are not good.

BEDFORDSHIRE CHAMPION: Very popular — scores over Ailsa Craig by being a good keeper. Large and globular, but very susceptible to downy mildew.

RIJNSBURGER: The catalogues list many strains — Balstora, Wijbo, Bola, etc. Large, globular, white-fleshed — earliness and keeping qualities depend on the strain you choose.

LANCASTRIAN: A large globe variety with golden skin — a good choice for show bench and kitchen.

HYGRO: An F₁ hybrid which is increasing in popularity. No faults — heavy, globular, and suitable for storage.

NORTH HOLLAND BLOOD RED: A red-skinned onion — a good choice if you want a colourful onion for exhibition.

BUFFALO: An F₁ hybrid which produces a very early crop from a spring or late summer sowing. Onions in June, claim the catalogues, but you won't be able to store them.

RED BARON: An early red-skinned onion with flattish bulbs which store well.

RELIANCE: Perhaps the best of the standard varieties for sowing in August. The flat bulbs are large and the keeping qualities are outstanding.

EXPRESS YELLOW: One of the earliest of the Japanese varieties. The flattish bulbs are yellow-skinned. Choose one of the other Japanese types if you want maximum yields.

KAIZUKA EXTRA EARLY: Like Express Yellow the bulbs are flattish, but the skins are paler and they mature a little later.

IMAI YELLOW: A Japanese variety which is globe-shaped and early.

SENSHYU: Rather similar to Imai Yellow, but a little flatter and later cropping.

Ailsa Craig

SALAD varieties

Thinnings of the bulb varieties can be used as salad or 'spring' onions, but there are several varieties which are grown specifically for salad use. These salad varieties, also known as scallions or bunching onions, are white-skinned and mild-flavoured.

WHITE LISBON: By far the most popular of the salad varieties. Quick-growing and silvery-skinned, a small patch of ground can provide salad onions for six months of the year.

ISHIKURA: Something new in salad onions. The long, straight stems do not form bulbs — simply pull out a few at a time and let the rest of the pencil-like plants grow on for harvesting later.

White Lisbon

PICKLING varieties

Several onion varieties are grown for their small silverskin bulbs (button onions) which are lifted in July or August and pickled for use as cocktail onions. These varieties should be sown in April in sandy soil — do not feed. The seedlings should not be thinned.

PARIS SILVER SKIN: The favourite pickling onion; lift when the bulb is the size of a marble.

BARLETTA: Another popular variety for making cocktail onions — no particular advantage or disadvantage compared with Paris Silver Skin.

Paris Silver Skin

ONION & LEEK TROUBLES

Although many plant disorders can attack onions, only four are likely to seriously trouble the gardener. They are onion fly, stem and bulb eelworm, neck rot and white rot. Plants grown from seed are more susceptible to onion fly, so raise onions from sets if you have been disappointed in the past. Leeks are much less prone to attack than onions.

	Symptom	Likely Causes
Seedlings	— eaten	**Cutworm** (see page 110)
	— killed	4
	— toppled over	**Damping off** (see page 110)
Sets	— lifted out of ground	**Frost** or **Birds**
	— two or more plants produced	6
Leaves	— tunnelled	12
	— eaten above ground level	**Cabbage moth** (see page 29)
	— eaten at ground level	**Cutworm** (see page 110) or **Wireworm** (see page 110)
	— diseased	7 or 8 or 11
	— yellow, drooping	1 or 13 or 14
	— green, drooping	2
	— white tipped	10
	— swollen, distorted	4
Plants	— abnormally thick-necked	9
	— run to seed	3
Bulbs in the garden	— tunnelled, maggots present	1
	— split at base	5
	— mouldy at base	13
	— soft, not evil-smelling	4 or 11 or 13
	— soft, evil-smelling inside	14
Bulbs in store	— soft, mouldy near neck	15
	— soft, evil-smelling	**Soft rot** (see page 85)

TUNNELLED BULBS

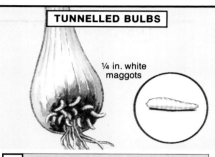

¼ in. white maggots

1 ONION FLY

Tell-tale signs are yellow drooping leaves. Worst attacks occur in dry soil in midsummer. The maggots burrow into the bases of the bulbs — young plants are frequently killed, older ones fail to develop properly.

Treatment: Lift and burn badly affected plants.

Prevention: Treat with pirimiphos-methyl shortly before sowing or planting. Destroy all thinnings, damaged leaves and infested bulbs — firm the soil around the plants. If onion fly is a regular problem grow onions from sets rather than seeds.

TWISTED, SWOLLEN LEAVES

4 STEM & BULB EELWORM

Swollen, distorted foliage indicates attack by this microscopic soil-living pest. Young plants are killed; older ones produce soft bulbs which cannot be stored.

Treatment: Lift and burn infected plants.

Prevention: Do not grow onions, peas, beans or strawberries, for several years, on land affected by stem and bulb eelworm.

2 DROOPING LEAVES

Leaves sometimes droop even though neither pest nor disease is present. If foliage is darker green than normal, then the usual cause is either too much fresh manure before planting or too much nitrogen in the soil. Watering with a potash-rich fertilizer, such as a tomato or rose fertilizer, will help.

BULBS SPLIT AT BASE

5 SADDLEBACK

Harvested onions are found to be split at the base. This disorder affects crops grown from sets, and it is always associated with heavy rain or watering after a prolonged period of drought.

Treatment: None. Use affected onions as soon as possible as they will not keep in store.

Prevention: Never keep the plants short of water during dry spells in summer.

3 BOLTING

Onions occasionally bolt (premature production of flower heads). When this happens cut off the flower stalks and lift bulbs in the usual way. Use as soon as possible as they will not store satisfactorily. Common causes are early sowing or planting in a cold spring and planting in loose soil.

6 SET DIVISION

Onions grown from sets may produce twin bulbs. The cause of this splitting is usually planting at the wrong time or growing the plants in poor soil. Prolonged dry weather can also induce set division.

7 SMUT

Black spots and blotches appear on leaves and bulbs. Only young plants are affected — the leaves become thickened and twisted. Leeks are more susceptible than onions.

Treatment: None. Lift and burn diseased plants.

Prevention: Do not grow leeks nor onions on infected land for at least 8 years.

SPOTS ON LEAVES

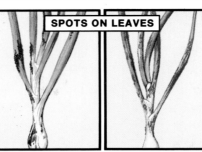

8 RUST

Orange spots and blotches appear on the surface of leaves. Uncommon, but effect can be fatal in a severe attack in summer. Leeks are more susceptible than onions.

Treatment: Remove and burn diseased leaves.

Prevention: Do not grow leeks nor onions on land affected by rust in the previous season.

WHITENED LEAVES

10 WHITE TIP

Leaf tips of leeks turn white and papery in autumn. Disease spreads downwards and growth is stunted.

Treatment: Spray with mancozeb as soon as the first signs are noticed. Lift and burn badly diseased plants.

Prevention: Do not grow leeks on land affected in the previous season.

9 BULL NECK (Thick Neck)

The production of abnormally thick necks is a serious complaint as the bulbs will not store properly. Bull-necked onions are often associated with the overmanuring of land and the use of too much nitrogen. Use a liquid feed during the growing season — choose one such as tomato fertilizer which contains more potash than nitrogen. Another possible cause is sowing seed too deeply.

MOULD ON LEAVES

11 DOWNY MILDEW

Downy grey mould covers leaves, which slowly die back and shrivel from the tips. Bulbs are usually soft and not suitable for storage. A serious disease in cool, damp seasons.

Treatment: Spray with carbendazim at the first signs of disease. Repeat every fortnight.

Prevention: Grow onions on a different site each year. Avoid badly-drained areas.

TUNNELLED LEAVES

12 LEEK MOTH

Pale green ½ in. caterpillars feed inside young onion leaves so that only outer skin remains. The foliage of leeks may also be attacked.

Treatment: Spray with a contact insecticide at the first signs of attack. Destroy badly affected leaves.

Prevention: No practical method available.

ROTTING BULBS IN STORE

15 NECK ROT

Grey mould appears near neck in store; bulbs turn soft and rotten.

Treatment: None. Examine stored bulbs frequently and remove rotten bulbs immediately.

Prevention: Dust seeds and sets with carbendazim before planting. Follow all the rules for correct storage — dry bulbs thoroughly and store only hard, undamaged ones in a cool well-ventilated place. Don't store onions with fleshy, green necks.

ROTTING BULBS IN THE GARDEN

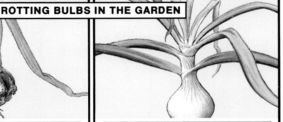

13 WHITE ROT (Mouldy Nose)

Foliage turns yellow and wilts. Fluffy white mould appears on the base of the bulbs, and round black bodies appear in this fungus. White rot is a serious disease, and is always worst in hot, dry summers.

Treatment: None. Lift and burn diseased plants.

Prevention: There is no chemical treatment you can use. Do not grow onions on infected land for at least 8 years.

14 SHANKING

Centre leaves turn yellow and collapse; outside leaves soon follow. Cut open a bulb; the tell-tale sign is evil-smelling slime within the scales. This disease is much less common than white rot.

Treatment: None. Lift and burn diseased plants.

Prevention: No practical method available. Do not grow onions on infected land for several years.

1 in. = 2.5 cm, 1 ft = 30 cm, 1 oz = 28 gm, 1 lb = 450 gm

PARSNIP

The popularity of parsnips continues to decline. They occupy the ground for a long time and when plain boiled provide a dish which is not to everybody's taste. Do think twice, however, before rejecting them. They need very little attention and you can sow a catch-crop of radish or lettuce between the rows. The roots can be left in the ground during winter and dug up as required, and there are several appetising ways of serving them. There are not many varieties from which to make your choice — pick a long one if your soil is good and you want to show off your skill, but a short variety is usually a better choice for most gardens.

SEED FACTS

Seed is very light — sow on a still day. Germination is slow in cold weather.

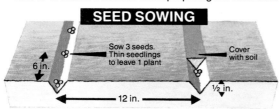

Actual size

Expected germination time:	10 – 28 days
Approximate number per ounce:	8000
Expected yield from a 10 ft row:	8 lb
Life expectancy of stored seed:	1 year
Approximate time between sowing and lifting:	34 weeks
Ease of cultivation:	Easy

SOIL FACTS

- If you want to grow long and tapering parsnips you will need a deep, friable and stone-free soil which has been well-manured for a previous crop.
- Any reasonable soil in sun or light shade will grow a good crop of one of the shorter varieties. Dig deeply in autumn or early winter and refrain from adding any fresh manure or compost. Lime if necessary. Break down clods and rake in Growmore fertilizer when preparing the seed bed.

SEED SOWING

6 in. | Sow 3 seeds. Thin seedlings to leave 1 plant | Cover with soil | ½ in. | 12 in.

- Use fresh seed every year. February is the traditional month for sowing parsnips, but it is better to wait until March when the weather will be warmer or even April if you are growing one of the shorter-rooted varieties.

CALENDAR

	JAN	FEB	MAR	APR	MAY	JUN	JUL	AUG	SEP	OCT	NOV	DEC
Sowing Time												
Lifting Time												

LOOKING AFTER THE CROP

- Parsnips seldom produce satisfactory roots after transplanting, so throw thinnings away.
- Hoe regularly to keep down weeds. Take care — never touch the crowns of the developing plants. The crop requires very little attention and it is not usually attacked by pests. The leaf-mining celery fly is occasionally a nuisance — squash the blisters between the fingers.
- The soil should not be allowed to dry out, but it will be necessary to water when there is a prolonged dry spell.

HARVESTING

- The roots are ready for lifting when the foliage begins to die down in autumn. It is claimed that the flavour is improved after the first frosts.
- Lift the crop as required, using a fork to loosen the soil. Leave the remainder in the soil for later harvesting. It is a good idea to lift some in November and store as for carrots (see page 40). In this way you will have a supply of parsnips when the soil is frozen or covered with snow. Lift and store any remaining roots at the end of February.

IN THE KITCHEN

Before the potato came to Britain from the New World it was the parsnip which accompanied roasts, game and fish. Nowadays it is regarded as too sweet and too strongly flavoured as an everyday dish, but part of the problem is due to the common habit of boiling it for 25 – 30 minutes and serving as a straight substitute for boiled potatoes. Parsnips deserve better treatment.

FREEZING Trim, peel and wash — cut into cubes and blanch for 5 minutes. Freeze in polythene bags.

STORAGE Store them in a polythene bag in the refrigerator — parsnips will stay fresh for up to 2 weeks.

COOKING Top and tail with a knife and remove any damaged or diseased parts. Scrub — avoid peeling if you can. Remove central hard core if roots are old. Parboil for 2 minutes and then place around a joint of meat for roasting. Alternatively cut into strips and fry as chips or cut into rings and fry as fritters after dipping in batter. Boil and mash with butter, nutmeg and carrots or go American and glaze them with brown sugar.

VARIETIES

GLADIATOR: An F_1 hybrid which has become popular — the wedge-shaped roots are smooth and white-skinned. Resistant to canker.

TENDER AND TRUE: Still the most popular long variety, widely recommended for exhibition. There is very little core and the resistance to canker is high.

HOLLOW CROWN IMPROVED: Another long variety for exhibition and kitchen use. As with all the long ones you will need a deep, clay-free soil or you will have to sow in specially-prepared soil pockets.

AVONRESISTER: One of the shortest — 5 in. cones which are resistant to canker and capable of growing in poor soils. Sow at 3 in. intervals — not the standard 6 in. Sweet-flavoured.

WHITE GEM: Similar to the old variety Offenham but resistant to canker. Easy to lift, excellent flavour — taking over from Offenham in the catalogues.

THE STUDENT: Medium-sized — thick and tapering. The one to choose for flavour.

TROUBLES

See pages 42-43

For key to symbols — see page 7

PEA

The garden pea was the first vegetable to be canned, and nowadays we spend over £100 million annually on tinned peas. Peas were also the first vegetable to be successfully frozen, and they are more popular today than any other type of frozen vegetable. These preserved products plus their shop-bought counterparts which are shelled at home provide a vital part of our national diet, but they don't taste as good as the peas we pick from the garden. The reason is quite simple — as soon as a pod is pulled from the plant, the sugar content of the peas within it starts to turn into starch. If you want to taste just how good peas can be then pick the pods when the peas are quite small and within an hour boil the shelled peas for about 10 minutes in a small amount of water to which a sprig of mint has been added. Unfortunately peas quite often cause disappointment as a garden crop. The yield can be quite small for the area occupied, and if the soil is poor or the weather hot it can seem that the amount obtained is not worth all the trouble. The answer is to read the rules for success before buying a packet of seed in spring and popping them into the ground. There are many types and their classification is complex at first glance — round or wrinkled; tall or dwarf; first early, second early or maincrop. Never plant peas in cold and wet soil, make sure that the soil is fertile, keep the birds away, spray when necessary and with space, skill and the right varieties you can have peas fresh from the garden from May until October.

TYPES

ROUND GARDEN PEA (dried)   **WRINKLED GARDEN PEA (dried)**   **MANGETOUT**   **PETIT POIS**   **ASPARAGUS PEA**

SEED FACTS

Treat with a fungicidal seed dressing if seed is to be sown in early spring.

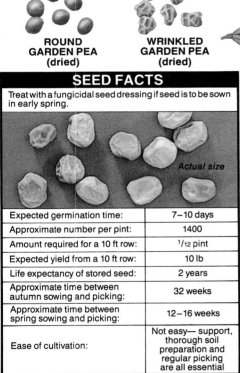

Actual size

Expected germination time:	7–10 days
Approximate number per pint:	1400
Amount required for a 10 ft row:	1/12 pint
Expected yield from a 10 ft row:	10 lb
Life expectancy of stored seed:	2 years
Approximate time between autumn sowing and picking:	32 weeks
Approximate time between spring sowing and picking:	12–16 weeks
Ease of cultivation:	Not easy— support, thorough soil preparation and regular picking are all essential

SEED SOWING

Press into soil surface. Firm down soil *lightly* after sowing. 3 in. 6 in. Expected height of crop. 2 in.

LOOKING AFTER THE CROP

- Immediately after sowing you must protect the row from birds. Do not rely on a chemical deterrent — use black cotton stretched between short stakes or plastic netting. You can place twiggy branches over the surface, but best of all are wire-mesh guards.
- Hoe regularly and carefully to keep weeds under control. When the seedlings are about 3 in. high insert twigs alongside the stems to provide support. Do not delay this operation — leaving the stems to straggle over the soil surface is likely to result in severe slug damage. Medium- and tall-growing varieties will need extra support — place a strongly erected screen of plastic netting at the side of each row.
- Water during dry spells in summer. Apply a mulch of weedkiller-free grass clippings between the rows in order to conserve moisture.
- Spray the plants with fenitrothion 7-10 days after the start of flowering to avoid maggoty peas.

HARVESTING

- A pod is ready for picking when it is well filled but while there is still a little air space between each pea. Start harvesting at this stage, beginning at the bottom of the stem and working upwards. Use two hands, one to hold the stem and the other to pick off the pod.
- Pick regularly — pods left to mature on the plant will seriously reduce the total yield. If you harvest too many to cook immediately, place the excess in the refrigerator or you can deep freeze them.
- When all the pods have been picked, use the stems for making compost. Leave the roots in the soil.
- To dry peas, allow the pods to mature on the stems — in wet weather lift the plants and hang in bundles indoors until the pods are ripe.
- Pick mangetout when they are about 3 in. long and the peas within are just starting to develop. Asparagus peas are ready when they are 1–1½ in. long.

SOIL FACTS

- Under poor soil conditions the yield will be very disappointing. The need is for good structure, adequate humus and enough lime to ensure that the soil is not acid. Avoid adding too much fertilizer — a heavy nitrogen dressing will do more harm than good.
- Choose an open spot which has not grown peas for at least 2 seasons. Dig the soil in autumn or early winter, incorporating 2 bucketsful of well-rotted manure or compost into each sq. yard of soil. Apply a light dressing of a general-purpose fertilizer shortly before sowing time.

1 in. = 2.5 cm, 1 ft = 30 cm, 1 oz = 28 gm, 1 lb = 450 gm

IN THE KITCHEN

As the textbooks will tell you, this vegetable has been popular since prehistoric times. An interesting fact which is not usually mentioned is that it was *dried* peas which were part of our staple diet in the old days. Pease pudding, made from dried peas, butter and eggs, was the traditional accompaniment to boiled bacon or pork. It was not until the 17th century that the wealthy and fashionable in Britain adopted the continental idea of cooking *fresh* peas. Today, of course, almost all of us prefer fresh peas. Pick before maturity and cook as soon as possible after picking. Do not overcook (10 minutes should be enough) and do not use too much water. The rule for shop-bought peas is different — you may need to boil them for 15 minutes.

FREEZING Use young peas. Shell and blanch for 1 minute. Cool, drain and freeze in polythene bags or rigid containers. Use within 12 months.

STORAGE Keep in a polythene bag in the refrigerator — peas will stay fresh for up to 3 days.

COOKING The standard method of boiling peas is given above — for a change you can try *petit pois a la francaise*. A petit pois variety is used, or an ordinary garden variety picked when the peas are small. These are gently cooked with lettuce and shallots or salad onions for about 10 minutes in a covered pan with a tablespoon or two of water, a little butter and a sprinkling of sugar. Boiled peas are usually served as a hot vegetable but they are also a useful salad ingredient when cold. For the thrifty, you will find a recipe for pea pod soup in many cookery books — the soup is mixed in a blender and then sieved to remove the fibre. With mangetout the pods are not a problem. You eat them pods and all — raw when small and fresh or boiled for 3 minutes and then tossed in butter. Asparagus peas, like mangetout, are not shelled before eating — boil or steam for 5 minutes.

CALENDAR

		JAN	FEB	MAR	APR	MAY	JUN	JUL	AUG	SEP	OCT	NOV	DEC
For a May/June Crop: Choose a sheltered site — expect some losses if the site is cold and exposed. Grow a round variety — Feltham First is reliable for both early spring and late sowing. Meteor has an excellent reputation for hardiness. Cover seedlings and plants with cloches.	Sowing Time		⬇	⬇							⬇	⬇	
	Picking Time					▓							
For a June/July Crop: For a mid March sowing choose a round variety or a First Early wrinkled variety such as Kelvedon Wonder, Beagle or Early Onward. For late March or April sowing pick a Second Early wrinkled type — Onward is the usual choice but Hurst Green Shaft is a good alternative.	Sowing Time			▓									
	Picking Time							▓					
For an August Crop: Use a Maincrop wrinkled variety — be guided by the height on the back of the packet rather than the pretty picture on the front. If space is limited choose a medium-height pea such as Senator — leave Alderman for the people who can spare 5 ft between the rows.	Sowing Time				▓								
	Picking Time								▓				
For an Autumn Crop: Fresh peas are especially welcome in September and October when the main picking season is over. June–July is the sowing season and you must choose the right type — a First Early wrinkled variety with good mildew resistance. Neither Kelvedon Wonder nor Pioneer will let you down.	Sowing Time						▓						
	Picking Time									▓	▓		
Mangetout & Petit pois: Sow seed when the soil has started to warm up in April — sowing can be delayed until May. Neither mangetout nor petit pois have become popular like the familiar garden peas — you may have to send off for seeds if your local garden shop does not carry them.	Sowing Time				▒	▓							
	Picking Time								▓	▓			
Asparagus Pea: Sow seed in mid or late May so that the seedlings will appear after the last frosts have gone. Make 1 in. deep drills about 15 in. apart and sow seeds at 6 in. intervals. The harvest period usually starts at the beginning of August and continues for many weeks.	Sowing Time					▓							
	Picking Time								▒	▓	▒		

For key to symbols — see page 7

VARIETIES

ROUND varieties

The seeds of these varieties remain smooth and round when dried. They are all First Earlies — hardier and quicker-maturing than other types and more able to withstand poor growing conditions than the wrinkled types. Round varieties are used for late autumn and early spring sowing.

FELTHAM FIRST: 1½ ft. An old favourite which requires little support, producing 4 in. long pointed pods 11-12 weeks after sowing.

METEOR: 1 ft. The baby of the group with a high reputation for succeeding in cold and exposed sites.

PILOT: 3 ft. Very popular as it combines earliness with a heavy crop. If you have the space, the best choice for a May/June crop.

DOUCE PROVENCE: 1½ ft. Perhaps you are looking for maximum sweetness rather than maximum yield. Douce Provence is the one to choose — it has all the robustness of Feltham First but the flavour is superior.

FORTUNE: 1½ ft. Quite similar to Feltham First — it matures rather later but the yields may be higher.

Feltham First

1 in. = 2.5 cm, 1 ft = 30 cm, 1 oz = 28 gm, 1 lb = 450 gm

WRINKLED varieties

Kelvedon Wonder

The seeds of these varieties are distinctly wrinkled when dried. These 'marrowfat' peas are sweeter, larger and heavier cropping than the round ones, and are therefore much more widely grown. They are, however, less hardy and should not be sown before March. These wrinkled varieties are classified in two ways. Firstly by height (there are the 1½–2 ft dwarfs and the 4–5 ft tall varieties) and secondly by the time taken from sowing to first picking. First Earlies take 11–12 weeks, Second Earlies 13–14 weeks and Maincrop 15–16 weeks. In catalogues and garden centres you will find a large choice from each group.

First Earlies
KELVEDON WONDER: 1½ ft. An excellent choice if you want to buy just one variety for successional sowings. A good one to pick for early sowing or for sowing in June for an autumn crop. Mildew resistance is high.

LITTLE MARVEL: 1½ ft. All the catalogues list it, but Little Marvel is not as popular as Kelvedon Wonder. The flavour is good and the blunt-ended pods are borne in pairs.

EARLY ONWARD: 2 ft. Look for its more famous brother in the Second Earlies section. This one has all the Onward characteristics, but matures about 10 days earlier.

BEAGLE: 1½ ft. Sometimes listed as Hurst Beagle — the earliest wrinkled variety. Blunt-ended pods — 8 peas per pod.

PROGRESS NO. 9: 1½ ft. Almost rivals Beagle in earliness — differs from it by bearing pointed pods.

PIONEER: 1½ ft. A useful variety for early sowing and also for June sowing as, like Kelvedon Wonder, it resists mildew. Unfortunately, you will have to search for it these days.

Second Earlies
HURST GREEN SHAFT: 2½ ft. All the catalogues sing its praises — pods with 10 peas borne in pairs at the top of the plant to make picking easier, pods which can win prizes at the show and peas to win praise in the dining room. Resistant to both mildew and fusarium wilt.

ONWARD: 2½ ft. The most popular garden pea. It crops heavily and has good disease resistance. The pods are plump, blunt-ended and dark green.

CAVALIER: 2½ ft. The long pointed pods are borne in pairs — yields are high and the flavour is good. Mildew resistance makes it suitable for summer, the only Second Early you can use.

BIKINI: 1½ ft. One of the new less-leaf, more-tendril varieties. It is claimed that the tendrils can be boiled and eaten as a second vegetable. Other less-leaf peas are Eaton and Poppet.

Maincrops
LORD CHANCELLOR: 3½ ft. Late-maturing — claimed by some to be the best Maincrop pea variety. A heavy cropper bearing dark green, pointed pods.

ALDERMAN: 5 ft. Quite a giant — popular with exhibitors. The large pods contain 11 large peas. Yields are high and the picking season is prolonged.

GRADUS: 3 ft. This one is for sowing in April for a July crop — pods are large and the crops are heavy. Support is necessary. The flavour is rated very highly.

SENATOR: 2½ ft. Highly recommended as the Maincrop for small gardens. The pods are borne in pairs — both flavour and yield are claimed to be exceptional.

MANGETOUT varieties

Oregon Sugar Pod

There are several names for this group — chinese peas, snow peas, sugar peas and eat-all. They are rather easier to grow than garden peas — pick before the seeds swell and cook the pods whole.

OREGON SUGAR POD: 3½ ft. A popular variety listed in many catalogues — pods can reach 4–4½ in., but pick at the 3 in. stage.

SUGAR DWARF SWEET GREEN: 3 ft. Another true mangetout — little to choose between it and Oregon Sugar Pod.

SUGAR SNAP: 5 ft. A dual-purpose pea — when the pods are young they are cooked like a true mangetout variety. More mature pods with peas inside can be 'stringed' and then cooked like french beans or shelled and cooked like peas.

EDULA: 3 ft. Like Sugar Snap, but more compact for the smaller garden.

PETIT POIS varieties

Waverex

Petit pois are not immature peas gathered from small pods of any garden pea variety — they are a small number of dwarf varieties which produce tiny (⅛–¼ in.) peas which are uniquely sweet.

GULLIVERT: 3 ft. Once the basic type, now replaced in the catalogues by Waverex. The pods and seeds were small, the peas were delicious, but the plants were rather tall for such a tiny pea.

WAVEREX: 2 ft. The petit pois you are most likely to find. Eat raw in salads or cook the French way described on page 78.

COBRI: 2 ft. An old variety which is still available. Typical petit pois for you to shell and cook — boil in the pods and shell before serving, advises the main supplier.

ASPARAGUS PEA variety

This variety is also known as the winged pea. It is not really a pea at all — it is a vetch which produces sprawling bushy plants. It is not frost-hardy, so sowing must be delayed until May. The red flowers which appear in summer are followed by curiously shaped winged pods — these must be gathered whilst they are still small or they will be fibrous and stringy. The small pods are cooked whole like mangetout.

TROUBLES
See pages 20–22

1 in. = 2.5 cm, 1 ft = 30 cm, 1 oz = 28 gm, 1 lb = 450 gm

POTATO

Some of the vegetables in this section, such as salsify and celeriac, need an introduction — potatoes do not. They remain our basic vegetable — the almost invariable partner for meat, fish or poultry. So the question is which type to grow and not whether to grow the vegetable — no worries here about gluts or turned-up noses! Your choice is between the Earlies and the Maincrops, the difference being in the time taken to reach the lifting stage. If you have a large plot the answer is simple — grow Earlies to provide 'new' potatoes in summer and also grow Maincrops to provide tubers for storage over winter. If space is limited then an Early variety should be your only choice. The yield will be lower than from a Maincrop, but it will take up less space, miss the ravages of blight and provide new potatoes at a time when shop prices are high. Potatoes are half-hardy — young leaves are killed by late frosts in spring and the stems are destroyed by the first frosts of autumn. During the period in between our most popular vegetable must put on all its growth and produce the underground tubers we use for food. Potato growing has a language of its own. We begin with *good quality seed* — small potatoes produced from plants which have been certified as virus-free. These potatoes are usually *chitted*, which means that they have been induced to develop small shoots before planting. From these planted seed potatoes the *haulm* (stems and leaves) is produced and below ground *bulking-up* takes place — swelling of the tubers in summer or early autumn. *Greening* must be avoided by *earthing-up* — the covering of the stem bases with soil. The reason is simple — green potatoes are poisonous.

SEED FACTS

Seed should be the size of a small hen's egg (1–2 oz). Do not plant diseased or soft seed potatoes. Large seed should not be cut in half.

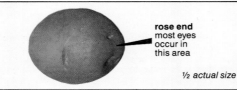

rose end most eyes occur in this area

½ actual size

Amount required for a 10 ft row:	1½ lb
Expected yield from a 10 ft row:	12 lb (Early varieties) 20 lb (Maincrop varieties)
Approximate time between planting and lifting:	13 weeks (Early varieties) 22 weeks (Maincrop varieties)
Ease of cultivation:	Not difficult — but high yields call for watering and spraying

SOIL FACTS

- Potatoes can be grown in practically every soil type. It is the best crop to grow in grassland or wasteland which is to be turned into a vegetable plot — earthing-up and the dense leaf canopy help to clean up new ground. In the established vegetable plot potatoes should not be grown on land which has been used for this crop within the past 2 seasons.
- Choose a sunny spot if possible and avoid frost pockets. Dig the soil in autumn and add peat or compost if the soil was not manured for the previous crop.
- Before planting treat the soil with pirimiphos-methyl if there is a wireworm problem, which is likely in newly-dug grassland. Break down any clods and sprinkle Growmore fertilizer over the surface.

PLANTING

- When you obtain your seed potatoes in February set them out (rose end uppermost) in egg boxes or in wooden trays containing a 1 in. layer of dry peat. Keep them in a light (not sunny) frost-free room and in about 6 weeks there will be several sturdy ½–1 in. shoots. Do not remove any of these sprouts. Chitting is vital for Earlies and useful for Maincrops.

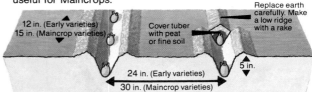

Replace earth carefully. Make a low ridge with a rake

12 in. (Early varieties)
15 in. (Maincrop varieties)

Cover tuber with peat or fine soil

24 in. (Early varieties)
30 in. (Maincrop varieties)

5 in.

LOOKING AFTER THE CROP

- If there is a danger of frost when the shoots have begun to emerge draw a little soil over them for protection.
- When the haulm is about 9 in. high it is time for earthing-up. First of all, break up the soil between the rows with a fork and remove weeds. Use a draw hoe to pile the loose soil against the stems to produce a flat-topped ridge about 6 in. high. Some people like to earth-up a little at a time, but there is little evidence that such a procedure gives better results than the one-step method.
- Water liberally in dry weather — this is most important once the tubers have started to form.

HARVESTING

- With Earlies wait until the flowers open or the buds drop. Carefully remove soil from a small part of the ridge and examine the tubers. They are ready for harvesting as new potatoes when they are the size of hens' eggs — insert a flat-tined fork into the ridge well away from the haulm and lift the roots forward into the trench.
- With Maincrops for storage cut off the haulm once the foliage has turned brown and the stems have withered. Remove the cut haulm and wait 10 days — then lift the roots and let the tubers dry for several hours. Place them in a wooden box and store in a dark, frost-free shed — they should keep until the spring.
- When harvesting remove *all* tubers from the soil, however small, to avoid problems next year.

IN THE KITCHEN

We cook potatoes every day and so the experienced housewife will probably not bother to read this section. Certainly a short summary cannot begin to describe the 500 ways of serving potatoes, but there are a few rules for the everyday methods which are frequently ignored. New potatoes are earlies lifted before the plant has reached maturity and before the skins of the tubers have set. Rub the skin of a raw potato gently — if it does not come off readily then it doesn't deserve the title 'new'. Serve them boiled — hot, or cold in salads. Use old potatoes (maincrops which have been allowed to set their skins) for the multitude of other uses — chipped, mashed, creamed, baked, sautéed, roasted and so on.

FREEZING Blanch whole new potatoes in water and chips in oil — blanching time 3 minutes. Cool and drain — then pack and freeze in rigid containers.

STORAGE Store in a cool, dark place. In the kitchen you can keep new potatoes in a polythene bag in the refrigerator — potatoes will stay fresh for up to 2 weeks.

COOKING First of all, new potatoes. Wash under running water and either leave skins on or rub off with your fingers. Boil for 12 minutes with a sprig of mint. Drain, and then toss in a little butter. Now for old potatoes — scrub under running water and scrape off the skin if you can — peeling removes much of the vitamin C which is just below the surface. For boiling, cut into chunks and cook for 15–20 minutes; for roasting parboil for 5 minutes and put around the roast for 45 minutes. Cooking the perfect chip is an art — cut ½ in. thick strips and wash in ice-cold water to remove the surface starch. Drain and dry thoroughly in a cloth, then fry until golden as a shallow layer in a frying basket in a pan one-third full of oil at 350°F. Drain and serve. Baking is much easier — wash, dry and prick the surface all over with a fork. Brush lightly with oil and bake for 1 hour at 400°F. In a microwave oven you will only have to wait for about 10 minutes. Potatoes *duchesse, anna, château, rösti, pont-neuf, dauphine* . . . you'll find them all in a good cookery book.

- **First Early varieties:** Plant seed potatoes in late March — a week or two earlier in southerly areas and a couple of weeks later in the north. Harvest in June or July.
- **Second Early varieties:** Plant in early–mid April and lift in July or August.
- **Maincrop varieties:** Plant in mid–late April. Some of the tubers can be lifted in August for immediate use but potatoes for storage should be harvested in September or early October.

CALENDAR

	JAN	FEB	MAR	APR	MAY	JUN	JUL	AUG	SEP	OCT	NOV	DEC
Planting Time			▓	▓								
Lifting Time						▓	▓		▓	▓		

For key to symbols — see page 7

VARIETIES

Potatoes are available in a wide range of shapes, sizes, colours and textures. The skin may be red, yellow or white and the flesh pale cream or yellow. Texture may be waxy or floury and the shape is round, oval or long. Variety is the basic deciding factor with regard to shape and quality but both soil type and weather play a part.

Round

Oval

Long

Duke of York

Pentland Javelin

ARRAN PILOT: Long; white flesh. An old favourite, now being replaced by modern varieties. A heavy cropper which does best in light soil in southern counties.

DUKE OF YORK: Oval; yellow flesh. This variety will succeed in nearly all areas and soil types, and is reputed to have the finest flavour among the First Earlies.

ROCKET: Round; white flesh. A variety of the 1980s bred in Cambridge. It has become popular — the yields are good and the egg-sized tubers have waxy flesh. Tuber blight can be a problem.

MARIS BARD: Oval; white flesh. The earliest of all, producing heavy crops of waxy, well-flavoured tubers. Scab resistance is slight, but resistance to virus is high.

ULSTER SCEPTRE: Long; white flesh. Nearly as early as Maris Bard — the other 'Ulster' you can buy is Ulster Chieftain.

EPICURE: Round; white flesh. An old variety which is chosen by people seeking an 'old-fashioned' flavour. Hardier than most on cold, exposed sites.

SHARPE'S EXPRESS: Long; white flesh. Once available everywhere — now pushed aside by the new varieties. Still a good choice for heavy soil. Rather late, but tubers store well.

VANESSA: Long; yellow flesh. This is the red-skinned First Early, late to mature but succeeds better than most in dry weather.

SUTTON'S FOREMOST: Oval; white flesh. This variety has an excellent reputation for high yields and flavour.

PENTLAND JAVELIN: Oval; white flesh. One of the modern varieties which is later than most First Earlies but produces heavy crops which are resistant to scab and some strains of eelworm. The texture is waxy.

1 in. = 2.5 cm, 1 ft = 30 cm, 1 oz = 28 gm, 1 lb = 450 gm

Wilja

Desiree

Pentland Crown

SECOND EARLY varieties

NADINE: Round; white flesh. This is one of the newer varieties which are steadily replacing the old favourites. The tubers are smooth and uniform, making them good exhibition potatoes. Flavour rating is also high. It is claimed that this variety is strongly resistant to eelworm.

STROMA: Oval; yellow flesh. A variety for people who prefer colour in their potatoes — pink skin and yellowish flesh with a mild flavour. It is claimed to have some resistance to slugs.

MARFONA: Round; creamy flesh. High yields of large round or short oval tubers are a feature of this Dutch variety. A good choice if your soil is sandy or if you like baked potatoes.

WILJA: Oval; pale yellow flesh. According to many experts this variety, Nadine and Estima are the ones to choose. High yields, excellent cooking qualities and reliability are the reasons for its growing popularity.

ESTIMA: Oval; pale yellow flesh. Another modern Dutch variety which is rapidly gaining in popularity because of its attractively-shaped tubers and heavy crops. Scab can be a problem.

MARIS PEER: Oval; white flesh. Good yields and some resistance to both scab and blight — but it will fail miserably in dry soil which is not irrigated.

CATRIONA: Long; creamy flesh. Popular with exhibitors.— its long yellow tubers with purple patches are eye-catching. Crops well but cannot be stored for long periods.

MAINCROP varieties

MARIS PIPER: Oval; creamy flesh. A rising star, taking over from the once popular Majestic. It has its problems — scab, slug and drought resistance are low, but it gives excellent yields and its cooking qualities are rated very highly.

MAJESTIC: Long; white flesh. Now more than 70 years old, it is less vigorous than it used to be. It has been pushed out of the recommended lists by modern varieties, but it still keeps its reputation as a fine potato for making chips.

DESIREE: Oval; pale yellow flesh. The combination of good characteristics found in this pink-skinned variety makes it hard to beat. It is a very heavy cropper and succeeds in all soil types. It has good drought resistance and the waxy-textured tubers have an excellent flavour.

PENTLAND CROWN: Oval; white flesh. This late Maincrop is claimed to produce higher yields than other popular varieties — grow it for its good resistance to blight, scab and virus but not for its keeping and cooking qualities, which are only moderate.

PENTLAND SQUIRE: Oval; white flesh. The nearest rival to Pentland Crown for the top yield title, but differs by being an early Maincrop with good keeping and cooking properties. The tubers are unusually large.

PENTLAND DELL: Long; white flesh. Another of the Pentlands — early, high yields and good flavour but it has its problems. It suffers in cold soil in the spring and the tubers tend to blacken when cooked.

KING EDWARD: Oval; creamy flesh. This red-blotched variety is one of the best known of all potatoes and is still grown by gardeners who are looking for cooking quality rather than quantity.

CARA: Round; creamy flesh. This high-yielding potato stores well and the pink-eyed tubers are excellent for baking. There is some blight resistance but it has a drawback — it is a late maturing variety.

STEMSTAR: Long; creamy flesh. One of the newer varieties with several good points — large tubers, high yields, good slug resistance and no discoloration after cooking. A good exhibition variety.

GOLDEN WONDER: Long; yellow flesh. The best-flavoured of all potatoes according to many books, but it is rarely a good choice. It needs well-manured soil and is susceptible to both drought and slugs. Tubers are small and yields are low.

PINK FIR APPLE: Long; yellow flesh. This peculiar variety is over a century old and is worth trying, although the yields may disappoint you. The long, irregular tubers are waxy and have a new-potato flavour — serve hot or cold.

KERR'S PINK: Round; white flesh. An early Maincrop, grown by people in wet and heavy soil areas who like a floury potato. An excellent chip potato.

ROMANO: Oval; white flesh. A new red-skinned variety with waxy-textured tubers. It stores and cooks well but you must water when the weather is dry.

CHRISTMAS POTATOES
New potatoes for Christmas Dinner — something of a gamble but worth trying if you want to beat the Jones's. When lifting your crop of First Earlies in July set a few tubers aside. Plant them in a warm spot in the garden and look after them in the normal way. In late September cover the plants with large cloches and then get busy with a fork on Christmas Eve.

POTATOES UNDER POLYTHENE
The practice of growing potatoes under plastic is becoming increasingly popular. After planting, the row is covered with a sheet of black plastic — before putting down the sheet scatter Slug Pellets along the mounded ridge. Push the edges of the plastic sheet into the soil with a spade. As the haulm emerges it will push against the polythene — at this stage cut a slit and pull through the young stems.

There are many advantages with this method of growing — the soil is warmer and moister, and potatoes can be harvested a few at a time simply by lifting up a section of the sheet. Weeds are suppressed and the chore of earthing-up is removed, but there are drawbacks. There is the cost of the polythene and the menace of slugs.

Many diseases, pests and disorders can attack potatoes and reduce yields, but only four are likely to be a serious threat. Three of these are pests — potato cyst eelworm, slugs and wireworm. The other one is a disease — potato blight. The virus diseases can be a menace and you should therefore buy seed which is known to be virus-free.

POTATO TROUBLES

	Symptom	Likely Causes
Seed potatoes	— thin, long sprouts	2
	— no sprouts	11
Leaves	— pale green or yellow	6 or 12 or 14 or **Drought**
	— pale green or yellow mottling	4 or 9
	— yellow or brown between veins	10
	— rolled, brittle	3
	— torn	9
	— brown patches	1
	— many small holes	7
	— tiny brown spots	7
	— greenfly clusters	6
Stems	— tunnelled	13
	— blackened at base	12
Roots	— covered with tiny cysts	14
Tubers	— abnormally small	3 or 4 or 12 or 14 or **Drought**
	— contain narrow tunnels	21
	— contain wide tunnels	15 or **Millepede** (see page 110) or **Cutworm** (see page 110)
	— hollowed out	23 or 26
	— split	22
	— scabby spots on surface	16 or 18
	— wrinkled area, small woolly growths	20
	— brown lines in flesh	17
	— brown areas under skin	19
	— flesh slimy, evil-smelling	25
	— sunken brown area on surface	26
	— cauliflower-like warty outgrowths	24
	— black at centre	8
	— poor flavour or texture	8
	— soft at lifting time	5

BROWN-BLOTCHED LEAVES

1 POTATO BLIGHT

Blight is the most serious potato disease, capable of destroying all the foliage during August in a wet season. The first signs are brown patches on the leaves. Look on the underside of the leaflets — each blight spot has a white mould fringe in damp weather.

Treatment: None, once the disease has firmly taken hold.

Prevention: Plant healthy seed tubers. Spray with mancozeb in July and repeat at fortnightly intervals if the weather is damp. If blight spots are already present, spraying will slow down the spread of the disease to other plants.

2 SPINDLY SPROUTS

By far the most common cause of spindly sprouts is keeping the tubers too dark or too warm prior to planting. If threadlike shoots form despite standing the tubers in a light, cool place then virus infection is a possible cause. Alternatively the tubers may have been slightly frosted. Always buy good quality seed potatoes and sprout them in a light, frost-free location.

5 SOFT TUBERS

Some of the tubers lifted after an extremely dry summer may appear to be perfectly sound on the outside but are soft and rubbery to the touch. This is not a disease; it is a disorder caused by the plant withdrawing water from the developing tubers. It can be prevented by watering thoroughly during drought.

ROLLED LEAFLETS

3 LEAF ROLL VIRUS

Leaf roll is one of the most serious virus diseases which attack potatoes. Leaflets roll upward and become hard and brittle. Affected plants are stunted and the yields are poor.

Treatment: None.

Prevention: Use virus-free seed. Spray with heptenophos to control the virus-carrying aphids.

MOTTLED LEAVES

4 MOSAIC VIRUS

There are several mosaic diseases, and the symptoms vary with the potato variety grown. The usual tell-tale sign is yellow or pale green mottling over the whole leaf surface. Brown streaks may also appear.

Treatment: None.

Prevention: Use virus-free seed. Spray with heptenophos to control the virus-carrying aphids.

POTATO TROUBLES continued

6 | APHID (Greenfly)

In a dry warm season the foliage may be heavily infested with greenfly. Plants are weakened and leaflets turn brown and may die. The most serious effect is the spread of virus diseases by these sap-sucking pests.

Treatment: Spray with permethrin or heptenophos.

Prevention: No practical method available.

INSECTS ON LEAVES

¼ in. greenish insects

7 | CAPSID BUG

Small brown spots which later turn into holes appear on the foliage. Young shoots may be distorted and the crinkling of small leaflets may be severe.

Treatment: Damage is usually too slight to affect yield. Spray the plants with permethrin or fenitrothion if attack is severe.

Prevention: No practical method available.

YELLOW-BLOTCHED LEAVES

9 | FROST

Late spring frosts can severely damage the young shoots, delaying the development of early varieties. A severe frost can turn the stems black; less severe frosts cause yellow patches and torn leaflets on the older foliage.

Treatment: None.

Prevention: Cover shoots of Earlies with newspaper if frosts are expected.

8 | POOR QUALITY

The cooking and eating qualities of tubers can sometimes be disappointing. Obviously all the tuber troubles described on the next page make kitchen use difficult or impossible, but several disorders do not show up until the potatoes are being cooked or eaten. A **soapy texture** is usually due to lifting the tubers before they are mature. It can also be caused by growing potatoes on chalky soil. A **sweet taste** is usually due to keeping the tubers too cold during storage. An **earthy taste** is caused by the presence of powdery scab or by growing the plants in soil treated with lindane. Potatoes sometimes have a **black heart** or turn **black when cooked**. The major causes are storage at over 100°F and potash deficiency.

11 | GAPPING

The failure of seed potatoes to develop sprouts is usually due to the presence of disease in the tuber. Another possible reason for this failure is the frosting of the seed tubers in transit or during storage. If such faulty seed is planted then a gap will occur where a plant should be.

BROWNING BETWEEN VEINS

10 | MAGNESIUM DEFICIENCY

The first symptom is a yellowing of the tissue between the veins of the leaflets. These yellow areas then turn brown and brittle. Growth is stunted.

Treatment: Apply a trace element spray. Repeat if necessary.

Prevention: Feed regularly during the growing season with a fertilizer, which contains magnesium as well as nitrogen, phosphates and potash.

BLACKENED STEMS

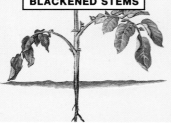

12 | BLACKLEG

Tell-tale sign is the blackening of the stems at and below ground level. The leaves turn yellow and wilt; eventually the haulm withers. This disease attacks early in the season and is worst in heavy soils and rainy weather.

Treatment: None. Lift and burn affected plants.

Prevention: Never plant seed tubers which are soft and rotten. The practice of making seed potatoes go further by cutting them increases the risk of attack.

TUNNELLED STEMS

1 in. bristly caterpillars

13 | ROSY RUSTIC MOTH

Potatoes grown in new gardens may have their stems hollowed out by these caterpillars. Affected plants die down earlier than normal.

Treatment: None. Dig out and destroy infested plants.

Prevention: No practical method available.

WITHERED LOWER LEAVES

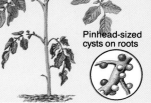

Pinhead-sized cysts on roots

14 | POTATO CYST EELWORM

Plants appear weak and stunted. Lower leaves wither away; upper leaves are pale green and wilt during the day. Haulm dies down prematurely. Marble-sized tubers are produced.

Treatment: None. Destroy infected plants and tubers.

Prevention: Practise crop rotation. Do not grow a susceptible variety on infected land for at least 6 years — grow a resistant variety instead.

1 in. = 2.5 cm, 1 ft = 30 cm, 1 oz = 28 gm, 1 lb = 450 gm

TUBER TROUBLES

15 SLUGS

Attacks begin in August — Main-crop potatoes grown in heavy soil can be ruined.

Treatment: None.

Prevention: Avoid susceptible varieties. Apply methiocarb in July. Lift the crop as soon as the tubers are mature.

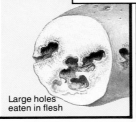

Large holes eaten in flesh

16 COMMON SCAB

Disease is only skin deep; eating qualities unaffected. Most severe on light soils under dry conditions.

Treatment: None.

Prevention: Dig in compost but do not lime before planting. Grow a resistant variety (e.g Wilja).

Ragged-edged scurfy patches

17 SPRAING

Tubers are normal on the surface — discoloured inside. There are several causes — viruses, trace element deficiency or water shortage.

Treatment: None.

Prevention: Practise crop rotation. Do not grow Pentland Dell, which is very susceptible.

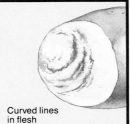

Curved lines in flesh

18 POWDERY SCAB

Much less frequent than common scab. Most severe on heavy soils under wet conditions. Scabs are powdery on the surface.

Treatment: None.

Prevention: Practise crop rotation. Do not grow susceptible varieties (e.g Cara, Estima and Pentland Crown).

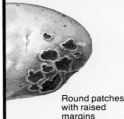

Round patches with raised margins

19 POTATO BLIGHT

Caused by blight spores from the leaves reaching the tubers. Affected potatoes rot in store.

Treatment: None. Do not store.

Prevention: Keep haulm well earthed-up. If there is blight on the leaves then cut off and destroy stems 10 days before lifting.

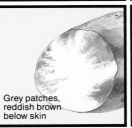

Grey patches, reddish brown below skin

20 DRY ROT

Dry rot occurs in store. Careless handling when lifting makes tubers more susceptible.

Treatment: None. Destroy tubers.

Prevention: Practise crop rotation. Store only sound, healthy tubers and keep them in a cool but not over-dry atmosphere.

Shrunken area, whitish pustules

21 WIREWORM

Wireworm is a serious pest in new gardens, especially in wet summers. Tubers are riddled with narrow tunnels.

Treatment: None.

Prevention: Apply pirimiphos-methyl to the soil before planting. Lift as soon as tubers are mature.

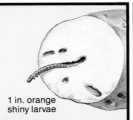

1 in. orange shiny larvae

22 SPLITTING

Deep cracks make the tubers difficult to peel. The affected potatoes are also very susceptible to rotting in store and so should be used immediately.

Treatment: None.

Prevention: Keep plants well watered during dry spells.

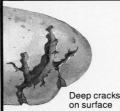

Deep cracks on surface

23 HOLLOW HEART

Affects large tubers. Caused by a prolonged wet spell after dry weather. Hollow-hearted potatoes may rot in store.

Treatment: None.

Prevention: Keep plants well watered during dry spells.

Hollow centre

24 WART DISEASE

Once very serious, now uncommon as nearly all modern varieties are immune.

Treatment: None. Destroy affected tubers. Ministry of Agriculture must be informed of the outbreak.

Prevention: Plant only immune varieties on infected land.

Black warty outgrowths

25 SOFT ROT

Soft rot is an infection which attacks damaged tubers. Affected tubers soon become slimy and putrid and are quite unusable.

Treatment: None. Destroy tubers.

Prevention: Store only sound, healthy tubers and make sure they do not become damp.

Soft, evil-smelling flesh

26 GANGRENE

Gangrene occurs in store. Inside of tuber becomes decayed and hollow.

Treatment: None. Remove from store.

Prevention: Store only sound, healthy tubers and make sure the store is airy and frost-free.

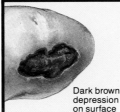

Dark brown depression on surface

1 in. = 2.5 cm, 1 ft = 30 cm, 1 oz = 28 gm, 1 lb = 450 gm

RADISH

Many of today's gardening experts began their outdoor horticultural careers with a packet of French Breakfast or Scarlet Globe. The summer or salad radish is an ideal starter vegetable for a child — it is practically trouble-free and the round or long roots are ready for salads or sandwiches in about a month. For the grown-up gardener the well-known red varieties are used to fill the space between rows of peas and carrots or as row markers mixed with slow-germinating seeds such as parsley, parsnips or onions. The radishes quickly germinate and so mark out the row and are ready for pulling before the main vegetable needs the space. It is a pity that so many people don't take their radish knowledge beyond this stage. There are unusual varieties — small yellow roots, giant Japanese types for pulling in summer and even a radish which is grown for its pods rather than its roots. The large winter radish remains a vegetable for the adventurous even though it is easily grown for winter use in salads or as a hot vegetable. As with all vegetables, there is always something new to learn and try . . .

SEED FACTS

Expected germination time:	4–7 days
Approximate number per ounce:	3000
Expected yield from a 10 ft row:	4 lb (Summer varieties) 10 lb (Winter varieties)
Life expectancy of stored seed:	6 years
Approximate time between sowing and lifting:	3–6 weeks (Summer varieties) 10–12 weeks (Winter varieties)
Ease of cultivation:	Easy

Actual size

SEED SOWING

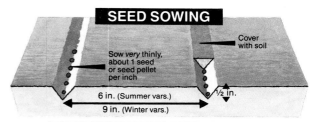

Sow *very* thinly, about 1 seed or seed pellet per inch

Cover with soil

6 in. (Summer vars.)
9 in. (Winter vars.)
½ in.

SOIL FACTS

● All the textbooks will tell you that radishes relish a reasonably fertile, well-drained soil which is adequately supplied with humus and free from stones, but summer radishes usually have to put up with an odd corner without any thought about soil preparation.

● Despite this lowly status, they should be given some soil preparation so as to ensure the quick growth which is essential for tenderness and flavour. Dig some peat or well-rotted compost into the soil if it was not manured for a previous crop — apply a fertilizer before sowing and rake to a fine tilth.

● Choose a sunny spot for spring sowing but the summer crop needs some shade — sow between other vegetables.

LOOKING AFTER THE CROP

● With the summer varieties little or no thinning should be necessary — if there is any overcrowding then thin immediately so that the plants are spaced at 1 in. (small radishes) or 2–4 in. intervals (larger and Japanese radishes). With the winter varieties thin to leave the plants 6 in. apart — make sure you carry out this thinning before the plants are overcrowded.

● Protect the crop against birds if they are a nuisance in your area. Spray with derris if flea beetles begin to perforate the leaves.

● Hoe to keep down weeds. Water if the soil is dry — rapid and uninterrupted growth is essential for top quality. Summer radish is not an easy crop to grow in July or August when the weather is hot and dry. Swelling is often unsatisfactory and the roots may be woody and peppery.

HARVESTING

● Pull the summer varieties when the globular ones are the diameter of a 10p coin and the intermediates are no longer than your thumb. They can, of course, grow much longer but overgrown specimens would be woody and hollow.

● Japanese varieties are best when pulled at the 6 in. stage but they can be allowed to grow longer if required for cooking.

● The winter varieties can be left in the soil and lifted as required, provided that you cover the crowns with straw, bracken or peat. It is better to lift them in November and store as for carrots (see page 40).

● **Summer varieties:** Sow under cloches in January or February or outdoors in March. For a prolonged supply sow every few weeks or try 'Mixed Radish' seed which contains varieties which mature at different times. Sowing after early June often gives disappointing results.

● **Winter varieties:** Sow in July or early August. Lift roots from late October onwards.

CALENDAR

	JAN	FEB	MAR	APR	MAY	JUN	JUL	AUG	SEP	OCT	NOV	DEC
Sowing Time												
Lifting Time												

1 in. = 2.5 cm, 1 ft = 30 cm, 1 oz = 28 gm, 1 lb = 450 gm

For key to symbols — see page 7

IN THE KITCHEN

Thinly-sliced summer radishes may be a satisfactory way of decorating a salad plate but they are not a suitable way of savouring this vegetable. The proper way was described hundreds of years ago — wash and trim each root, then cut off the foliage so as to leave the bottom 1 in. of the stalks to serve as a handle. You hold the handle and eat with coarse bread, butter, salt, cheese . . . and alcohol. Radishes have been used as an appetiser since the dawn of history and the Ancient Egyptians fed them to the pyramid-makers. Despite this long history of the radish as a health-giver and sustainer of the poor, it will remain primarily a garnish for salads. To make radish roses, cut off the stalk end and make a number of cuts from the stalk end to the root. Place the cut radishes in iced water for ½ hour and the 'petals' will open.

STORAGE Keep in a polythene bag in the refrigerator — radishes will stay fresh for up to 1 week.

COOKING Summer radishes are for eating raw and the Winter varieties are for cooking or pickling, according to the general rule. After peeling, boil the sliced or cubed radish in lightly salted water for about 10 minutes. Drain thoroughly and serve with parsley sauce or tossed in butter. This is not the only or even the best way to cook radish — thin slices or strips of a winter variety or one of the larger summer types can be stir-fried. This means that despite the general rule the Japanese-type of summer radish is suitable for cooking — and to break the rule still further the winter radishes can be peeled and then grated or sliced for eating raw in salads. The texture is somewhat coarse and the flavour is rather pungent, but how else can you enjoy fresh radishes from the garden with your Christmas Dinner?

VARIETIES

  **SUMMER varieties**

Globular **Intermediate** **Long**

Scarlet Globe

This is by far the more popular group — the radishes which garnish the salad plate. Most (but not all) are small and the usual colour is all-red or a red/white mixture. There are variations — the Japanese types which can grow 1 ft long and the yellow and all-white varieties which have never become really popular.

CHERRY BELLE: Globular; all-red. A very popular radish — cherry-coloured on the outside and white, crisp and mild inside. It will remain in the ground for a considerable time without going pithy.

SCARLET GLOBE: Globular; all-red. Another popular round radish with bright red skin. A quick-maturing variety for early spring sowing.

PRINZ ROTIN: Globular; all-red. One of the modern radishes for which it is claimed that the roots remain crisp and mild when they are double or treble the diameter of a normal round radish. A good choice if you plan to sow in the difficult midsummer period.

HELRO: Globular; all-red. A high quality radish which is suitable for sowing outdoors in spring/summer or under glass in winter.

PINK BEAUTY: Globular; pink. Useful for bringing an additional colour to the salad bowl — a change from the usual white and red radishes.

SPARKLER 3: Globular; red/white. Very quick growing, with no other outstanding virtues.

FRENCH BREAKFAST: Intermediate; red/white. One of the most popular of all radishes. The cylindrical roots are crisp and mild when pulled at the proper time but hot and woody if harvesting is delayed.

CRYSTAL BALL: Globular; all-red. Sow this one in January or February under glass for very early crops. Sow outdoors from early March onwards — similar varieties include Robino and Saxa.

LONG WHITE ICICLE: Long; white. An excellent choice, producing in a few weeks 3 in. long roots which are crisp and nutty-flavoured. It has never become popular as we expect radishes to be red.

MINOWASE SUMMER: A Japanese-type radish, producing roots up to 12 in. long. Sow in May and begin pulling when the roots are 6 in. long — harvesting can continue for about a month. Excellent for filling the summer period.

APRIL CROSS: A mooli or Japanese radish — like Minowase Summer will reach 12 in. or more. Can be sown in spring.

MUNCHEN BIER: The odd one of the group, both in name and use. It grows about 2 ft high and it is the pods (eaten raw or boiled) and not the roots which are harvested.

French Breakfast

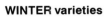 **WINTER varieties**

The Cinderella group, rarely grown and only a few varieties are listed in the catalogues. The roots are large, measuring a foot or more and weighing up to several pounds. They have white, black or pink skins and a flavour which is usually stronger than the summer varieties.

CHINA ROSE: Not really a giant — the oval roots are about 5 in. long and 2 in. wide. The skin colour is deep rose, the flesh crisp and white.

BLACK SPANISH ROUND: A large globular variety, black-skinned and white-fleshed. Like China Rose it appears in most catalogues — others are not as easy to find.

BLACK SPANISH LONG: Similar to Black Spanish Round apart from its shape — 1 ft long and tapered like a parsnip.

MINO EARLY: Foot-long cylindrical roots with a flavour which is milder and perhaps more acceptable for salads than the other winter varieties.

TROUBLES

See page 107

China Rose

RHUBARB

Most people regard rhubarb as a 'fruit', but it squeezes into this and many other vegetable books because it is so often grown on allotments. It is usually neglected, although it will repay just a little care by providing you with succulent stalks ('sticks') from February until midsummer. All it needs is a sunny spot, an annual dressing with well-rotted compost or manure and division of the roots every five years. The sticks can be left to develop naturally for pulling in spring or the plants can be forced by covering them in late winter so as to provide a February or March crop. The leaves are poisonous — dispose of them on the compost heap.

PLANT FACTS

Can be raised from seed sown in April, but results are sometimes disappointing. Much better to lift mature roots ('crowns') and divide into pieces ('sets') bearing one or more buds.

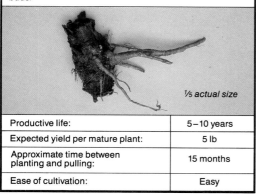

⅕ actual size

Productive life:	5–10 years
Expected yield per mature plant:	5 lb
Approximate time between planting and pulling:	15 months
Ease of cultivation:	Easy

SOIL FACTS

- Not fussy at all, provided that the soil is not subject to prolonged waterlogging in winter.
- Pick an open site which is not shaded. Dig deeply in autumn, incorporating a liberal amount of compost or well-rotted manure. Rake in Growmore fertilizer shortly before planting.

PLANTING

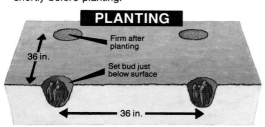

Firm after planting

36 in.

Set bud just below surface

36 in.

CALENDAR

	JAN	FEB	MAR	APR	MAY	JUN	JUL	AUG	SEP	OCT	NOV	DEC
Planting Time												
Pulling Time												

LOOKING AFTER THE CROP

- Keep the plants well watered. Remove any flowering shoots which may appear.
- Feed the plants with a liquid fertilizer during the summer. If this is not done, sprinkle a general-purpose fertilizer around the crowns once the harvesting season is over.
- Place a mulch of compost or well-rotted manure over the crowns in January or February.

HARVESTING

- Begin pulling the sticks in April — hold the stalk close to the ground and then pull upwards with a twisting motion. Never strip a plant — always leave at least 4 stalks. Do not remove any stalks after July.
- Allow new plants to become established during the first year — pulling can begin 12–18 months after planting.
- Force one or two plants for a February or March crop — cover each crown in January with an upturned bucket or plastic bin which should be covered with compost or straw. The forced sticks will be ready in about 6 weeks — do not force these plants again for at least 2 years.

IN THE KITCHEN

The thin, pale sticks of forced rhubarb need less preparation and less sugar than the stalks gathered later in the season. Stewing with or without water is the usual method of cooking and custard is the usual accompaniment, but there are many other ways of using the crop. Pies, crumbles, jams, chutneys, fools, mousses . . . there is a long list of traditional recipes.

FREEZING Place a layer of rhubarb sections in an open freezer tray and freeze for an hour. Pack into polythene bags — store for up to 1 year.

COOKING Simply cut off the leaves of forced rhubarb, wash and cook slowly with sugar (no water) in a pan until the flesh is tender. Do not overcook. Older sticks should be peeled to remove the stringy skin. Improve the flavour by adding orange juice and cinnamon.

VARIETIES

CHAMPAGNE EARLY: Deep red stems make this one of the most attractive varieties. Reliable and early — sometimes listed as Early Red.

GLASKIN'S PERPETUAL: In more seed catalogues than the others because it can be cut in the first year.

VICTORIA: A very popular variety although it is the last one to produce its stalks in late spring.

TIMPERLEY EARLY: The opposite to Victoria — thin stems which are ideal for forcing in early spring.

TROUBLES

CROWN ROT

The terminal bud rots and the tissue below the crown decays. The sticks are spindly and dull-coloured. There is no cure, so badly infected plants should be dug out and burnt. Do not re-plant the affected area.

HONEY FUNGUS

Tell-tale sign is the presence of white streaks in the brown, dead tissue of the crown. Orange toadstools appear around the affected plants. Dig out and burn diseased roots.

SALSIFY & SCORZONERA

You will find these two root vegetables in all the seed catalogues but in very few gardens. They have been around for centuries, but they still remain oddities in Britain. Salsify looks rather like a poorly-grown parsnip — long, rather thin and slightly corky. The flavour, however, is much superior to the parsnip — a delicate taste which has been likened to both asparagus and oysters — hence the alternative name 'oyster plant'. Its black-skinned relative is scorzonera, which has an ugly appearance and an awkward name but a delicious flavour.

SEED FACTS

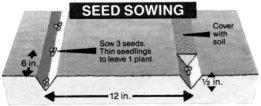

Salsify **Scorzonera**

Actual size

Expected germination time:	12–16 days
Approximate number per ounce:	2000
Expected yield from a 10 ft row:	4 lb
Life expectancy of stored seed:	2 years
Approximate time between sowing and lifting:	25 weeks
Ease of cultivation:	Easy — but careful weeding is necessary

SOIL FACTS

- These vegetables grow best in deep, friable and stone-free soil which has not been recently manured.
- Dig deeply in autumn or early winter and refrain from adding any fresh manure or compost. Lime if necessary. Break down clods and rake in Growmore fertilizer when preparing the seed bed.

SEED SOWING

Cover with soil

Sow 3 seeds. Thin seedlings to leave 1 plant

6 in.

½ in.

— 12 in. —

LOOKING AFTER THE CROP

- Salsify and scorzonera will not produce satisfactory roots after transplanting, so throw thinnings away.
- Weed carefully around each plant. If using a hoe, avoid at all costs touching the crown of the plant.
- The crop requires very little attention and is rarely attacked by pests. Water in dry weather and apply a mulch in summer.

HARVESTING

- The roots are ready for lifting from mid October onwards. They are hardy and can be left in the soil until April.
- Lift as required, taking great care not to snap the brittle, foot-long roots. You will not be able to harvest them in frosty weather, so lift some in November and store as for carrots (see page 40).
- Some books recommend that the tops should be cut off some of the roots in autumn and the fresh shoots which appear in spring used as greens in May. This is not really advisable — these vegetables produce superior-tasting roots but only average-flavoured leaves.

IN THE KITCHEN

Salsify and scorzonera can be cooked in a variety of ways — baked, puréed, dipped into batter and fried, or served *au gratin* (with cheese and breadcrumbs). According to some culinary experts the delicate flavour should not be masked — simple boiling is recommended. The young shoots ('chards') can be blanched like chicory and served raw in salads.

STORAGE Keep in a polythene bag in the refrigerator — roots will stay fresh for up to 1 week.

COOKING The secret for top flavour appears to be peeling after and not before boiling. Scrub the roots thoroughly under the tap and trim the ends. Cut into 2 in. lengths and cook for 25 minutes in boiling salted water to which lemon juice has been added. Drain and squeeze off skins — toss with a little melted butter and chopped parsley.

VARIETIES

There are only 2 or 3 varieties of salsify and there are no particular merits to help you make your choice. Just buy the one you are offered.

MAMMOTH-SANDWICH ISLAND: Some suppliers call it Mammoth — in other catalogues it is listed as Sandwich Island. This variety of salsify has been around since the beginning of the century.

GIANT: The only other variety you are likely to find — just as reliable as Mammoth-Sandwich Island.

RUSSIAN GIANT: The most popular variety of scorzonera — you might be offered Long Black instead but there is little to choose between them.

TROUBLES

WHITE BLISTER

Shiny white blisters on the leaves; growth is stunted and root development is limited. Cut off and burn diseased foliage.

CALENDAR

	JAN	FEB	MAR	APR	MAY	JUN	JUL	AUG	SEP	OCT	NOV	DEC
Sowing Time												
Lifting Time												

SEED SPROUTS

Most of us began our horticultural education by growing mustard and cress on damp blotting paper in a saucer. After a week or two the seedlings were cut and used in salads or sandwiches — a proud moment for the budding gardener. Unfortunately our involvement in sprouting seeds for kitchen use usually ended there, despite a large amount of modern research which has shown that the sprouts of seeds are surprisingly rich in vitamins, minerals, proteins and polyunsaturated oils. Even if nutritional values do not interest you, there must still be something appealing about vegetables which can be raised indoors at any time of the year and which can be eaten raw or cooked to provide flavours ranging from bland to peppery. Bean sprouts are a popular item in every Chinese restaurant, but there are many other seeds which can be sprouted for the table. It is, however, best not to experiment. Many sprouts are tasteless, some are bitter and a few (e.g. tomato) are positively harmful — so choose one from the list on page 91. You can buy a special propagator but there really is no need to do so — all you require is either a shallow tray or a jar and a few days' patience. Raising seed sprouts is a simple task and an ideal one for children, but it is not *quite* as foolproof as the books sometimes suggest. The crop will fail if you allow the seeds to dry out and the seedlings will go mouldy if you keep them too wet. The rules may be straightforward but they must be followed to ensure success.

BEFORE YOU START

Weigh out the amount of seeds you propose to sprout and wash them in cold water. Drain thoroughly and then let them soak overnight in a bowl of tepid water. Next day allow the seeds to drain and then use the appropriate sprouting technique.

IN THE KITCHEN

Wash and dry the harvested sprouts, and then use as quickly as possible — do not store for more than 2 days. They can be served raw in salads — some are soft (e.g. mustard and cress) and others, such as mung beans, are crunchy. Bean sprouts are, of course, a basic ingredient in Oriental cooking and are used in a variety of ways. The basic method of preparing them is by stir-frying. Heat a little vegetable oil in a pan and add the bean sprouts — stir quickly for about 2 minutes and serve immediately.

SPROUTING TECHNIQUES

Jar Method

- Place soaked seeds in a clean jam jar — remember that their volume will increase four or five times by harvest time. Cover the top with a square cut from a pair of old tights and secure with a rubber band. Fill the jar with water and pour off.
- Put the jar in a bowl, propped up as shown below to ensure that the seeds will not stand in water.

- If the seeds require **forcing**, place the bowl in a cupboard from which all light is excluded. A temperature of 55–70°F is required — an airing cupboard is often ideal. If the seeds require **greening**, place the bowl in the dark until the seeds have germinated. Move to a well-lit spot away from direct sunlight 1–2 days before harvesting.
- It will be necessary to rinse the seeds twice daily. To do this, half fill the jar with water and then drain it away through the cloth at the top. Replace the jar in the bowl when the rinsing process has been completed.

Tray method

- Place several sheets of kitchen paper towelling at the bottom of a shallow waterproof tray. Dampen this absorbent layer thoroughly, pour off any excess water and then scatter the soaked seeds evenly over the surface.

- If the seeds require **forcing**, put the tray inside a polythene bag and place in a cupboard from which all light is excluded. A temperature of 55–70°F is required — an airing cupboard is often ideal. If the sprouts require **greening**, place the tray in the dark until the seeds have germinated. Move to a well-lit spot away from direct sunlight 1–2 days before harvesting.
- It will be necessary to inspect the tray regularly to ensure that the absorbent layer remains damp. Moisten as necessary, but make sure that there is no free water standing at the base of the tray.

ADZUKI BEAN

The Japanese form of the Chinese bean sprout. The adzuki (or aduki) bean is chestnut brown and the short white sprouts have a crisp, nutty flavour. Eat raw or use as directed in Oriental recipes.

Propagation: Requires forcing by the tray or jar method. Harvest when sprouts are 1 in. long — this will take 3–6 days.

FENUGREEK

Smell the seeds and you will know that they are a constituent of curry powder. All sorts of medicinal properties have been ascribed to them, but the sprouts are now used solely for their spicy flavour in salads, soups or stews.

Propagation: Requires greening by the jar method. Harvest for a strong curry flavour when the sprouts are ½ in. long — for a mild flavour leave until they are 3 in. long. This will take 4–8 days.

MUSTARD AND CRESS

The old favourites for salads, garnishing and sandwiches. There are two types of cress — curly-leaved and plain, and the mild-flavoured rape seed is sometimes substituted for the rather peppery white mustard.

Propagation: Requires greening by the tray method. Sow cress seed evenly and thickly and 3 days later sprinkle mustard seed over or alongside the emerging cress seedlings. Move to a well-lit spot when the leaves start to unfold. Harvest when the seedlings are 2 in. high — this will take 10–15 days. Remove by cutting the base of the stems with scissors.

MUNG BEAN

The familiar Chinese bean sprout, now widely available in supermarkets. The green beans produce long and plump sprouts which can be eaten raw with a suitable dressing or cooked in a variety of ways. Soya beans are sometimes used as a substitute but the flavour is inferior.

Propagation: Requires forcing by the tray or jar method. Harvest when sprouts are 2 in. long — this will take 4–6 days.

ALFALFA

Grown to maturity by farmers for cattle food, but the young sprouts have a sweet, pea-like flavour and crisp texture when served raw in salads. Rich in minerals and Vitamin B.

Propagation: Requires greening by the jar method. Harvest when sprouts are 1–2 in. long — this will take 3–5 days.

RADISH

Radish is present on nearly every vegetable plot but a rarity on the seed sprouter's list. Strange, because radish seeds readily sprout and provide a pleasant and peppery taste to sandwiches and salads. Any variety is suitable.

Propagation: Requires greening (½ day) by the jar method. Harvest when sprouts are ½–1 in. long — this will take 3–4 days.

TRITICALE

A hybrid of wheat and rye. The protein-rich sprouts can be used in several ways — salads, soups, stews or as a constituent of bread dough.

Propagation: Requires forcing by the tray or jar method. Harvest when sprouts are 2 in. long — this will take 2–3 days.

1 in. = 2.5 cm, 1 ft = 30 cm, 1 oz = 28 gm, 1 lb = 450 gm

SPINACH

The experts will tell you that it is possible to pick spinach every day of the year from your garden . . . but who would want to? The average family regards spinach as an uncomplicated and unattractive vegetable — green leaves which turn into gritty, slimy and strong-tasting mush when cooked. However, it is eaten occasionally because of its remarkably high content of iron. All of these points, however, are incorrect. First of all, it is certainly not uncomplicated — the classification of spinach is complex. There are two types of true spinach — they are both annuals which are either picked in summer (round-seeded varieties) or during winter and spring (mostly prickly-seeded varieties). The half-hardy New Zealand spinach is not spinach at all although its leaves are used in the same way, and perpetual spinach (spinach beet) is really a type of beetroot (see page 23). Secondly, it is prolonged storage, poor preparation and bad cooking which give rise to the grittiness and sliminess. Finally, spinach does not deserve its Popeye image — the iron content is not much higher than occurs in fresh peas, and its oxalic acid content makes it unsuitable for feeding in large quantities to children.

SEED FACTS

Spinach seed is either round (smooth-surfaced) or prickly (rough-surfaced).

Actual size

Expected germination time:	12–20 days
Approximate number per ounce:	1500
Expected yield from a 10 ft row:	5–10 lb
Life expectancy of stored seed:	4 years
Approximate time between sowing and picking:	8–14 weeks
Ease of cultivation:	Not easy to grow well — rich soil and regular watering are required

SOIL FACTS

- Spinach is sometimes described as an easy vegetable to grow, but it will not succeed if the soil and position are poor. The ground must be rich and contain plenty of organic matter — starved spinach produces a bitter-tasting crop.
- The ideal place for summer spinach is between rows of tall-growing vegetables — the dappled shade will reduce the risk of running to seed. Sow winter spinach and New Zealand spinach in a sunny spot.
- Dig deeply in winter and apply lime if necessary. Apply Growmore fertilizer about 2 weeks before sowing time.

SEED SOWING

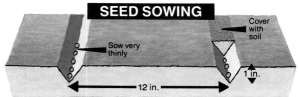

- New Zealand spinach needs more space. Sow 3 seeds about ¾ in. below the surface, spacing the groups 2 ft apart. Thin to 1 plant per station.

LOOKING AFTER THE CROP

- The seedlings of summer and winter varieties should be thinned to 3 in. apart as soon as they are large enough to handle. A few weeks later remove alternate plants for kitchen use — do not delay thinning.
- Hoe to keep down weeds. Water copiously during dry spells in summer.
- Winter varieties will need some sort of protection from October onwards unless you are lucky enough to live in a mild area. Use cloches or straw to cover the plants.

HARVESTING

- Start picking as soon as the leaves have reached a reasonable size. Always take the outer leaves, which should still be at the young and tender stage.
- The secret is to pick continually so that fresh growth is encouraged. With summer varieties you can take up to half the leaves without damaging the plants — with winter varieties pick much more sparingly. Take care when harvesting. Pick off the leaves with fingernails — don't wrench them off which could damage the stems or roots.
- The rules for New Zealand spinach are different — pull off a few young shoots from the base of the plant at each harvesting session. A single sowing will last throughout the summer if you pick little and often.

- **Summer varieties:** Sow every few weeks from mid March to the end of May for picking between late May and the end of October.
- **Winter varieties:** Sow in August and again in September for picking between October and April.
- **New Zealand variety:** Sow in late May for picking between June and September.

CALENDAR

	JAN	FEB	MAR	APR	MAY	JUN	JUL	AUG	SEP	OCT	NOV	DEC
Sowing Time												
Picking Time												

1 in. = 2.5 cm, 1 ft = 30 cm, 1 oz = 28 gm, 1 lb = 450 gm

For key to symbols — see page 7

IN THE KITCHEN

Young spinach leaves can be used for salad making but this vegetable is usually cooked before serving. A boiled or steamed mound between the potatoes and meat on the dinner plate should not be its only role — try it for filling an omelette or quiche, as a base for poached eggs (eggs florentine) or as an ingredient in soup. The summer varieties are the most tender and delicately flavoured — winter spinach is darker and coarser.

FREEZING Use young leaves. Wash well and drain, then blanch for 2 minutes. Cool and press out all excess moisture. Pack into polythene bags and squeeze out air before sealing.

STORAGE Try to cook spinach on the same day as picking — the flavour deteriorates rapidly with age. If you must store it, place washed leaves in a polythene bag in the refrigerator — spinach will stay fresh for up to 2 days.

COOKING Thorough washing to remove grit is the first essential step. Place the leaves in a large bowl of cold water, shake them and then remove. Change the water in the bowl and repeat the process — once or twice depending on the amount of grit and sand present. Trim the leaf bases of summer varieties — the coarser winter types should have the midribs removed. The best way to cook the leaves is to steam and not boil them. Place the washed leaves in a large pan and sprinkle with salt, pepper plus a small knob of butter or margarine. Add no extra water. Steam for 5–10 minutes and then squeeze out as much water as you can with a potato masher. Add grated nutmeg or chopped mint, say the culinary experts.

VARIETIES

SUMMER varieties

These varieties have round seeds and will grow quickly under good conditions to provide an early and tender crop. The major problem is their dislike of hot and dry weather, and some varieties rapidly run to seed during a prolonged warm spell in summer.

MEDANIA: This popular variety has several plus points — vigorous growth, good mildew resistance and it is slow to bolt.

KING OF DENMARK: An old favourite — the round leaves are borne well above the ground but the resistance to bolting is not good.

BLOOMSDALE: A deep green variety which has earned a good reputation for resistance to bolting. Certainly worth a trial.

LONG-STANDING ROUND: A popular variety, highly recommended for early spring sowing. Noted for its flavour, but a late-sown crop may quickly run to seed.

SIGMALEAF: Perhaps no other summer variety goes on cropping for quite so long without running to seed. That is not its only advantage — Sigmaleaf can be sown in autumn as a winter variety.

SYMPHONY: An F_1 hybrid with an impressive list of virtues. Early, erect, large-leaved, and high resistance to both mildew and bolting.

SPACE: Like Symphony an F_1 hybrid with similar virtues. Other F_1 varieties include Triathlon, Trinidad, Sporane, Triade, Sprint and Splendour.

NORVAK: A typical example of the advance in plant breeding which has occurred. Norvak is high yielding and slow to bolt even in midsummer.

Norvak

WINTER varieties

Most of these varieties have prickly seeds but there are exceptions, such as Sigmaleaf, which have smooth seeds. These plants provide a useful harvest of greens from October to April. Pick regularly and use only young leaves for cooking — pick old leaves and leave them in the kitchen for a few days and you will soon discover just how unpleasant spinach can taste!

BROAD-LEAVED PRICKLY: The name refers, of course, to the seeds and not the leaves. A standard winter variety — the foliage is dark and fleshy and the plants are slow to bolt.

LONG-STANDING PRICKLY: Quick to grow and slow to run to seed — an old favourite which is losing its place in the catalogues.

DOMINANT: One of the old favourites which is now being replaced in the catalogues by newer varieties as a summer spinach. It has less competition as a winter crop for autumn sowing. Good resistance to bolting.

MONNOPA: A fine-flavoured variety which has a low oxalic acid content. Grow it if you propose to use some of the crop as baby food.

SIGMALEAF: See 'Summer varieties' above.

NEW ZEALAND variety

This is not a true spinach. It is a dwarf and rambling plant with soft, fleshy leaves which are used as a spinach substitute. It is sensitive to frost and so it should be raised indoors and planted out in May or sown outdoors when the danger of frost has passed. Soak seed overnight before sowing and pinch out the tips of young plants to induce bushiness. The flavour is milder than true spinach — its advantage is the ability to flourish in hot and dry conditions without running to seed.

New Zealand Spinach

SPINACH TROUBLES

There are only three troubles which are likely to affect spinach, but they can make this a difficult crop to grow. Downy mildew, bolting and spinach blight are the major troubles, and if you have had problems with annual spinach in the past then try the much easier types — New Zealand spinach (page 93) and spinach beet (page 23).

	Symptom	Likely Causes
Seedlings	— eaten	**Birds** or **Millepede** or **Slugs & Snails** (see page 110)
	— toppled over	**Damping off** (see page 110)
Leaves	— yellow between veins; acid soil	**Magnesium deficiency** (see page 31)
	— yellow between veins; chalky soil	②
	— holed	**Slugs & Snails** (see page 110)
	— spotted	④
	— infested with blackfly	**Black bean aphid** (see page 20)
	— infested with greenfly	**Aphid** (see page 110)
	— rolled	⑤
	— blistered	**Mangold fly** (see page 26)
	— yellow patches above	①
	— greyish purple mould below	①
	— inner leaves narrow, yellow	⑤
Plants	— run to seed	③
	— early death, leaves deformed	⑤
	— early death, leaves not deformed	**Too hot and dry** or **Overcropping**

YELLOW PATCHES

1 DOWNY MILDEW

Watch for downy mildew if the weather is wet and cold. It begins on the outer leaves — yellow patches above and greyish purple mould below. As the disease progresses affected patches turn brown.

Treatment: Pick off diseased leaves. Spray with carbendazim at the first sign of attack.

Prevention: Practise crop rotation. Make sure the soil is well drained and avoid overcrowding by thinning the crop promptly.

2 MANGANESE DEFICIENCY

Yellow blotches appear between the veins, and the margins tend to curl up slightly. The symptoms are most pronounced in midsummer. Manganese deficiency is associated with poorly-drained soils, which can make successful spinach growing difficult in such areas.

Treatment: Apply a trace element spray containing manganese to the soil. Spraying with a foliar feed may help.

Prevention: Avoid growing spinach in poor soil. Do not overlime.

YELLOWED LEAVES

3 BOLTING

The commonest spinach trouble in home gardens is bolting, which results in the premature flowering of the plants. The danger is greatest in hot, settled weather and it will occur if the plants have been kept short of either water or nutrients. Avoid trouble by preparing the soil properly by digging in compost and raking in a general purpose fertilizer. Choose a variety which is described as bolt-resistant. Thin the seedlings early, and water in dry weather. In some soils bolting occurs year after year, and the best plan here is to grow New Zealand spinach.

SPOTTED LEAVES

4 LEAF SPOT

Numerous ¼ in. spots appear in the foliage — in a bad attack the spots join up and the leaf is destroyed. Central area of each spot is pale brown and may drop out — outer ring is dark brown or purple.

Treatment: Pick off and burn diseased leaves. Spray with mancozeb.

Prevention: Practise crop rotation. Apply a balanced fertilizer, such as Growmore, before sowing seed.

ROLLED LEAVES

5 SPINACH BLIGHT

Young leaves are affected first. The tell-tale signs are narrow and small leaf blades, inrolled margins and a puckered, yellow surface. The cause of this serious disease is the cucumber mosaic virus.

Treatment: Destroy infected plants — there is no cure.

Prevention: Keep down weeds. Spray with heptenophos or permethrin to control greenfly, which carry the virus.

1 in. = 2.5 cm, 1 ft = 30 cm, 1 oz = 28 gm, 1 lb = 450 gm

SWEDE

The introduction of disease-resistant varieties has made this winter vegetable even easier to grow. All you have to do is sprinkle some seeds in late spring or early summer, thin a few weeks later and then lift the large, globular roots as you need them from autumn until spring — few other crops are quite so straightforward. Swedes are closely related to turnips (the name is an abbreviation of 'Swedish turnip') but the flesh is generally yellow and the flavour both milder and sweeter. There are other differences — the plants are hardier, the yields are greater and the growing period is longer.

SEED FACTS

Actual size

Expected germination time:	6–10 days
Approximate number per ounce:	8000
Expected yield from a 10 ft row:	30 lb
Life expectancy of stored seed:	3 years
Approximate time between sowing and lifting:	20–24 weeks
Ease of cultivation:	Easy

SOIL FACTS

- Swedes are brassicas (see page 27) and like other members of the family need a firm, non-acid soil which has reasonable drainage.
- Pick a sunny spot and dig in autumn. Lime if necessary. In spring apply Growmore fertilizer — prepare the seed bed about a week later. Apply a nematode-based insecticide if cabbage root fly is known to be a problem.

SEED SOWING

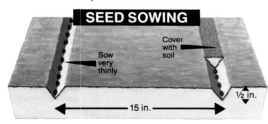

Sow very thinly

Cover with soil

½ in.

15 in.

LOOKING AFTER THE CROP

- Thin out the crop as soon as the seedlings are large enough to handle. Do this in stages until the plants are 9 in. apart.
- Keep the soil hoed and remember to water in dry weather — failure to do so will result in smaller and woodier roots. Rain following a dry spell can cause roots to split.
- Spray with derris at the first signs of flea beetle damage.

HARVESTING

- Begin lifting as soon as the roots are large enough to use. This will be from early autumn onwards, and there is no need to wait until they reach their maximum size. You can leave them in the soil and lift with a fork as required until spring, but it may be more convenient to lift and store them indoors in December for later use.
- The storage technique is to twist off the leaves and place the roots between layers of dry peat or sand in a stout box. Store in a cool shed.

IN THE KITCHEN

Swede is generally acceptable as an ingredient for stews, casseroles and soups, but for many people the memory of the yellow mush from schooldays has outlawed this vegetable as an accompaniment to meat or fish. Give it another try — lift some roots when they are the size of a large grapefruit and make the swede and potato mixture described below.

STORAGE Keep unpeeled in a cool and dry place — swedes will stay fresh for up to 5 days.
COOKING Remove the tops and roots — peel thickly until the yellow flesh is reached. Boiling and mashing is the traditional method of cooking — the 'bashed neeps' of Scotland. Cut the flesh into slices or cubes and boil for 30 minutes. Drain, and then mash with butter, cream, pepper and either ginger or nutmeg. This dish is a little watery for some palates — mixing it with an equal quantity of leftover potatoes at mashing time makes it more acceptable to English swede-haters. You can use swede fingers instead of parsnips for roasting around the joint.

VARIETIES

MARIAN: This is the swede to buy. It has all the plus points — high yields, good flavour and texture with the bonus of resistance to club root and mildew.

BEST OF ALL: You will find this purple-skinned, yellow-fleshed variety in many catalogues. Very hardy and reliable.

LIZZY: This recent introduction is claimed to have a better flavour than the other varieties. Slow to run to seed.

RUBY: Like Lizzy this new swede has been bred for extra sweetness. More resistant than most to powdery mildew.

WESTERN PERFECTION: The reputation of this variety is based on its quick-growing nature. Roots will be ready for lifting in September. The purple-topped roots have yellow flesh.

ACME: Another purple-topped variety which is quick growing like Western Perfection.

TROUBLES

See page 107

CALENDAR

	JAN	FEB	MAR	APR	MAY	JUN	JUL	AUG	SEP	OCT	NOV	DEC
Sowing Time												
Lifting Time												

SWEET CORN

Sweet corn is a type of maize which has been bred for its high sugar and low starch content. Once the cob has been picked the sugar in the kernels is steadily converted into starch, which is why the flavour of home-grown sweet corn cooked within an hour of picking is so much better than the taste of shop-bought corn. The 6–8 in. cobs are borne on 4–6 ft stems — the tassels at the top of the adult plant are the male flowers; the female flowers are the 'silks' above the immature cobs. The plants are decorative as well as useful, but are regarded as semi-tropical by many. There is still a widespread view that sweet corn cannot be grown outside the southern counties, but this is no longer true. Choose one of the early F_1 hybrids which have revolutionised the reliability of sweet corn in this country. In April raise the seedlings indoors in peat pots for planting outdoors once the danger of frost has passed. Set them out in a sheltered, sunny spot and it would have to be a poor summer for this crop to disappoint even as far north as Lancashire or Yorkshire.

SEED FACTS

Use a seed dressing before sowing outdoors. A minimum soil temperature of 50°F is required for germination.

Actual size

Expected germination time:	10–12 days
Amount required for a 10 ft row:	$\frac{1}{12}$ oz
Expected yield from a 10 ft row:	10 cobs
Life expectancy of stored seed:	2 years
Approximate time between sowing and picking:	14 weeks
Ease of cultivation:	Not difficult if you can provide the necessary growing conditions

SOIL FACTS

- There are two basic soil requirements — good drainage and enough humus to ensure that the ground will not dry out too quickly. Ideally it should be slightly acid, reasonably fertile and deep, but the situation is more important than the soil type.
- Choose a spot in full sun which is sheltered from the wind. Dig in winter, incorporating peat or old compost if the previous crop was not manured. Rake in Growmore fertilizer about 2 weeks before sowing or planting.

SOWING & PLANTING

Sow 2 seeds. Remove weaker plant
18 in.
18 in.
1 in.

- Sweet corn must be sown or planted in rectangular blocks, not as a single row. This will ensure effective wind pollination of the female flowers.
- Outdoor sowing may be reliable in the south but in other areas sow under cloches or preferably in pots indoors. Root disturbance must be avoided so use 3 in. peat pots — not clay or plastic ones. Sow 2 seeds about 1 in. deep in seed compost — remove weaker seedling. Harden off before planting outdoors — leave 18 in. between transplants.

LOOKING AFTER THE CROP

- Remove cloches when the foliage touches the glass. Protect seedlings with black cotton if birds are a nuisance. Keep down weeds but do not hoe close to the plants.
- Roots will appear at the base of the stem — cover them with soil or a mulch of old compost. The side shoots ('tillers') which may develop should not be removed.
- Water in dry weather — this is especially important at flowering time. Stake if the plants are tall and the site is exposed.
- Tapping the tassels at the top of each stem when they are fully developed in late June or July will help pollination. Liquid feed when the cobs begin to swell.

HARVESTING

- Each plant will produce 1 or 2 cobs. Test for ripeness when the silks have turned chocolate brown. Pull back part of the sheath and squeeze a couple of grains between thumbnail and fingernail. If a watery liquid squirts out then the cob is unripe. If the liquid is creamy then the cob is just right for picking but if the liquid is thick and doughy you have waited too long.
- Carefully twist off the ripe cob from the stem. Do this just before it is required for cooking.

Southern counties: Sow outdoors in mid May — the cobs should be ready for picking in late August or September. For extra reliability and an earlier crop (late July onwards in mild areas) sow under glass as described below.

Other counties: Sow seeds under glass in mid April–early May and plant out in late May–early June. Alternatively sow outdoors under cloches in mid May — place cloches in position about 2 weeks before sowing.

CALENDAR

	JAN	FEB	MAR	APR	MAY	JUN	JUL	AUG	SEP	OCT	NOV	DEC
Sowing Time (Outdoors)					🌱							
Sowing Time (Indoors)				🪴🪴	🌱🌱							
Picking Time									▓	▓		

1 in. = 2.5 cm, 1 ft = 30 cm, 1 oz = 28 gm, 1 lb = 450 gm

For key to symbols — see page 7

IN THE KITCHEN

Country sayings emphasise the need to cook sweet corn as soon as possible after picking. According to the Americans, "walk slowly to pick it, run back to the kitchen to cook it". Nearer home, the advice is to "take a pan of boiling water with you when you pick the cobs". Freshness, then, is all-important for top flavour and so are two other tips — never add salt to the water and never boil for more than a few minutes if the cobs have been freshly picked. To prepare the cob, strip off the outer leaves, cut off the stalk and pull off the silks.

FREEZING Blanch prepared cobs for 4–6 minutes, depending on their size. Cool and drain thoroughly, then wrap individually in foil or cling film before freezing.

STORAGE If storage is unavoidable, place cobs in the refrigerator — sweet corn will stay fresh for up to 3 days.

COOKING Place the cobs in a pan of boiling unsalted water for 5–8 minutes. They are ready when a kernel can be easily detached with a fork from the cob. Drain thoroughly and serve with melted butter and coarse salt. If you want to do things properly, serve each cob in a long dish with corn holders inserted at each end. It may be more satisfying to the viewer (but less satisfying to the eater) to serve the separated kernels in a dish — they can be easily stripped off the cooked cob for this purpose. Boiling is not the only cooking method — if you are having a barbecue wrap the cobs in buttered foil and place amongst the ashes for 10 minutes. Corn fritters are an American favourite but it would be a pity to waste home-grown sweet corn on them — use tinned corn instead. Deep fry spoonfuls of a mixture of mashed corn, salt, flour, milk and egg for 1–2 minutes or until golden brown.

VARIETIES

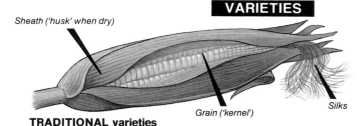

Sheath ('husk' when dry)

Grain ('kernel')

Silks

TRADITIONAL varieties

The open-pollinating varieties are not as reliable in our climate as the modern F₁ hybrids and so they have almost disappeared from the catalogues. With these F₁ varieties favoured mild areas are no longer essential as they have been specially bred for our northern conditions. There are early-, midseason and late-maturing types — the late-maturing ones are tall and the cobs are large but always choose an early-maturing type if conditions are less than ideal.

FIRST OF ALL: One of the very early ones — highly recommended for table and exhibition, especially for areas north of the Midlands. The medium-sized cobs are about 6 in. long.

EARLIKING: Medium height with large cobs. An early variety with a good reputation for sweetness — a popular choice, especially in northern areas.

KELVEDON GLORY: A popular midseason variety. It is a heavy cropper, producing well-filled 7–8 in. cobs. The kernels are pale yellow. Recommended for its flavour.

SUNDANCE: An F₁ hybrid which is an improvement on the old favourite Kelvedon Wonder. Received the RHS Award of Garden Merit.

MINOR: A mini-corn for harvesting when the cobs are about 4 in. long. Boil, steam or stir-fry and eat whole. The stems grow about 5 ft high.

EARLIBELLE: An early-maturing variety — the cobs are long and well-filled. Stands up well to poor weather conditions.

Kelvedon Glory

SUPERSWEET varieties

A recent innovation has been the introduction of the supersweet varieties. These contain about twice the amount of sugar as the traditional types, but their benefit in the dining room does not extend to the garden. They lack the vigour of traditional varieties, so they should not be sown until early June and the seed should be treated with a fungicide. Do not grow near traditional varieties, as cross-pollination will spoil the flavour.

EARLY XTRA SWEET: One of the first of the supersweet varieties. Early and very tasty, but the cobs are not as well-filled as First of All, etc.

DICKSON: An outstanding supersweet. The plants reach 6 ft or more and the cobs are up to 8 in. long. Very early.

SWEET 77: A midseason type with very large cobs. Yields and vigour, however, are only moderate.

CANDLE: An early variety which matures in about 125 days after sowing. It is noted for the length of its cobs and their heavy weight as well as for the sweetness of the kernels.

CONQUEST: A supersweet with more cold weather resistance than most varieties in this group. Early with 7–8 in. long cobs.

TROUBLES

SMUT

Large galls ('smut balls') appear on the cobs and stalks in hot and dry weather. These galls should be cut off and burnt as soon as they are seen, or they will burst open and release a mass of black spores. Burn all plants after harvesting and do not grow sweet corn on the site for at least 3 years.

FRIT FLY

Frit fly maggots bore into the growing points of corn seedlings which then develop twisted and ragged leaves. Growth is stunted and undersized cobs are produced. Control measures are not generally worthwhile but the crop can be protected by using seed dressed with an insecticide or by dusting the seedlings with HCH.

Sweet 77

1 in. = 2.5 cm, 1 ft = 30 cm, 1 oz = 28 gm, 1 lb = 450 gm

TOMATO, GREENHOUSE

You will find tomato plants in the majority of greenhouses during the summer months, producing a succession of succulent fruit from the end of June until October. We seem to have an irrepressible urge to grow them, and this is a little surprising when you remember the problems involved. They need constant care, and in summer it is necessary to water growing bags or pots at daily intervals. A wide range of pests and diseases find the tomato an ideal host, and the flavour is not *all* that much better than the supermarket ones, now that you can buy tasty varieties such as Gardener's Delight in the shops. Perhaps the key is the fascination of watching tiny green pinheads swell into bright red fruits, plus the constant need we have in most households for both raw and cooked tomatoes. The greenhouse varieties are cordon (single-stemmed) plants which reach 6 ft or more if not stopped, and it is unfortunate that many gardeners refuse to be adventurous. Each spring they sow Alicante, Ailsa Craig or Moneymaker, but there are so many exciting new ones to try.

SEED FACTS

Expected germination time:	8–11 days
Expected yield per plant:	8 lb
Life expectancy of stored seed:	3 years
Approximate time between sowing and picking:	16 weeks
Ease of cultivation:	Not easy — growing tomatoes under glass is time-consuming

Actual size

SOIL FACTS

- Tomatoes can be grown in border soil — raised beds give better results than beds at ground level. Prepare the soil in winter — dig in peat and a small amount of compost or manure. Rake in Growmore fertilizer shortly before planting. Unfortunately border soil soon becomes infested with soil pests and root diseases, so the soil must either be sterilised or changed after a couple of seasons.

- Because of the difficulties with border soil, other growing systems have been evolved. Ring culture and growing on straw bales have lost their popularity as they can be tricky, but growing in 9 in. pots filled with soilless potting compost is simple.

- Growing bags have taken over as the most popular growing system with both the professional nurseryman and amateur gardener. Good and reliable … if you master the watering technique.

SOWING & PLANTING

- If you need a large number of plants, then follow the conventional technique of sowing thinly in trays or pans filled with Seed and Cutting Compost. Cover lightly with compost — keep moist but not wet at about 65°F. When the seedlings have formed a pair of true leaves prick them out into 3 in. peat pots filled with potting compost.

- If only a few plants are required, it is easier to sow a couple of seeds in each 3 in. peat pot of compost, removing the weaker seedling after germination. Alternatively, buy plants from a reputable supplier (see page 100).

- Plant out into growing bags, pots or border soil when the seedlings are 6–8 in. tall and the flowers of the first truss are beginning to open. Water the pot thoroughly before planting. In border soil plant 18 in. apart.

LOOKING AFTER THE CROP

- Tie the main stem loosely to a cane or wind it up a well-anchored but slack vertical string. Side shoots will appear where the leaf stalks join the stem. Cut or pinch them out when they are about 1 in. long.

- When the plants are about 4 ft tall, remove the leaves below the first truss. Remove yellowing leaves below fruit trusses as the season progresses, but never overdo this deleafing process. Use a sharp knife to remove this unwanted foliage.

- Water regularly to keep the soil moist — irregular watering will cause blossom end rot or fruit splitting. Feed with a soluble tomato fertilizer every time you water. If using growing bags you *must* water frequently.

- Mist plants and tap the supports occasionally to aid pollen dispersion and fruit set. Ventilation is essential in summer — shade the glass with Coolglass when temperature reaches 80°F. When plants have reached the top of the greenhouse or when 7 trusses have set, remove the tip at 2 leaves above the top truss.

HARVESTING

- Follow the rules set out for outdoor tomatoes — see page 100.

- In a heated greenhouse kept at a minimum night temperature of 50–55°F, tomato seed is sown in late December and planted out in late February or early March for a May–June crop.

- Most gardeners, however, grow tomatoes in an unheated ('cold') house. Sow seed in early March and plant out in late April or early May. The first fruit will be ready for picking in July.

CALENDAR

	JAN	FEB	MAR	APR	MAY	JUN	JUL	AUG	SEP	OCT	NOV	DEC
Sowing & Planting (Heated greenhouse)	▣	❧ ❧										▣
Sowing & Planting (Cold greenhouse)			▣ ▣	❧ ❧								
Picking Time												

VARIETIES

ORDINARY varieties

MONEYMAKER: One of the popular varieties for the amateur. Large trusses of medium-sized fruits are produced and crops are heavy, but the flavour is bland.

AILSA CRAIG: Another popular variety, producing brightly coloured, medium-sized tomatoes. It matures early, but its main claim to fame is the excellent flavour.

ALICANTE: Moneymaker type — heavy cropping and reliable, but Alicante has distinct advantages. It is resistant to greenback and the fleshy fruits have a fine flavour.

This group of red salad tomatoes contains several old favourites which are grown for reliability (Moneymaker), flavour (Ailsa Craig) or earliness (Harbinger).

HARBINGER: An early-cropping variety which is now a little more difficult to find than the trio of favourites — Moneymaker, Ailsa Craig and Alicante. Apart from earliness it has no outstanding advantages.

MONEYCROSS: If you are a Moneymaker fan, choose this selected strain for a change. It is resistant to leaf mould and rather earlier than the basic variety.

CRAIGELLA: An improved version of Ailsa Craig — the flavour has been maintained but the danger of greenback has been removed.

GARDENER'S DELIGHT: see
SWEET 100:   page
RED ALERT: 101

Ailsa Craig

F₁ HYBRID varieties

EUROCROSS: A good choice for the heated house — large fruits borne on leaf-mould resistant plants. It is immune to greenback.

SUPERCROSS: The fruit are the same shape and size as Moneymaker, but it is even more disease resistant than its close relative Eurocross. Tolerance to mosaic virus has been added.

ESTRELLA: Good disease resistance is the prime feature of this variety.

SHIRLEY: Few varieties have more plus points — resistant to leaf mould, virus and greenback plus heavy yields and early cropping. It is not troubled by a cold spell and the space between leaves is short — an advantage if your greenhouse has a low roof.

GRENADIER: A heavy-cropper which produces fairly large fruits. They have good keeping qualities and are free from greenback. Resistant to leaf mould.

This group bears fruit which is similar in appearance to the ordinary varieties, but these modern crosses have two important advantages — they are generally heavier yielding and also have a high degree of disease resistance.

HERALD: The F₁ hybrid to choose for top flavour, according to some experts. Early and resistant to leaf mould.

TUMBLER: This variety can be grown in a pot on the patio or put in a hanging basket with lobelias. Cherry-sized fruits are borne on pendent stems.

CHERRY BELLE: An excellent cherry tomato — this F₁ hybrid has good disease resistance and crops heavily. The taste is rated as outstanding.

DANNY: A high-yielding variety for growing in an unheated greenhouse. Fruit may be misshapen in a heated house.

TYPHOON: The plus points include strong growth, early cropping, good yields and high quality fruits.

Shirley

BEEFSTEAK varieties

This group produces the large and meaty tomatoes which are so popular in the U.S. and on the Continent. They are excellent for sandwiches but only you can decide whether their flavour is superior to our familiar salad varieties. There are three types of giants — the true beefsteaks such as Dombito, the large F₁ hybrids such as Big Boy, and the Marmandes (page 101) which are suitable only for outdoor growing. Stop the plants when the fourth truss has set and provide support for the fruit if necessary.

BIG BOY: The most popular giant, producing fruit which weighs 1 lb or more. For this sort of size disbud to three fruits per truss.

DOMBITO: A true beefsteak, bred in Holland. The fruits weigh about ¾ lb with thick, fleshy walls and few seeds. Disease resistance is good.

DOMBELLO: One of the best beefsteaks. It does not get to quite the size of Dombito but the large flattened globes are borne early in the season and the flavour is very good.

MARGLOBE: You can try this Marmande-type variety in an unheated house — flesh is thick and meaty.

Big Boy

NOVELTY varieties

GOLDEN SUNRISE: The usual choice for the gardener who wants a yellow tomato. The fruit is medium-sized with a distinctive taste.

GOLDEN BOY: The variety to grow if you want very large yellow fruits which are meaty rather than juicy.

YELLOW PERFECTION: This yellow tomato is reputed to be earlier and sweeter than the others listed.

Catalogues sing the praises of the yellow, orange and striped varieties but they remain distinctly unpopular. The first tomatoes sent to Europe were gold-coloured and not red, but that was a long time ago.

SAN MARZANO: The popular 'Italian' tomato — distinctly egg-shaped with firm flesh. Use for soups, spaghetti sauce etc.

TIGERELLA: An oddity — an early-maturing tomato which bears red and yellow stripes when mature. The flavour is good and so is the yield.

Yellow Perfection

TOMATO, OUTDOOR

In many areas of Britain the tomato crop requires protection — you can grow the plants in a greenhouse or cultivate dwarf varieties in frames or under cloches. If, however, you live in a mild area and there is some shelter from cold winds then you can expect a satisfactory crop in the open garden in most summers. The outdoor crop has its benefits — the flavour of the fruit is generally better, and the bush varieties take much of the hard work out of tomato growing. There are, however, a number of pitfalls for the unwary even if your site is warm and sheltered. First of all, you must choose a variety which is recommended for growing outdoors — don't buy seedlings without checking that they are suitable. You must also prepare the ground properly — tomatoes need well-drained, humus-rich soil. Finally, remember to remove the growing point of a cordon variety whilst the plant is still quite small (see below) — leaving it to grow to its natural height will prevent the tomatoes from ripening. As you will see on page 101, there are many varieties which are suitable for outdoor growing.

SEED FACTS

Actual size

Expected germination time:	8–11 days
Expected yield per plant:	4 lb
Life expectancy of stored seed:	3 years
Approximate time between sowing and picking:	20 weeks
Ease of cultivation:	Not easy — tomatoes in growing bags need regular attention

SOIL FACTS

- Outdoor tomatoes are a tender crop, so choose a warm spot in front of a south-facing wall if you can. During the winter dig thoroughly and incorporate garden compost plus peat. Shortly before planting rake in a general fertilizer.
- If you are growing only a few plants or if you have no land available, then outdoor tomatoes can be grown in 9 in. pots or in compost-filled growing bags. These can be placed on the open ground or on balconies and patios. Remember that container growing will call for much more frequent watering. Regular feeding will be essential.

SOWING & PLANTING

- If you want to raise your own seedlings, follow one of the techniques described on page 98. Alternatively, you can buy tomato seedlings for planting out. Look for ones which are dark green, sturdy and about 8 in. tall. These young plants should be pot grown.

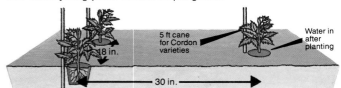

- Plant out into growing bags, pots or the vegetable plot when the flowers of the first truss are beginning to open. Water the pot before planting out and ensure that the top of the soil ball is set just below the soil surface.
- You will get a better crop if you spread black polythene sheeting over the soil surface and plant the tomato seedlings through X-shaped slits.

LOOKING AFTER THE CROP

- If a cordon variety is grown, loosely tie the stem to the cane. Make the ties at 12 in. intervals as the plant grows.
- Side shoots will appear where the leaf stalks join the stem. Pinch them out when they are about 1 in. long. Remove yellowing leaves below fruit trusses as the season progresses, but never overdo this deleafing process.
- Water regularly in dry weather to keep the soil moist — alternating dryness with flooding will cause blossom end rot or fruit splitting. If using growing bags you *must* water frequently as noted on the instructions. Feed regularly with a tomato fertilizer. When small tomatoes have developed on the 4th truss remove the tip at 2 leaves above this truss.

HARVESTING

- Pick the fruits when they are ripe and fully coloured. Hold the tomato in your palm and with your thumb break off the fruit at the 'knuckle' (swelling on the flower stalk).
- At the end of the season the stems can be removed from the canes and laid under cloches on a bed of straw. An easier way to ripen green fruit is to place them as a layer in a tray and put them in a drawer. Next to the tray set a couple of ripe apples to generate the ripening gas ethylene.

- The standard time for sowing seed under glass is in late March or early April. The young plants are hardened off during May and planted out in early June, or late May if the weather is favourable and the danger of frost has passed. Plants to be grown under cloches are planted out in the middle of May.
- Under average conditions the first tomatoes will be ready for picking in mid August.

CALENDAR

	JAN	FEB	MAR	APR	MAY	JUN	JUL	AUG	SEP	OCT	NOV	DEC
Sowing & Planting Time			🪴	🪴	🌱🌱							
Picking Time												

IN THE KITCHEN

It is true that a tomato picked from the plant will taste better than the fruit of the same variety bought in the supermarket, but a home-grown Moneymaker will have none of the 'real' tomato taste of shop-bought Gardener's Delight. Variety is all-important and you should check that your choice is recommended for its flavour. Most garden tomatoes are used for salads or for grilling and frying — simple methods of preparation for one of our favourite vegetables. Bite-sized tomatoes should be served whole but slicing or quartering are the usual methods of presentation on the salad plate. Simply add French dressing or else make a tomato salad fit for a gourmet — sprinkle salt and freshly ground pepper over the slices, add a little sugar and then cover with chopped basil or a mixture of parsley and chives.

FREEZING Skin and remove core of ripe fruit. Simmer for about 5 minutes and then sieve through a nylon strainer. Cool, pack in a rigid container and freeze.

STORAGE Keep in a polythene bag at the bottom of the refrigerator — tomatoes will stay fresh for up to 1 week.

COOKING For grilling, cut in half and coat exposed surface with oil, pepper and sugar — grill for 5 minutes. Stuffed tomatoes are delicious and may be served hot or cold — use a large, meaty variety rather than a small juicy one. Many recipes call for skinned tomatoes — peeling is simple if you first put the fruits in a bowl and cover with boiling water for about a minute. Tomatoes are used in many, many ways such as stews, omelettes, sauces, soups, sandwiches and so on. However, the tomato juice and the tomato soup you make at home will not taste like the canned versions — these commercial products are made from special varieties grown in sunny climes.

VARIETIES

CORDON varieties

These varieties are grown as single stems and they have to be trimmed and supported. As described on page 100, the stem is stopped after the 4th truss has set so as to hasten ripening before the autumn frosts. There are many red varieties, varying in size from giants to bite-sized fruits, and there are also yellow, orange and striped tomatoes.

AILSA CRAIG:	GOLDEN SUNRISE:	see	MONEYCROSS:	TIGERELLA:
ALICANTE:	HARBINGER:	page	MONEYMAKER:	YELLOW
CRAIGELLA:	TUMBLER:	99	DANNY:	PERFECTION:

Sweet 100

GARDENER'S DELIGHT: An old favourite, but the one to choose in the opinion of many experts. A heavy crop of bite-sized tomatoes is produced with a tangy flavour which puts the bland taste of some greenhouse varieties to shame.

SWEET 100: A rival to Gardener's Delight — the cherry-sized fruits are delicious and you can expect to pick several hundred from a well-grown plant.

MARMANDE: The other end of the scale to Gardener's Delight and Sweet 100 — the irregular-shaped fruits are very large and fleshy with few seeds. These are the well-known Continental tomatoes, but the full flavour does not develop under our cooler conditions.

SAINT PIERRE: Another large tomato, irregularly-shaped and deep red in colour. The flavour is good and yields are high.

OUTDOOR GIRL: One of the earliest tomatoes to ripen — widely recommended as one of the best outdoor varieties. It is a heavy cropper bearing slightly ribbed fruits with a good flavour.

HISTON EARLY: This one was introduced before the F_1 hybrids appeared but it is still grown for its heavy crops of bright red fruits. Size is good and so is the flavour.

GEMINI: Outdoor Girl has a good reputation for succeeding in cool summers and so does Gemini. Its fruits are medium-sized and sweet.

Marmande

BUSH varieties

These varieties make outdoor tomato growing much easier. They are either bushes 1–2½ ft high or creeping plants less than 9 in. tall. They do not require supporting, trimming or stopping, and are excellent for cloche culture. One drawback is that the fruits tend to be hidden, which makes harvesting more difficult than with cordon varieties. Straw or plastic sheeting must be laid around the plants as many fruits are at ground level.

THE AMATEUR: A popular but perhaps not the best variety of bush tomatoes. The 1½ ft plant produces a heavy crop of medium-sized tomatoes.

RED ALERT: A modern introduction which has become a favourite. It is very early and the small fruits have a better flavour than any other bush variety.

SLEAFORD ABUNDANCE: Despite the small amount of leaf borne by this variety the crop is heavy for a bush tomato.

ALFRESCO: An excellent variety, vigorous and high-yielding with good resistance to disease.

PIXIE: The plant is small and compact but staking may be necessary. The fruits are small and the flavour is good — a favourite with many gardeners but the crop can be disappointing in an indifferent summer.

SIGMABUSH: A good choice — the open growth habit allows the crop to ripen in dull weather. It is noted for its earliness and quality.

TOTEM: An early cropper with medium-sized fruits — grow it in bags or pots.

TORNADO: This variety is quite similar to Red Alert but a little later to come to fruit. The stems are vigorous, foliage is sparse and yields are high.

TINY TIM: A dwarf bush variety which you can plant in a windowbox. The cherry-like fruits are bright red and almost seedless.

ROMA: This is the one to grow if you want an outdoor bush which produces plum-shaped fruit. May need support.

Tiny Tim

1 in. = 2.5 cm, 1 ft = 30 cm, 1 oz = 28 gm, 1 lb = 450 gm

Diseases and disorders are much more important than insect pests — outdoor tomatoes are much less susceptible than crops grown under glass. Keep a careful watch and treat plants immediately symptoms appear. Tomatoes require regular feeding with a specific fertilizer which is rich in potash in order to prevent undersized fruit on the upper trusses. Don't overfeed — little and often is the secret.

TOMATO TROUBLES

	Symptom	Likely Causes
Seedlings	— eaten or severed	**Woodlice** or **Slugs** or **Cutworm** (see page 110)
	— toppled over	**Damping off** (see page 110)
	— gnawed roots	**Millepede** (see page 110)
Stems	— tunnelled	22 or **Wireworm** (see page 110)
	— grey mouldy patches	4
	— brown zone near soil level	6 or 7
Leaves	— blue tinged	**Too cold** or **too dry**
	— yellow between veins	12
	— grey mould	4
	— papery patches	17
	— brown patches on upper surface	13
	— yellow patches on upper surface	3
	— mottled	1 or **Red spider mite** (see page 56)
	— curled	1 or 2 or 8 or 9
	— wilted	5 or 6 or 7 or 10 or 11
	— fern-like	1 or 8
	— infested with greenfly	**Aphid** (see page 110)
	— tiny moths, sticky surface	9
	— holed, caterpillars present	22
Roots	— brown, corky	5
	— covered with cysts or galls	10
Fruits	— flowers drop before fruits form	16
	— form, but drop before maturity	4
	— form, but remain tiny	19
	— sticky, covered with black mould	9
	— soft rot	23
	— discoloured spots or patches	14 or 15 or 17 or 18 or 20 or 25
	— hollow	8 or 21
	— split or tunnelled	22 or 24

DISTORTED OR DISCOLOURED LEAVES

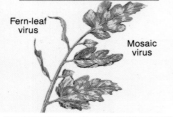

Fern-leaf virus

Mosaic virus

1 VIRUS

There are several important virus diseases which affect tomatoes. Leaves may be mottled and curled, stems may bear dark vertical streaks, foliage may be thin and distorted and growth may be stunted. Affected fruit is often mottled and bronzed.

Treatment: None. Destroy affected specimens. Feed remaining plants.

Prevention: Try to buy virus-free plants. Spray to control greenfly. Do not handle immediately after smoking.

2 LEAF ROLL

Unlike potatoes, rolled tomato leaves do not indicate disease. The inward curling of young leaves is usually taken as a good sign if they are dark green. The rolling of older leaves is usually due to excess deleafing or a wide variation between day and night temperatures. Provided that pests and disease are absent, there is no need to take action.

5 ROOT ROT

Poor drainage can lead to root disease. Below ground the roots become brown and corky, above ground the plants tend to wilt in hot weather. Rots cannot be cured once they have taken hold — mulch around the stems with moist peat to promote the formation of new roots. Next year grow plants in bags, fresh compost or sterilised soil.

BROWN MOULD PATCHES

3 TOMATO LEAF MOULD

Purplish brown mould patches appear on the underside of the foliage — the upper surface bears yellowish patches. Lower leaves are attacked first.

Treatment: Remove some of the lower leaves. Spray with carbendazim at the first signs of attack.

Prevention: Ventilate the greenhouse, especially at night.

GREY FURRY PATCHES

4 GREY MOULD (Botrytis)

Grey mould usually starts on a damaged area of the stem. Other parts of the plant may then be infected — diseased flower stalks cause fruit drop.

Treatment: Cut out diseased areas and dust wound lightly with carbendazim.

Prevention: Reduce humidity by adequate ventilation. Remove decaying leaves and fruit. Avoid overcrowding. Spray regularly with carbendazim.

6 FOOT ROT

Foot rot is generally a disease of seedling tomatoes, but mature plants can be attacked.

Treatment: None if diseased area is large. Lift plant and burn. If plant is only slightly affected mulch stem base with moist peat and water with Cheshunt Compound; some fruit may be obtained.

Prevention: Use sterilised soil or compost for raising seedlings. Avoid overwatering. Never plant into infected soil.

BROWN STEM BASES

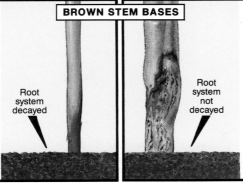

Root system decayed

Root system not decayed

7 STEM ROT (Didymella)

Stem rot is a disease of mature plants. Lower leaves turn yellow and a sunken brown canker appears at the base of the stem. Black dots develop in this cankered area. Disease may spread to other parts of the stem.

Treatment: None. Destroy badly affected plants and spray carbendazim on to the stem bases of the remaining plants. If plant is only slightly affected cut out diseased area and paint with carbendazim solution.

Prevention: Sterilise greenhouse and equipment between crops.

FERN-LIKE LEAVES

8 HORMONE DAMAGE

Traces of lawn weedkiller can cause severe distortion. Leaves are fern-like and twisted, stems and leaf stalks are also twisted. Similar in appearance to a virus disease, but spiral twisting is more pronounced. Fruit is plum-shaped and hollow. Avoid trouble by treating the lawn on a still day and by never using weedkiller equipment for other plants.

TINY MOTHS UNDER LEAVES

9 GREENHOUSE WHITEFLY

The most widespread of all tomato pests. Both the adults and larvae suck sap from the leaves which become pale and curled. Foliage and fruit are rendered sticky — black mould grows on this honeydew, thereby disfiguring the surface.

Treatment: Not easy to control. Spray with permethrin at 3 day intervals until the infestation has been cleared. Spray in the morning or evening.

Prevention: Hang yellow Flycatcher Cards above the plants.

SWELLINGS ON ROOTS

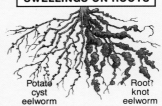

Potato cyst eelworm

Root knot eelworm

10 EELWORM

Growth is stunted and leaves are discoloured and wilted. Foliage may be purplish on the underside. Roots bear either tiny white cysts (potato cyst eelworm) or large brown swellings (root knot eelworm).

Treatment: None. Destroy plants.

Prevention: Do not grow tomatoes or potatoes in infested soil for at least 6 years.

BROWN-STREAKED TISSUE

11 VERTICILLIUM WILT

Leaves wilt in hot weather, appearing to recover on cool evenings. Lower leaves turn yellow. If you cut open the lower stem the tell-tale signs of wilt are revealed. Brown streaks run through the stem tissue.

Treatment: There is no chemical treatment — mulch around stem so new roots can form. If possible keep at 75°F for about 2 weeks.

Prevention: Do not grow tomatoes in infected soil — grow in compost.

YELLOWING BETWEEN VEINS

12 MAGNESIUM DEFICIENCY

Discoloration begins on lower leaves and moves upwards until all foliage is affected. Yellow areas may turn brown. A common and serious disorder which is made worse, not better, by standard feeding.

Treatment: Spray with Epsom Salts (½ oz/pint) or use a foliar spray containing magnesium.

Prevention: Use a fertilizer which contains magnesium (Mg).

DARK BROWN BLOTCHES

13 POTATO BLIGHT

Blight can be a devastating disease of outdoor tomatoes in wet weather. The first signs are brown areas on the edges of the leaves. The patches spread until the leaves are killed. Stems show blackened patches.

Treatment: None, once the disease has firmly taken hold.

Prevention: Spray with mancozeb as soon as the plants have been stopped. Repeat every 2 weeks if the weather is damp.

TOMATO TROUBLES continued

FRUIT TROUBLES

14 BLOSSOM END ROT

Leathery dark-coloured patch occurs at the bottom of the fruit. It is a frequent problem where growing bags are used.

Treatment: None.

Prevention: Never let the soil or compost dry out, especially when the fruit is swelling.

15 BLOTCHY RIPENING

Parts of the fruit remain yellow or orange and fail to ripen. The cause is usually too much heat or too little potash.

Treatment: None.

Prevention: Apply Coolglass and control heat. Feed with a potash-rich fertilizer. Water regularly.

16 BLOSSOM DROP

Flowers sometimes wither and break off at the knuckle. Pollination has not taken place, and the cause is usually dryness at the roots and in the air.

Treatment: None.

Prevention: Water regularly and spray flowers in the morning. Tap plants to aid pollination.

Knuckle

17 SUN SCALD

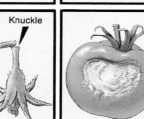

Pale brown, papery-skinned depression on the side of fruit facing the glass. Papery patches on leaves. Exposure to bright sun is the cause.

Treatment: None.

Prevention: Paint glass with Coolglass. Damp down adequately, but do not spray the plants at midday.

18 GHOST SPOT

Grey mould spores fall on or splash on to fruit. Small, transparent rings ('water spots') are formed.

Treatment: None. Affected fruit can be eaten.

Prevention: Provide good ventilation. Do not splash developing fruit when watering. Control grey mould.

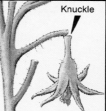

19 DRY SET

Growth of the fruitlet ceases when it reaches the size of a match-head. The trouble is due to the air being too hot and dry when pollination is taking place.

Treatment: None.

Prevention: Spray the plants daily with water in the morning or evening.

20 GREENBACK

Area around the stalk remains hard, green and unripe. The cause is too much sunlight or too little potash.

Treatment: None.

Prevention: Apply Coolglass. Control heat of greenhouse. Feed regularly with a potash-rich fertilizer. Resistant varieties are available.

21 HOLLOW FRUIT

There are several causes of hollow fruit — poor conditions for pollination (air too hot, too cold or too dry), too little potash in the soil or damage by a hormone weedkiller.

Treatment: None.

Prevention: Avoid factors listed above.

22 TOMATO MOTH

Large green or brown caterpillars tunnel into fruit and stems. Young caterpillars eat holes in leaves.

Treatment: Too late for effective treatment at this stage. Destroy fruit.

Prevention: Spray with permethrin or fenitrothion when small caterpillars and holes appear on leaves.

23 POTATO BLIGHT

Brown, shrunken area appears on fruit. The affected tomato is soon completely rotten. Infection may develop during storage.

Treatment: None. Destroy fruit.

Prevention: Protect fruit by spraying against potato blight as soon as it appears on the leaves (page 103).

24 SPLIT FRUIT

A common complaint, both outdoors and under glass. It is caused by heavy watering or rain after the soil has become dry around the roots. The sudden increase in size causes the skin to split.

Treatment: None.

Prevention: Keep roots evenly moist.

25 BUCKEYE ROT

Brown concentric rings around a grey spot on unripe fruit. Spores splash up from soil on to trusses.

Treatment: None. Remove and destroy infected fruits.

Prevention: Tie up lower trusses to prevent splashing. Apply a peat mulch. Water carefully.

TURNIP

Do not be misled by the overgrown, woody roots you may have bought from the greengrocer for stews or casseroles — home-grown turnips have much more to offer. There are Early or bunching varieties which are sown in spring and then pulled when they are the size of golf-balls for eating raw in salads or for boiling whole for the dinner plate. Round is not the only shape for these Early turnips — there are also flat and cylindrical ones. There is not much variation in the globular Maincrop types sown in summer, but you can choose the yellow-fleshed Golden Ball. Finally, turnips can be sown in the autumn and the tops cut for spring greens once winter is over — a green vegetable which is more nutritious than spinach. Turnips are an easy-to-grow and quick-maturing crop, but remember that the Early varieties are more demanding than the Maincrop varieties — any check due to starvation, poor drainage, dryness at the roots, etc. will drastically reduce both tenderness and flavour.

SEED FACTS

Expected germination time:	6–10 days
Approximate number per ounce:	8000
Expected yield from a 10 ft row:	7 lb (Early varieties) 12 lb (Maincrop varieties)
Life expectancy of stored seed:	3 years
Approximate time between sowing and lifting:	6–12 weeks
Ease of cultivation:	Easy

Actual size

SOIL FACTS

- Turnips are brassicas (see page 27) and like other members of the family need a firm, non-acid soil which has reasonable drainage.
- Early varieties require fertile soil — choose another crop if your soil is sandy or shallow.
- Pick a reasonably sunny spot and dig in autumn. Lime if necessary. In spring apply Growmore fertilizer and prepare the seed bed about a week later. You will have to take preventative measures (page 28) if cabbage root fly is known to be a problem.

SEED SOWING

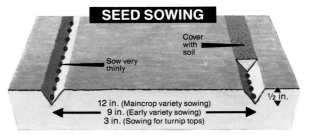

Cover with soil
Sow very thinly
12 in. (Maincrop variety sowing)
9 in. (Early variety sowing)
3 in. (Sowing for turnip tops)
½ in.

LOOKING AFTER THE CROP

- Thin out turnips grown for roots as soon as the seedlings are large enough to handle. Do this in stages until the plants are 9 in. (Maincrop varieties) or 5 in. (Early varieties) apart. Do not thin turnips grown for their tops.
- Keep the soil hoed and remember to water in dry weather — failure to do so will result in smaller and woodier roots. Rain following a dry spell can cause roots to crack if the soil has not been watered.
- Spray with derris at the first signs of flea beetle damage.

HARVESTING

- The roots of Early varieties are pulled like radishes rather than levered out with a fork like swedes. Pull whilst the roots are still small — golf-ball size if they are to be eaten raw or between golf-ball and tennis-ball size if they are to be cooked.
- Begin lifting Maincrop turnips as soon as they are large enough to use — remember that tenderness and flavour decrease with age. Harvesting normally begins in October and in most areas you can leave the turnips in the soil and lift them out with a fork as required. In cold and wet areas it is preferable to lift in early November — twist off the leaves and place the roots between layers of dry peat or sand in a stout box. Store in a cool shed.
- Turnips grown for spring greens should have their tops cut in March or April when they are about 5 in. high. Leave the plants to resprout — several cuts should be obtained.

- **Early turnips:** Sow Purple-top Milan under cloches in February and other Early varieties outdoors during March–June for a May–September crop.
- **Maincrop turnips:** Sow Maincrop varieties in mid July–mid August for cropping and storage from mid October onwards.
- **Turnip tops:** Sow a Maincrop variety in August or September for spring greens in March and April.

CALENDAR

	JAN	FEB	MAR	APR	MAY	JUN	JUL	AUG	SEP	OCT	NOV	DEC
Sowing Time												
Lifting Time			TOPS ONLY									

IN THE KITCHEN

Early turnips can be eaten raw — merely wash, remove the tops and roots, and peel thinly. Cut into slices or grate before adding to your favourite summer salad. Some people find raw turnips rather indigestible — in that case boil them whole for about 25 minutes and toss in butter and chopped parsley before serving. Maincrop turnips are more fibrous and need to be treated rather differently, as described below.

FREEZING Use small turnips — wash, trim off the tops and roots, and cut into slices or cubes. Blanch for 3 minutes, cool and then drain thoroughly. Freeze in a rigid container.

STORAGE Keep in a polythene bag in the refrigerator — turnips will stay fresh for up to 2 weeks.

COOKING After trimming maincrop turnips the outer fibrous layer should be removed by peeling thickly. Cut the roots into chunks and boil for about 30 minutes. Drain thoroughly and decide on your method of serving this hot vegetable. You can toss the chunks in melted butter and parsley or you can mash them with butter, cream, pepper and a little lemon juice. Some people prefer to mix them with boiled carrots or potatoes before mashing. Stews, casseroles and soups are the usual home for turnips, but you can also parboil them for roasting around the Sunday joint. Turnip tops are cooked in the same way as spinach — place the leaves in a pan and add salt, pepper and a small knob of butter or margarine. Add no water — simply steam for about 10 minutes in the water left on the leaves after washing. Drain thoroughly in a strainer, squeeze out excess water with the back of a spoon.

VARIETIES

EARLY varieties

Flat

Cylindrical

Globular

These varieties are quick maturing and should be pulled when the roots are still young and tender. They cannot be stored and should be used within a few days of harvesting.

PRESTO: Grow this one for golf-ball sized roots which are pulled about a month after sowing.

SNOWBALL: Quick-growing, globular, white-fleshed — considered by many to be the best Early turnip for both table and exhibition use. It is popular and you will find it at your local garden centre — choose it for growing under cloches for a May–June crop.

EARLY WHITE STONE: Also known as Early Six Weeks, another white-fleshed globular turnip which is similar to but no better than Snowball.

PURPLE-TOP MILAN: Something different — a flat, white turnip with a purple top. This is the earliest of the popular turnips.

RED GLOBE: The roots are globular and medium-sized — the flesh is white and the outside white with a red top.

GOLDEN PERFECTION: A flat variety with tender, yellow flesh. You may have to search to find it.

TOKYO CROSS: An unusual turnip — an Early (that is, quick-maturing) variety which is sown late. A May–August sowing produces small white globes ready for pulling in about 6 weeks.

SPRINTER: A selected strain of Purple-Top Milan. Slightly smaller and even earlier, according to the suppliers.

Snowball

MAINCROP varieties

White

Yellow

Green-top

These varieties are larger and slower to mature than the Early types. They are also hardier and have good keeping qualities — they can be lifted and stored in November for use throughout the winter and spring.

GREEN-TOP WHITE: The variety recommended for use as spring greens. If left to mature the roots are large and green-topped, as the name suggests. Very similar (or identical) varieties are Marble-Top Green, Green Top and Green Globe.

MANCHESTER MARKET: A typical green-top, producing large, white-fleshed turnips with a mild flavour. Manchester Market is especially recommended for winter storage.

GOLDEN BALL: The best of the Maincrops, according to some experts. The plants are compact and the yellow-fleshed roots are tender. It has good keeping qualities and is widely grown for exhibition but it is not quite as hardy as Manchester Market.

CHAMPION GREEN-TOP YELLOW: A yellow-fleshed variety like Golden Ball — both can be stored for a long period. Unlike Golden Ball it appears in few catalogues.

Green-Top White

TURNIP, SWEDE & RADISH TROUBLES

The brassica family is notorious for the frightening number of pests and diseases which can attack the plants. The root-producing members are no exception, as the extensive table on the right clearly shows, but in practice the troubles you are likely to encounter in the garden are very few. Flea beetle is the only serious problem of the radish crop — turnips and swedes have to face a few additional ones, including club root, powdery mildew and soft rot. Gall weevil and cabbage root fly are occasionally a nuisance, but the root brassicas are generally much healthier than the leafy ones such as cauliflower and brussels sprouts.

	Symptom	Likely Causes
Seedlings	— eaten	**Birds** or **Slugs** (see page 29) or **Flea beetle** (see page 30) or **Cutworm** (see page 31)
	— toppled over	**Damping off** (see page 110)
	— peppered with small holes	**Flea beetle** (see page 30)
	— severed at ground level	**Cutworm** (see page 31)
Leaves	— swollen, distorted ('Crumple leaf')	**Swede midge** (see page 30)
	— white floury coating	**Powdery mildew** (see page 21)
	— greyish mould on underside	**Downy mildew** (see page 28)
	— white spots	**White blister** (see page 29)
	— yellowing; black veins	4
	— dark green, raised spots	1
	— infested with greenfly	**Mealy aphid** (see page 30)
	— holed	**Cabbage caterpillar** (see page 29) or **Slugs** (see page 29) or **Flea beetle** (see page 30) or **Diamond-back moth** (see page 31)
Roots	— tunnelled, maggots present	**Cabbage root fly** (see page 28)
	— swollen outgrowths	**Club root** or **Gall weevil** (see page 28)
	— covered with purple mould	**Violet root rot** (see page 43)
	— scabby patches	**Common scab** (see page 85)
	— side shoots around crown ('Many neck')	**Swede midge** (see page 30)
	— split	**Splitting** (see page 43)
	— bitter, stringy	3
	— woody	**Short of water or fertilizer** or **Delayed harvesting**
	— inner black ring	4
	— wet rot starting at crown	2
	— brown markings in flesh	3

DARK GREEN SPOTS

1 TURNIP MOSAIC VIRUS

An infectious and damaging disease of turnips, which is fortunately uncommon. Young leaves are twisted and mottled; it may be fatal to young plants. Tell-tale sign is the presence of dark green, raised spots on the leaves.

Treatment: There is no cure. Destroy affected plants, as this disease can lead to soft rot.

Prevention: Spray with permethrin or heptenophos to control the greenfly which are the carriers of the disease.

2 SOFT ROT

A wet and slimy rot, beginning at the crown, can occur in both the growing crop and in stored roots. The outer skin of the roots remains firm. A tell-tale sign is the collapse of the foliage. Soft rot can be serious, especially in a wet season, and it is essential to remove affected plants immediately. To avoid trouble next season make sure the soil is well drained, avoid over-manuring, be careful not to injure roots when hoeing and never store damaged turnips or swedes. Practise crop rotation.

BROWN MARKINGS

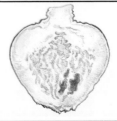

3 BROWN HEART

Greyish-brown rings run through the flesh. Affected areas become water-soaked. This disease is much more likely to attack swedes than turnips, and is usually restricted to light soils in a dry season. Affected roots are bitter. The cause is boron deficiency.

Treatment: None.

Prevention: If soil is known to be boron deficient, apply 1 oz borax per 20 sq. yards before planting — take care not to overdose.

OUTER BLACK RING

4 BLACK ROT

Above ground the symptoms of black rot are yellow leaves with black veins (see page 29). If an affected root is cut across a tell-tale ring of black dots can be seen just below the skin. Attacks are worst in a warm, wet summer on poorly drained soil.

Treatment: None. Lift diseased plants and burn.

Prevention: Practise crop rotation. Make sure the soil is well drained.

1 in. = 2.5 cm, 1 ft = 30 cm, 1 oz = 28 gm, 1 lb = 450 gm

CHAPTER 3

VEGETABLE TROUBLES

One of the most distressing sights in gardening is to see a whole crop of vegetables destroyed — eaten by pests rather than by you. Insects and other small creatures cause damage in the flower garden which is unsightly — on food plants they are destroyers. Diseases, too, can cause havoc. Most diseases are caused by fungi, and these can often be prevented by spraying with a fungicide. The others, caused by bacteria and viruses, can rarely be controlled in this way.

Not all vegetable troubles are caused by pests and diseases — split tomatoes, blown sprouts and bull-necked onions do not appear in the pest charts but they are still the effects of important disorders. The purpose of this chapter is to tell you how to avoid troubles of all types and to help you to identify and control the pests, diseases and disorders which can attack a wide range of plants. Specific problems of individual vegetables are dealt with on the pages describing each crop, and so a vast array of enemies is listed.

It is not the intention of this book to frighten you — no matter how long you garden you will never see all of these troubles. The role of these guides is to take away the worry of the unidentified problem, and to provide you with the knowledge to deal with the trouble speedily and correctly.

Prevent trouble before it starts

● **Choose wisely.** Read about the crop before you buy — don't rely solely on the seed packet. Make sure that the variety is suitable for the chosen sowing date and don't leave your purchase to the last minute — many select varieties sell out early. Sometimes you will need to buy seedlings instead of seeds for transplanting into the plot. Choose carefully — the plants should be sturdy, free from disease and discoloration and there should be a good root system. Here you must leave it to the last minute because there should be as little delay as possible between buying and planting.

● **Prepare the ground properly.** Good drainage is vital — a plant in waterlogged soil is likely to succumb to root-rotting organisms. Follow the rules for the correct way to manure, feed and lime the soil — remember that vegetables vary widely in their soil needs. The time for digging is autumn or early winter if you plan to sow in spring.

● **Rotate your crops.** Soil troubles and nutrient deficiencies can build up if you grow the same crop year after year on the same site. Crop rotation is necessary for successful vegetable production — see the rules on page 4.

● **Avoid overcrowding.** Sow seed thinly. Thin the seedlings as soon after germination as practical — overcrowding leads to crippled plants and high disease risk. Do not leave thinnings on the plot — put them on the compost heap or burn if instructed to do so.

● **Get rid of weeds and rubbish.** Weeds rob the plants of water, food, space and light. Rubbish, like weeds, can be a breeding ground for pests and diseases.

● **Get rid of badly infected plants.** Do not leave sources of infection in the garden. Remove and destroy incurable plants when this book tells you to do so.

● **Feed and water correctly.** Some plant troubles are due to incorrect feeding and soil moisture problems. Use a balanced fertilizer containing nitrogen, phosphates and potash — follow the instructions. Never let the roots get dry but daily sprinklings instead of a good soaking may do more harm than good.

Deal with trouble as soon as you can

● **Keep a small plant-aid kit.** It is a good idea to keep a small selection of pesticides in the garden shed for emergency use. You will need heptenophos, permethrin and carbendazim for above-ground pests and diseases, and methiocarb for slugs and some below-ground pests.

● **Spray when necessary.** Inspect the plants regularly and at the first sign of trouble look up the cause in the appropriate section of this book. Once you have put a name to the problem, act quickly — many pests and diseases can be checked quite easily if treated promptly, but may be difficult or impossible to control if left to get out of hand.

There are a few simple rules to ensure effective, safe and economical pest control. Read the label carefully and make sure that the product is recommended for the plants you wish to spray. Follow the instructions — do not make the solution stronger than recommended and never use equipment which has contained a weedkiller.

Try to pick a day when the weather is neither sunny nor windy and apply a fine forceful spray until both sides of the leaves are covered and the liquid has just started to run off. After spraying, wash out equipment and wash hands and face. Store packs in a safe place and do not keep unlabelled or illegible bottles or boxes. Never decant pesticides into old lemonade bottles, etc. If you have a large plot you may be tempted to buy professional packs, but their use is illegal for the amateur gardener.

Correct timing is important. Insecticides are normally applied at the first sign of attack. Systemic products such as heptenophos go inside the sap stream and protect parts not reached by the spray. Fungicides usually work as protectants and so they need to be applied *before* trouble appears.

Some problems (red spider mite, whitefly, diseases, etc.) need repeated spraying. Once again follow the instructions on the label. Finally, choose a product with a suitable harvesting interval — during the picking season choose a chemical with a 0–2 day interval between spraying and gathering.

GENERAL DISORDERS

Some vegetable troubles attack a single or small group of crops — examples are potato blight, carrot fly and pea moth. Other problems can attack a wide range of plants and these are the general disorders (described on this page) and general pests and diseases (see page 110).

WIND

Wind is often ignored as a danger, yet a cold east wind in spring can kill in the same way as frost. More frequently the effect is the browning of leaf margins. Another damaging effect is wind rock, which can lead to rotting of the roots.

FROST

A severe late frost will kill half-hardy vegetables. The shoots of asparagus and potatoes are blackened, but healthy shoots appear after the frosts have passed. The general symptoms of moderate damage are yellow patches or marginal browning of the leaves. The basic rule is to avoid sowing or planting before the recommended time unless you can provide protection. If your garden is on a sloping site, open part of the lower boundary to air movement so as to prevent the creation of a 'frost pocket'.

TOO LITTLE WATER

The first sign is a dull leaf colour, and this is followed by wilting of the foliage. Discoloration becomes more pronounced and growth is checked. Lettuces become leathery, roots turn woody and some plants run to seed. Flowers and young fruit may drop off. If water shortage continues, leaves turn brown and fall, and the plant dies. Avoid trouble by incorporating organic matter, by watering thoroughly and by mulching.

TOO MUCH WATER

Waterlogging affects the plant in two ways. Root development is crippled by the shortage of air in the soil. The root system becomes shallow, and also ineffective as the root hairs die. Leaves often turn pale and growth is stunted. The second serious effect is the stimulation of root-rotting diseases. Good drainage is therefore essential, and this calls for thorough autumn digging. Incorporate plenty of organic matter into heavy soil — the correct timing for humus addition depends on the crop being grown.

HEAVY RAIN FOLLOWING DROUGHT

The outer skin of many vegetables hardens under drought conditions, and when heavy rain or watering takes place the sudden increase in growth stretches and then splits the skin. This results in the splitting of tomatoes, potatoes and roots. Avoid by watering before the soil dries out.

TOO LITTLE PLANT FOOD

The major plant foods are nitrogen, phosphates and potash, and a vigorous crop acts as a heavy drain on the soil's resources. Nitrogen shortage leads to stunted growth, pale leaves and occasional red discoloration. Potash shortage leads to poor disease resistance, marginal leaf scorch, and produce with poor cooking and keeping qualities. Before sowing or planting apply a complete fertilizer, such as Grow-more fertilizer, containing all the major nutrients.

Apply one or more dressings to the growing plants. Backward vegetables are helped by spraying dilute liquid fertilizer over the leaves.

SHADE

In a small garden deep shade may be the major problem. Straggling soft growth is produced and the leaves tend to be small. Such plants are prone to attack by pests and diseases. Grow leaf and root types rather than fruit and pod vegetables.

TRACE ELEMENT SHORTAGE

Vegetables often show deficiency symptoms such as yellowing between the veins and leaf scorch. The most important trace elements are magnesium, manganese, iron, molybdenum and boron. Make sure the soil is well supplied with compost or manure. If your soil is known to have a trace element deficiency problem, undoubtedly the best answer is to water the ground early in the season with a sequestered trace element product which will supply the minor nutrients needed by the plants.

TOO LITTLE ORGANIC MATTER

The soil must be in good heart and this calls for liberal amounts of organic matter. Not all materials are suitable; peat may increase aeration and water retention but the need is for an active source of humus. Good garden compost and well-rotted manure are ideal. Timing is all-important — look up individual crops in this book for details.

GENERAL PESTS & DISEASES

APHID

The weakening effect of greenfly and blackfly on leaves and shoots is obvious. There are, however, other damaging results. Sticky honeydew is deposited, and the sooty moulds which grow on it are unsightly and block the leaf pores. Even worse is the danger of virus infection, as aphids are the prime carriers. For these reasons aphids should be tackled quickly. Outdoors spray with heptenophos or permethrin — under glass use permethrin.

EARWIG

The leaves of beetroots, parsnips and carrots may be skeletonized by this pest. Spray with permethrin when they are first noticed.

BIRDS

Birds are a joy in the garden and most of them do no harm. A few species, however, are a serious nuisance to seeds, seedlings and some mature crops, and netting is necessary.

CATS

Cats often choose seed beds for toilet purposes, and usually avoid their own gardens. This is a difficult problem — it is worth trying a cat repellent dust or spray where cats are a nuisance.

SOIL PESTS
GROUP 1: Controlled by methiocarb

Methiocarb is an alternative to metaldehyde for the control of slugs. It has the advantage of being effective in wet as well as dry weather. Research has shown that a light sprinkling raked into the soil surface will control woodlice, millepedes and leatherjackets.

SLUGS & SNAILS

Extremely troublesome pests especially in wet weather. Seedlings may be killed; leaves, stems and roots of older plants are damaged. Look for the tell-tale slime trails.

LEATHERJACKET

Dark grey grubs, about 1 in. long. Most active in light soils and wet weather. Stems are attacked, lower leaves devoured. Root crops are tunnelled.

MILLEPEDE

Pink or black grubs which curl up when disturbed. They attack underground parts of plants, often extending areas damaged by other pests. Most troublesome under cool, damp conditions. Not easy to control.

WOODLICE

Hard-coated pests found in greenhouses. Seedlings and young plants are attacked. They hide during the day.

SOIL PESTS
GROUP 2: Controlled by nematode-based insecticide

These products contain living organisms rather than chemicals. Inside the package there are millions of microscopic nematodes (eelworms) which kill the larvae of several common soil pests. Cabbage root fly, vine weevil, leatherjacket, as well as cutworm and chafer grub are all vulnerable. This non-chemical approach obviously appeals to the environmentally-minded, but it does not work when the temperature falls below 50°F and the shelf-life is quite short.

CUTWORM

Fat grey or brown caterpillars, 1½–2 in. long. They live near the surface and eat young plants at ground level. Stems are often severed.

CHAFER GRUB

Large curved grubs, over 1 in. long. They feed throughout the year on roots and are often a serious pest in newly broken-up grassland.

DAMPING OFF

Germinating seedlings can be attacked by the damping off fungi, withering and blackening at the base before toppling over. Indoors use sterilized compost, sow thinly, water carefully, ventilate properly and provide adequate light. Outdoors avoid sowing in cold wet soil, sow thinly and do not overwater. If the disease does occur remove the affected seedlings immediately and water remainder with Cheshunt Compound.

PESTICIDE	Minimum Interval between Spraying and Harvesting
sulphur	0 days
permethrin	0 days
horticultural soap	0 days
pyrethrum	0 days
copper sulphate	0 days
copper oxychloride	0 days
bifenthrin	0 days
B. thuringiensis	0 days
derris	1 day
heptenophos	1 day
malathion	1–4 days
carbendazim	2–21 days
pirimicarb	3 days
methiocarb	7 days
pirimiphos methyl	7 days
mancozeb	7–21 days
fenitrothion	14 days
lindane (HCH)	14 days

CHAPTER 4

UNUSUAL VEGETABLES

Vegetable plots and allotment gardens from Caithness to Cornwall present a familiar scene. Depending on the season, rows of beans, peas, brassicas, carrots and onions ... a block of potatoes and the saladings (lettuces, radishes, etc.) pushed in where space allowed. Nothing strange, and that is what you would expect. The purpose of the plot is to raise food for the family, and it would be foolish indeed to waste all that money and effort to produce vegetables which turned out to be unpalatable.

On the other hand, it is silly never to try anything new, and the soundest advice is to devote a small area or even a single row to a rarity — a vegetable you have never grown before and perhaps never even seen before in a garden.

It is easy to make out a strong case for growing rarities. After all, it will only cost you the price of a packet of seeds and some are no more difficult to grow than potatoes and a lot easier than peas. After harvest you can impress your friends by serving vegetables which they have never seen before ... but there are snags.

The reason why a vegetable has failed to achieve popularity is generally due to a clear-cut fault. Some, such as corn salad and the culinary dandelion, are flavourless or somewhat bitter and so add little to the range of tastes available from the everyday greens we all grow. Others (seakale, cardoon, etc.) are troublesome to cultivate as they require blanching, and there are others such as the chinese artichoke which are troublesome to prepare in the kitchen. Perhaps the main reason for the disappearance of many once-popular vegetables from the seed catalogues is the simple truth that fashions change and the old is replaced by the new. Examples described in this chapter are good king henry, nasturtium leaves and seakale — others not listed include purslane, skirret and rampion. Strange names indeed, but these were the vegetables to be found in the old catalogues when tomatoes and runner beans were regarded as oddities.

Obviously it would be foolhardy to devote a large area to the growing of a wide range of oddities, only to find that the family found them distasteful. The golden rule is to try to taste an unknown vegetable before you decide to grow it. Still, gardening without some degree of risk and venture into the unknown would be a dull hobby, so follow the route outlined below.

First of all, grow an unusual variety of a popular vegetable. You can try the turnip-sized Black Spanish Round or the giant Minowase Summer instead of the humble red radish, or you can sow eat-in-the-pod mangetout peas in place of the Onward or Kelvedon Wonder you sow every year. There are purple-podded french beans, red brussels sprouts, striped tomatoes and bronze-coloured lettuces ... something different without venturing into new and perhaps unacceptable tastes. There are the baby varieties which are now becoming quite popular —on page 116 you will find varieties of cauliflower and sweet corn which will fit comfortably in the palm of your hand. For the unusual varieties of usual vegetables your best sources of information are the catalogues produced each autumn by the major seed houses.These and the garden magazines will tell you about the latest novelties which are available for the home gardener.

Your next step into the unknown should be to sow one or more of the less usual vegetables in Chapter 2. Seeds are available from most large nurserymen and there is nothing really 'peculiar' about any of them. Good examples are globe and jerusalem artichokes, celeriac, kohl rabi, salsify and scorzonera. Once again, buy a few from the supermarket and get the family's approval before devoting space and time to them on the vegetable plot. If you have a greenhouse, you can try aubergine or capsicum alongside the ever-popular tomato and cucumber.

Finally, for the truly adventurous there are the rarities described and illustrated in this chapter. In nearly all cases you will have to search through the catalogues to find a supplier — the outstanding exception is the nasturtium which can be bought everywhere and grown anywhere. For a list of suppliers of the really unusual ones you should consult *The Fruit & Veg Finder* which can be ordered from your local bookshop. Some are certainly worth growing — florence fennel should not be missed if you like the taste of aniseed, land cress is an excellent substitute for watercress and nasturtium leaves add more zest to a green salad than soggy lettuce leaves. Hamburg parsley provides leaves for garnishing and roots for cooking, and a clump of welsh onions will provide 'spring onions' year after year. Maybe you won't be quite as enthusiastic as the writer after you have tried these rarities ... but what have you got to lose?

CARDOON

The cardoon was once in the recommended vegetable lists, but it is a rarity nowadays. This is not really surprising — it takes both trouble and space to grow, and the end-product is not particularly exciting as a vegetable. If, however, the unusual appeals to you or if you are interested in the flavours of the past, cardoons are worth a trial. The thistle-like plants grow up to 6 ft tall and are more suited to the back of the herbaceous border than the vegetable plot.

Sow seeds in April in groups of 3 about 2 in. deep — leave 2 ft between the groups. Thin to a single seedling at each station and water copiously during summer. In September tie the leaves into a bush and blanch as for celery (see page 47). Dig up the plants after 5 weeks, cut off the roots and remove the outer leaves.

Cardoon produces flower-heads which look like small globe artichokes but it is grown for its blanched stems. Treat as tough and stringy celery. It cannot be eaten raw and should be cooked by first cutting into pieces, stripping off the outer strings and then boiling until tender — at least 30 minutes.

CHINESE ARTICHOKE

Amongst the root artichokes, the jerusalem variety (page 9) is an unusual sight on the allotment or vegetable plot, but the other one, the chinese artichoke, is distinctly rare. From the cultivation standpoint this is rather odd — the chinese artichoke is easier to grow, requiring neither staking nor earthing-up. The reason for the unpopularity of this vegetable is the nature of the tubers — small, convoluted and indented, so that it is the cook rather than the gardener of the family who finds this vegetable frustrating.

If you can locate a supplier of tubers, plant in the same way as jerusalem artichokes, 6 in. deep in February or March. Use closer spacings — 1 ft intervals in drills 1½ ft apart. Growth is not vigorous, so do all you can to promote maximum tuber development. Plant in humus-rich soil and in summer water and feed regularly. Lift, as required, between November and early spring. Cover the plant with straw, leaves or compost in winter. At the end of the season make sure that *all* the tubers have been removed.

The flavour of chinese artichokes is both delicate and delicious — treat as jerusalem artichokes for cooking.

CORN SALAD

Corn salad (lamb's lettuce) will never win any prizes in a gourmet contest, despite what the over-optimistic catalogues may tell you. Its sole advantage over lettuce is that its small leaves can be picked outdoors between November and January when home-grown saladings are distinctly rare.

It will grow in nearly all soils and situations but you may need to guard against birds and slugs at the early stages. Sow in August or September, ½ in. deep in drills 6 in. apart. Use the thinnings in the kitchen and leave plants at 4–6 in. spacings to mature. During winter pick a few leaves from each plant when you harvest — never strip a stem bare. A trouble-free plant, but you will have to ensure that weeds do not swamp this lowly vegetable.

In the kitchen wash the leaves thoroughly to remove grit. Use them as a substitute for lettuce — if you find the flavour a little too bitter, blanch the leaves before the next picking by covering the plants with a box or pot for a few days.

DANDELION

Dandelions have no place in the lawn or flower bed but they have had a place in the vegetable garden since mediaeval times. The leaves are blanched by excluding light completely from the plant and they are then cut and used as a salad ingredient. The roots can be roasted and ground as a coffee substitute — very cheap but not very good.

Ordinary wild dandelions can be used for blanching but it is better to buy a variety which has been specially bred to produce large and succulent leaves. Sow in April in fertile soil and semi-shade — the rows should be 1 ft apart and the seedlings thinned to 9 in. In the following spring cover each plant with a box or pot which is light-proof. About 10 days later the leaves will be white and ready for use in a salad — do not blanch plants after June as they need to put on leaf in summer to build up reserves for next year's crop.

You can make your own salad combination — the classic mix is blanched dandelion leaves, parsley and chives with a garlic, oil-and-vinegar dressing.

FLORENCE FENNEL

Florence fennel, or finocchio, is a highly decorative plant for the vegetable plot. It is grown for its swollen bulb-like base which has a distinct taste of aniseed and as an added bonus the feathery foliage can be used as a substitute for fennel (see Chapter 8). Unfortunately, it is not an easy plant to grow — a warm summer is required for proper bulb development and any check to growth results in the plant running to seed.

Well-drained sandy soil is needed, in which humus has been incorporated during winter digging. Sow ½ in. deep in drills 1½ ft apart in late April and thin the seedlings to 1 ft. Water when the weather is dry and earth-up the bulb when it is the size of a golf ball. Continue this earthing-up until the bulb is as large as a tennis ball (July-September), then harvest by cutting the base with a sharp knife.

Slice for serving raw in salads or boil for 30–40 minutes. Serve in melted butter, white sauce or cheese sauce after draining.

GOOD KING HENRY

Good king henry has many other names — mercury, lincolnshire spinach, poor man's asparagus and so on, and it has been grown as a vegetable in cottage gardens for hundreds of years. But fashions change, and now this dual-purpose vegetable is a rarity.

It is a perennial which reaches about 2 ft high. Pick a fertile, sunny spot which is free from perennial weeds and sow the seeds in April in drills which are ¼ in. deep and 1½ ft apart. Thin the seedlings to 1 ft — do not transplant. You must not expect too much in the first season — keep the plants regularly hoed, well watered and each time you harvest pick just a few leaves from each plant for cooking.

Cut down the foliage in autumn and mulch with peat, leafmould or well-rotted compost. Cropping can begin in the spring — cut some of the new shoots as they appear from April until June and cook like asparagus. Cutting should then cease and all shoots must be allowed to develop. The succulent triangular leaves are picked a few at a time until the end of August and cooked like spinach.

HAMBURG PARSLEY

Leaves which can be used like parsley, roots which taste like well-flavoured parsnips with a hint of celery, and a constitution which allows it to succeed in shade … and yet hamburg parsley is hardly ever grown in Britain.

Dig the soil thoroughly in winter — work in well-rotted compost. Sow in mid March if you can cover the soil with cloches for a few weeks prior to sowing — otherwise choose a suitable day in mid April. Sow ½ in. deep in drills 1 ft apart and thin seedlings to 9 in. apart. Keep the land hoed and watered, and in November the first roots will be ready for lifting. They will be about 8 in. long and can be left in the ground over winter for you to dig up as required. Alternatively you can lift and store the roots in the same way as parsnips.

Remove the stalks and fine roots — scrub thoroughly but do not peel before cooking. Cook them in the same way as parsnips — if they are to be cubed or sliced sprinkle with lemon juice to prevent discoloration. The tastiest way to cook hamburg parsley is by roasting or frying them as chips.

LAND CRESS

Watercress, rich in vitamins and peppery-flavoured, is a favourite garnish but unfortunately requires more water than the ordinary gardener can provide. Land cress (american cress) is a practical and quick-growing alternative for the home plot — all you need to provide is a shady spot and a thorough watering when the weather turns dry.

Incorporate a plentiful supply of compost or well-rotted manure into the soil when digging. Sow the seeds ½ in. deep in drills 1 ft apart — a March sowing will provide a summer crop and putting out seeds in September will provide leaves for winter. Thin the seedlings to 8 in. spacings when they are large enough to handle and the first pickings can start about 8 weeks after sowing. Pick the outer leaves from young plants and the heart leaves from old ones. Remove flower stalks as they appear and cover with cloches in autumn.

Land cress is a wholly satisfactory substitute for watercress. Use it for garnishing and as a salad or sandwich ingredient. It can also be cooked like spinach or be turned into an excellent soup.

NASTURTIUM

You may be surprised to find nasturtium in a vegetable book, yet both its leaves and flowers have been used as saladings for centuries. Now that the cottage garden is no longer the basic source of greenstuff for the kitchen, the use of this flowering plant as a vegetable has greatly declined. It is a pity — the leaves have a peppery taste, rather like watercress, and can add zest to flavourless butterhead lettuce.

There is, of course, no need to grow nasturtium on the vegetable plot — raise them in the flower bed as usual. Sow a climbing variety, such as Tall Mixed, or a semi-trailer like Golden Gleam. Nasturtium thrives best in a poor, sandy soil — sow seeds in April, ½ in. deep and 1 ft apart. Pick young and fresh leaves for salads and sandwiches — make sure that blackfly are removed before use. Flowers can also be added to salads but they have less flavour — seeds are used for pickling as a substitute for capers. To make nasturtium salad, mix nasturtium leaves with an equal quantity of shredded lettuce in a garlic-rubbed bowl. Add quartered hard boiled eggs, dress with a vinaigrette dressing and garnish with nasturtium flowers.

SEAKALE

Vegetables which require forcing by being shielded from the light are not popular — chicory and endive are examples and so is seakale. This was not always so — seakale was widely grown in Victorian times when gardeners were plentiful. It is grown for its shoots, which after blanching in spring are cooked like asparagus.

It is fussy about soil — a fertile, sandy site is needed and both lime and humus are necessary. Use crowns and not seeds for planting — rub off all the buds but one from each crown which should be set 18 in. apart with a covering of 2 in. of soil. During summer water regularly, feed occasionally and remove all flowering stems as they appear. In autumn cut down the yellowing foliage and fork over the ground. In November cover each plant with a pot or bucket (all light must be excluded) and surround with a layer of leaves or compost for insulation. Cut the blanched shoots in April when they are about 8 in. tall. After removing the pots apply a mulch and allow growth to develop normally to build up the reserves for next year. You can blanch year after year — a great advantage compared to rhubarb.

SORREL

The French cannot understand our total disregard for this vegetable. Sorrel for them is a basic ingredient for many soups, such as *potage santé* (health soup), for livening up omelettes and for the classic green sauce which is served with fish. French sorrel is the cultivated version of the garden weed — you will either love or hate its sharp taste.

It is a perennial, propagated by means of seed or division, and requires a soil enriched with humus and fertilizer. Sow seeds in April in drills ¼ in. deep and 1½ ft apart — thin the seedlings to 9 in. spacings. Little attention is needed, but you should water in dry weather and must remove flower-heads as they appear. Pick a few leaves from each plant as soon as they are big enough to use — small leaves are much less bitter than large ones. Once the plants are established the harvesting season lasts from March until November each year.

Chop a few leaves to add zest to a salad or omelette, or cook like spinach.

WELSH ONION

The flavour of onion is required for all sorts of dishes, and we rely on the varieties listed on pages 71–73 or on chives (see Chapter 8). There are, however, other types of onion which can be used but have never become popular. Welsh onion (japanese bunching onion) is a perennial producing clumps of hollow leaves up to 2 ft tall — an excellent evergreen substitute for spring onions. A similar but smaller plant raised from bulbs rather than seeds is the everlasting or everready onion. These are leaf onions. If you want unusual bulbs then you can do no better than grow the tree onion — a perennial which produces its bulbs at the top and not at the bottom of the stems!

Sow welsh onion seed in March in drills ½ in. deep and 1 ft apart. Thin the seedlings to 9 in. spacings and remove leaves as required. The clumps will increase in size each year but quality deteriorates — lift, divide and replant every 3 years.

Use the leaves of the welsh onion as a substitute for spring onions or chives.

1 in. = 2.5 cm, 1 ft = 30 cm, 1 oz = 28 gm, 1 lb = 450 gm

CHAPTER 5
BABY VEGETABLES

A common sight in supermarkets these days are small trays of miniature vegetables — tiny cobs of sweet corn for stir frying or putting in stews, slender french beans which do not require cutting before cooking and bite-sized tomatoes for eating whole. These products are quite expensive, so it is nice to know that you can grow your own.

The terms 'baby vegetable' and 'mini vegetable' have been coined to describe these items — carrots no longer than your thumb and a cauliflower no larger than a tennis ball are obviously miniatures, but you should realise at the outset that there are two distinct types of baby vegetable.

First of all there are standard varieties which produce baby vegetables by being grown closely together and then harvested at an early stage. They are generally quick-maturing varieties — good examples are short-rooted Early carrots such as Amsterdam Forcing and Early turnips such as Snowball. The leek King Richard can be widely spaced and left to mature to produce foot-long thick white shanks, but it can also be grown in close rows and the thin stems pulled after 12 weeks as a substitute for spring onions.

Secondly there are a number of varieties which have been bred specifically as baby vegetables and you will find these described and illustrated in a separate section in some seed catalogues. These baby varieties are a fascinating group. Mini-cauliflowers are sown in March and in June the firm heads are cut — each one small enough to fit in the palm of your hand. The Savoy cabbage Protovoy is not much larger — sow it in April for small pointed heads in autumn.

Thus there are two types of baby vegetable — the standard varieties which are harvested at an early stage and the specific baby varieties which are true miniatures. Both these types are grown more closely together than standard varieties grown in the standard way. The usual distance between the rows is 6 in., but you will need more space for bigger plants such as sweet corn and courgettes. The distance between the plants after thinning is 1 in. for roots (carrot, beetroot, turnip, etc.), 6 in. for lettuce and cabbage and 12 in. for sweet corn.

With these greatly reduced plant distances baby vegetables are extremely useful where space is limited. They make growing your own food in pots, troughs, tiny beds and window boxes a practical proposition, but there is one point you must remember. Baby vegetables need to be grown quickly, so grow them in a reliable brand of compost or humus-rich soil and feed them regularly. Water the plants thoroughly when the weather is dry.

Cauliflower Idol

Kale Showbor

Parsnip Lancer

BABY VEGETABLE VARIETIES

Included here are varieties which have been specifically bred as baby vegetables, together with some standard varieties which can be harvested at an early stage.

VEGETABLE	VARIETY
BEETROOT	Pronto Monaco Nero Detroit 2 — Little Ball
BRUSSELS SPROUT	Energy
CABBAGE (RED)	Primero
CABBAGE (SAVOY)	Protovoy
CAPSICUM	Minibell
CARROT	Amini Ideal Suko Parmex
CAULIFLOWER	Idol
COURGETTE	Supremo Patriot
CUCUMBER	Petita
FRENCH BEAN	Masai Safari
KALE	Showbor
KOHL RABI	Logo Rolando
LEEK	King Richard Jolant
LETTUCE	Blush Minigreen Sherwood Tom Thumb
ONION	Shakespeare Imai Senshyu
PARSNIP	Arrow Lancer
SPINACH	Teton
SQUASH	Sunburst Peter Pan
SWEET CORN	Minipop
TOMATO	Tumbler Tiny Tim Gardener's Delight Sweet 100 Red Alert
TURNIP	Arcoat Tokyo Cross

Turnip Tokyo Cross

Cabbage Protovoy

Leek King Richard

Brussels sprout Energy

Sweet corn Minipop

Carrot Amini

CHAPTER 6

WHERE TO GROW VEGETABLES

Until quite recently there were basically just two ways in which people grew their vegetables. In the garden they were grown in long rows in a vegetable plot or they were cultivated on an allotment — neat lines of cabbages, peas, lettuce, carrots and so on with walkways in between. In addition to the vegetable plot there was the greenhouse at the bottom of the garden, and here the crop chosen by nearly everybody was the tomato.

In recent years alternative ways of growing vegetables have become increasingly popular for several reasons. There are millions of households which just do not have the space or are no longer willing to devote a section of the garden exclusively to vegetables, and for them there is the cottage garden approach of growing some vegetables in the flower bed or shrub border. Then there are others who don't want all the hard work associated with the traditional plot, and so they are turning increasingly to the bed system or containers. The potager is an advance on the simple bed system — a decorative effect is important here as well as the yield of produce. Finally there are the humble pots of herbs on the windowsill — so useful when winter rain and cold make a trip to the vegetable plot an unpleasant experience.

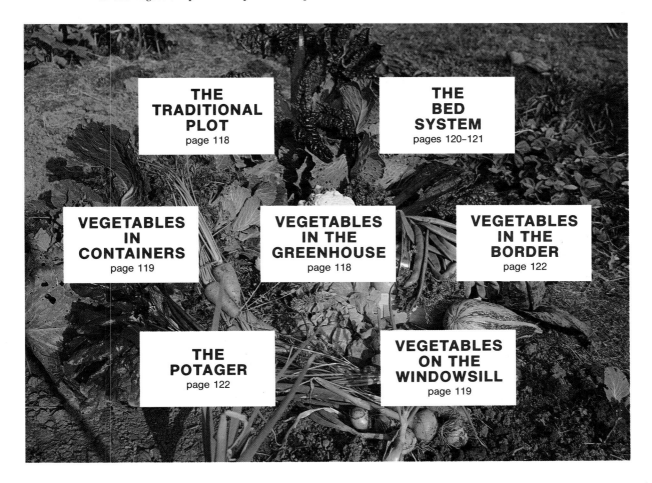

THE TRADITIONAL PLOT
page 118

THE BED SYSTEM
pages 120–121

VEGETABLES IN CONTAINERS
page 119

VEGETABLES IN THE GREENHOUSE
page 118

VEGETABLES IN THE BORDER
page 122

THE POTAGER
page 122

VEGETABLES ON THE WINDOWSILL
page 119

THE TRADITIONAL PLOT

The traditional plot remains the standard way of growing vegetables at home. The whole of the area is cultivated and the plants are grown in rows, apart from a small patch for permanent plants such as asparagus or rhubarb. Strips of bare earth are left between each row or group of rows so that the gardener is able to walk along for watering, weeding, feeding, picking, etc. The planting or final thinning out distance between the seedlings in the rows and between the rows is sufficiently large to enable the plant to develop to its full potential. By this method the longest beans, the heaviest cabbages and the largest onions are produced, and the textbooks (including this one) assume that you are going to follow this method when giving you cultural instructions.

Despite its popularity the traditional plot may not be the best method of growing vegetables for you, unless you want to grow bigger vegetables than your neighbour or want to win a prize at the local show. It is extremely laborious — the tramping down of the soil along the pathways means that there is the chore of digging over the plot every autumn. In addition the bare pathways and the large spaces left between the plants encourage weeds and that means regular hoeing. This is obvious to every gardener who has tended an allotment or large vegetable plot — less obvious is the fact that the overall crop yield per sq. ft of growing area is less than the harvest obtained by using the bed method.

VEGETABLES IN THE GREENHOUSE

The usual reason for growing vegetables in a greenhouse is the ability to grow those types which are unpredictable outdoors and even impossible in some districts — aubergines, capsicum and tomatoes are typical examples. In addition there is the satisfaction of harvesting produce before the outdoor crop is ready — early potatoes, early carrots and so on. There is another advantage which is important but does not appear in the standard textbooks — the ability to sow, care for the plants and harvest the crop without having to worry about wind, rain and snow.

A large number of ornamentals need a cool (minimum temperature 45°F) or a warm (minimum temperature 55°F) greenhouse for satisfactory development, but all the popular vegetables can be grown in an unheated greenhouse. This can be more productive than an area with just a few growing bags of tomatoes — remember that there are also cucumbers, aubergines, winter lettuce, okra, etc. Early in the season the space between tomatoes and cucumbers can be utilised for quick-growing catch crops such as carrots. Always check that the variety of tomato, cucumber or lettuce is recommended for greenhouse growing.

The greenhouse has another role to play. It can be used to give outdoor varieties an early start in life by sowing them in a propagator, pricking out into pots and then planting outdoors to give them several weeks' advantage over garden-sown specimens.

VEGETABLES IN CONTAINERS

Growing plants outdoors in containers has become very popular during the past 20 years. Pots, troughs, growing bags, etc. are now accepted as one of the answers to growing vegetables if you have no space in the garden for a vegetable plot, and the *only* answer if you have a balcony but no garden. Some experts stress the advantages of growing in containers. No poor soil problems if you use shop-bought compost, no weeding and digging worries, and no soil pest problems. Growing bags on the patio can be filled with all sorts of vegetables and tender types can be moved to the most sheltered part of the garden. There are other experts, however, who are not so keen. They point out the amount of produce you can grow by this method is strictly limited and the plants are usually non-decorative or downright ugly if you plan to have the containers close to the house. Perhaps the main drawback is the need for regular watering and feeding.

Any pot, tub or trough deeper than 8 in. will do — make sure that the container is raised above the ground. For most people there is little point in growing 'ordinary' vegetables by this method. You can choose decorative ones (see Vegetables in the Border on page 122 for suggestions) or you can grow tender types such as aubergines, sweet peppers or bush tomatoes against a south-facing wall. Another approach is to raise salad crops in growing bags in order to provide fresh produce without having to walk to the vegetable plot.

VEGETABLES ON THE WINDOWSILL

If you are keen on herbs in cooking then you can have a line of pots on the windowsill in the kitchen and fill them with basil, rosemary, lemon balm, sage, thyme and so on for use during the winter months. You will be able to pick your favourite seasonings without having to trudge through the mud or snow. The kitchen window is an excellent place for plants — the air is often steamy and you can't help noticing if they are in need of watering.

For most people such an extensive herb garden indoors is not a good idea. It is better to restrict your windowsill allotment to just a few herb and salad crops which you eat regularly, because if the plants are left uncut they become leggy and unattractive. So don't be too ambitious at the start. Fill a few pots with seed compost — the pressed-down surface should be about ½ in. below the rim. A typical arrangement consists of a mint pot (plant a rooted clump from the garden), parsley (sow seed), chives (again a clump from the garden or garden centre) and spring onions (sow seed). Water in the plants or seeds, and when they are growing water once or twice a week.

Cut the mint, parsley and chives as required and pull the spring onions. Don't forget to mist the leaves once or twice a week. From these simple beginnings you can become more adventurous. Lettuce growing is the next step — raise the seedlings in shallow plastic trays. If you have space for a 6 in. pot you can grow a miniature variety of tomato — Tiny Tim is the usual choice.

THE BED SYSTEM

The basic principle is to create a series of rectangular beds which are divided by permanent paths. These paths are covered with gravel or bark chippings and the beds must be narrow enough so that all the plants can be reached from the path. Construct the beds so that they run North-South if possible. Organic matter is added to the soil and it should be left to settle for at least a couple of weeks before sowing or planting. The yearly round begins in autumn or early winter when a layer of organic matter such as rotted manure or garden compost is worked into the surface with a fork. Digging is not necessary as you have not trodden down the surface by walking on it.

Choose your vegetables from the A–Z guide on pages 7-107. As a general rule it is a good idea to choose dwarf and early-maturing types — yield per individual plant is of course less than you would expect by the traditional long row method, but surprisingly the yield per sq. ft of cultivated land is often higher. On page 121 is a list of easy-to-grow vegetables which are ideal for the bed system — note that the plants are grown at the same distance from each other in both directions. This space is quite close so that the leaves of adjacent plants touch when they are mature.

Looking after the crop during the growing season is usually a relatively simple job. There are no muddy walkways between the plants and the closeness of the vegetables smothers most weeds.

FLAT BEDS

The flat bed is the easiest type to create but you do need free-draining soil. Use the dimensions given for raised beds in the drawing below. Turn over the soil and work in a 1 in. layer of organic matter.

RAISED BEDS

10 ft maximum

2–3 ft

4 ft

1½ ft

Pathway covered with gravel or coarse bark chippings. Put black plastic sheeting under-neath to prevent weed growth

The raised bed is the type to create if drainage is poor and the ground gets waterlogged in winter. You will have to build retaining walls — see the drawing above. Railway sleepers, bricks or blocks can be used but 1 in. thick pressure-treated wooden planks attached to 2 in. square corner posts are the usual choice. The raised bed should be at least 4 in. high — fork over the bottom and then fill with a mixture of 2 parts topsoil and 1 part organic matter.

Easy Vegetables for the Bed System

NAME	SOW	DEPTH	PLANT	DISTANCE BETWEEN PLANTS	HARVEST	TIME TAKEN (weeks)
BEAN, BROAD	February –April	2 in.	—	6 in.	July –August	16S → H
Begin picking when pods are 3 in. long — cook whole						
BEAN, FRENCH	May –June	2 in.	—	6 in.	July –September	10S → H
Pencil-podded or Continental varieties (e.g Sprite) are now popular						
BEETROOT	April –June	1 in.	—	3 in.	June –October	11S → H
Grow a globe variety — harvest when no larger than a tennis ball						
CALABRESE	April –May	½ in.	June –July	15 in.	August –September	15S → H
Express Corona is a good choice — ready for cutting 50 days after planting						
CARROT	March –July	½ in.	—	4 in.	July –October	14S → H
Pick a quick-maturing short-rooted variety such as the round Early French Frame						
COURGETTE	May –June	1 in.	—	18 in.	July –September	10S → H
Cut when 3–4 in. long. Gold Rush (yellow) is a colourful variety						
KALE	May	½ in.	July	15 in.	December	30S → H
Pentland Brig is the variety to grow. Pick young leaves in winter						
LETTUCE	March –July	½ in.	—	9 in.	June –October	12S → H
Grow a miniature e.g Tom Thumb or Little Gem or a loose-leaf variety (e.g Salad Bowl)						
ONION	—	Tip showing	March –April	3 in.	August	20P → H
Grow sets rather than seed — harvest 2 weeks after stems topple over						
POTATO	—	5 in.	March –April	12 in.	June –July	13P → H
Grow an early variety for new potatoes in early summer						
RADISH	March –July	½ in.	—	2 in.	May –September	6S → H
Nothing is easier to grow. All varieties are suitable						
TOMATO	—	—	June	18 in.	August –September	12P → H
An easy crop in mild areas, but only if you choose a bush variety						
TURNIP	March –June	½ in.	—	6 in.	May –September	10S → H
Early varieties (e.g Snowball) are sown in spring and picked at golf-ball size						

KEY

DISTANCE BETWEEN PLANTS

These spacings are the recommended distances between rows and mature plants in the rows. See Chapter 2 for spacings recommended for the traditional plot.

TIME TAKEN (weeks)
S : Sowing
P : Planting
→ : to
H : Harvest

VEGETABLES IN THE BORDER

There are several reasons why many gardeners reject the idea of devoting a plot entirely to vegetables. One argument is that there is too much work involved, although the bed system (page 120) makes vegetable growing much easier. Others argue that they cannot possibly use all the cabbages, lettuce, sprouts, etc. from the plot and it is a shame to see them go to waste. A more frequently-expressed view is that the garden should be solely for ornamental plants.

This final point should not be an argument for growing no vegetables at all. There are numerous vegetables which are distinctly ornamental and can be used as such as occasional specimens among flowers, shrubs, bulbs, roses and so on.

You will find examples in this book. Runner beans can be grown as climbing annuals at the back of the border — there are red-, pink- and white-flowered varieties and also the bi-coloured Painted Lady. The pods have little visual appeal but the yellow- and purple-podded varieties of french bean are decorative. For eye-catching leaves there is leaf beet — look for the swiss chard type for white veins and stalks or rhubarb chard for red ones. If red leaves or stalks appeal to you there are beetroot, Lollo Rossa lettuce and red varieties of celery and brussels sprouts. Among the herbs there are eye-catchers such as purple sage and yellow marjoram — with fruiting vegetables think about capsicum, globe artichoke and cherry-type tomatoes.

THE POTAGER

'Potager' is the french word for kitchen garden, but in this country it has acquired a more specialised meaning. It describes a plot in which vegetables, herbs and fruit are grown and where the ornamental aspect is just as important as the practical and productive one. To heighten this ornamental aspect a variety of flowers, bulbs, roses or shrubs are often included, but it is not the same as the mixed border described above. There the vegetables are the poor relations — in the potager they are the main feature.

There are other differences. In the potager the arrangement of the plants is formal and they are grown in a group of beds — these beds form a geometric pattern and are often enclosed by dwarf hedging. The pathways between the beds are made of paving slabs or gravel and archways draped with roses, beans, grapes, etc. are often constructed along the paths.

It is usual for some if not all of the vegetables and herbs to be ornamental ones — see Vegetables in the Border above. Apart from these plants quite ordinary types can look attractive in the right setting — there are the ferny leaves of carrots and the yellow flowers of courgettes. Use flowers, shrubs, etc. with care — good potager subjects include climbers for arches and walls, bright patches of flowers or bulbs, dwarf edging shrubs and annuals for cutting. Non-food crops should always be in the background — do not create large flower beds or borders in the potager.

CHAPTER 7

LOOKING AFTER VEGETABLES

Growing vegetables successfully takes time, effort and skill. The skill factor relates to doing the right thing at the right time, and the importance of proper timing cannot be exaggerated. Consider one of the simplest crops — the humble radish. You will, of course, thin the seedlings but if you don't do it early enough then the crop will suffer. Some weeks later you pull up the plants for the kitchen, but if you wait too long then the roots will be woody and hollow. With less robust crops correct timing of cultural operations is even more important.

THINNING

Germination may be inhibited if the surface forms a crust-like cap due to heavy rain followed by drying winds. If this happens water gently to keep the surface soft until germination has taken place.

Despite the often-repeated recommendation to sow thinly you will usually find that the emerged seedlings are too close together. Thinning is necessary, and this is a job to be tackled as soon as the plants are large enough to handle. The soil should be moist — water if necessary. Hold down the soil around the unwanted seedling with one hand and pull it up with the other. If the seedlings are too close together to allow this technique, merely nip off the top growth of the unwanted ones.

After thinning, firm the soil around the remaining seedlings and water gently. This thinning is often done in stages before the final spacing is reached.

TRANSPLANTING

Transplanting involves moving seedlings to their permanent quarters. These transplants may have been raised in a seed bed in the garden, bought from a reliable supplier or grown indoors in pots or trays of compost. It is a temptation to lift thinnings in an overcrowded row of seedlings in the garden and plant them elsewhere, but you must remember that transplanting is not suitable for all vegetables. It is firmly recommended for most brassicas (see page 27), acceptable for some popular crops such as peas and beans and definitely not recommended for many others such as lettuce and root crops.

Water both the seedlings and the site where they are to be planted on the day before transplanting. Use a trowel (or a dibber for brassicas) to set the plants at the depth they were in the seed bed or pot. Firm the soil around the plants and water in to settle the roots.

Transplanting is a critical time in the plant's life. Cold, wet soil can be fatal and so can late frosts for half-hardy vegetables. Water if there is a dry spell after planting.

WEEDING

Weeds are a threat and must be kept at bay. Apart from looking untidy they compete for space, food, water, etc. and can harbour pests and diseases.

There is no single miracle cure — there are a number of tasks you will have to carry out. The first one begins before the crop is sown — at digging time remove all the roots of perennial weeds you can find and bury small annual weeds by completely inverting each spadeful of soil.

If the plot has been neglected and is a sea of grass and other weeds then you have a problem on your hands. The best plan is to spray with glyphosate before soil preparation.

However thoroughly you remove weeds before sowing or planting, additional weeds will appear among the growing plants. Hoeing is the basic technique to keep the problem under control — it must be carried out at regular intervals in order to keep annual weeds in constant check and to starve out the underground parts of perennial ones. Hoeing can do more harm than good in careless hands — keep away from the stems and do not go deeper than an inch below the surface.

Chemicals have a part to play, but must be used with care as they cannot distinguish between friend and foe. Use diquat/paraquat to burn off weed growth between plants — paint leaves of perennial weeds with glyphosate.

FEEDING

Manure or fertilizer — the age-old argument. Actually there is nothing to argue about; both are vital and neither can be properly replaced by the other. The role of bulky organic matter is to make the *soil* good enough to support a vigorous and healthy crop. The role of fertilizer is to provide the *plants* with enough nutrient to ensure that they reach their full potential.

There are a number of vital nutrients — nitrogen for leaf growth, phosphorus for root development and potash for strengthening resistance to disease and poor conditions. This group is required in relatively large amounts and compound fertilizers contain all three. You will find a statement of the nutrient content on the package.

One of the most important uses for compound fertilizers is to provide a **base dressing** just before sowing or planting. A granular or powder formulation is used, and Growmore is the old favourite.

Crops which take some time to mature will need one or more **top dressings** during the growing season. These can be in powder or granular form, but you must take great care to keep such dressings off the leaves. It is better to use a soluble fertilizer which is diluted and then applied through a watering can. As an alternative to liquid feeding you can use a slow-release fertilizer — the granules , blocks or cones steadily release nutrients into the soil or compost for about 6 months.

Foliar feeding is an interesting technique which can be used when root feeding is ineffective. It is useful when the soil is shallow and when a pest or disease attack has taken place. The response is rapid and root activity is restored — use a hose-end dilutor and apply a liquid feed as directed.

WATERING

A prolonged dry spell can result in a small crop or even no crop at all. Heavy rain after drought causes the splitting of tomatoes and roots. Unfortunately, watering is usually dealt with very briefly in most handbooks on vegetable growing. The reason is simple — until the series of summer droughts in recent years many gardeners were able to succeed without watering their kitchen garden apart from sprinkling around transplants.

The first step is to incorporate adequate organic matter into the soil — this increases the water-holding capacity. Next, the top 9 in. of soil should be thoroughly and evenly moist but not waterlogged at sowing or planting time. Finally, put down a mulch (see page 125) in late spring.

You will have done all you can to ensure a good moisture reservoir in your soil — the rest is up to the weather. If there is a prolonged dry spell then water will be necessary, especially for tomatoes, cucumbers, marrows, beans, peas, celery and onions.

The rule is to water the soil gently and thoroughly every 7 days when the weather is dry during the critical period. This is between flowering and full pod development for peas and beans, and from seedling to maturity for leaf crops. Apply 2 gallons per square yard when **overall watering**, and try to water in the morning rather than at midday or in the evening. Remember to water slowly and close to the base of the plants. A watering can is often used but you really do need a hosepipe if watering is not to be a prolonged chore. One of the most effective methods of watering is to use lay-flat perforated tubing or a leaky-pipe watering system between the rows. Simple ... but expensive. Where there is a limited number of large plants to deal with, you would do better to use a technique known as **point watering**. This involves inserting an empty plant pot or creating a depression in the soil around each stem. Water is then poured into the pot or depression.

The main reason for failure or disappointment with growing bags is due to trying to follow the traditional technique used for watering the garden. Keeping the compost in a growing bag properly moist is a different technique, and you should follow the maker's instructions carefully.

1 in. = 2.5 cm, 1 ft = 30 cm, 1 oz = 28 gm, 1 lb = 450 gm

MULCHING

Mulching is an in-season method of manuring. A 1–2 in. layer of peat, well-rotted compost or leaf mould is spread between the young plants once they are established in spring. Cultivate and water the surface to make sure that it is moist, weed-free and friable before application.

The mulch will reduce water loss, increase nutrient content, improve soil structure and suppress weeds.

SPRAYING

People who claim that they *never* need to spray are lying, lucky or living on poor vegetables. Both pests and diseases attack well-grown as well as sickly plants — strength and vigour do not produce immunity in plants any more than in humans.

So keep a sprayer handy and a broad-spectrum spray recommended for vegetables. Read Chapter 3 to win the war against pests.

PROTECTED CROPPING

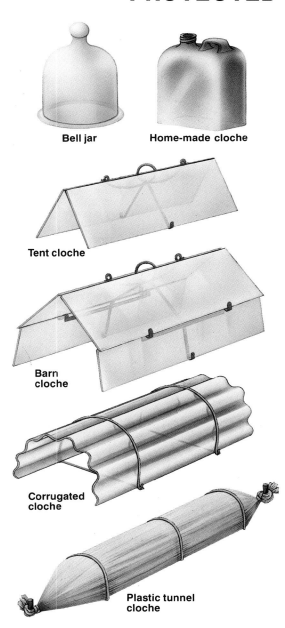

Bell jar

Home-made cloche

Tent cloche

Barn cloche

Corrugated cloche

Plastic tunnel cloche

Gardening writers have done their best to convince vegetable growers that cloches are as vital on the plot as a fork, hoe or the garden line. Sowing or planting of many vegetables can take place weeks earlier than on unprotected ground and that means early harvesting when shop prices may still be high. Half-hardy crops such as aubergines and capsicums can be grown successfully in unfavourable areas and leafy vegetables in winter are kept warm despite the rain and frosts. These benefits arise from the ability of glass or plastic to protect plants from the wind or rain and to raise the temperature of the air and soil around the plants. Despite these often-listed virtues, less than 20 per cent of gardeners possess a cloche.

The hey-day was in earlier centuries when professional gardeners used heavyweight bell jars placed over plants growing on hot beds to provide out-of-season vegetables for their masters' tables. The modern-day version of the old bell jar is the clear plastic container with its bottom cut off — a simple home-made cloche.

If you decide to buy a number of cloches you will be stuck for choice. A few rules to help you choose wisely — match the height to the expected size of the plants, as leaves should not touch the sides. Tent cloches for small plants, barn cloches for larger ones. Choose plastic for lightness, safety and cheapness — choose glass for clarity, permanence, maximum heat retention and resistance to blowing over. The corrugated PVC cloche is an excellent all-purpose cloche but if you wish to cover large areas cheaply the answer is the plastic tunnel cloche made from wire hoops and polythene sheeting. One of the major drawbacks with polythene sheet is that it deteriorates in a few years.

With all cloches some ventilation must be provided — increase the amount as temperatures rise. Provide ventilation by leaving gaps between cloches, not by leaving the ends open. There is no need to remove the cloches before watering — the water will run down the sides and into the soil. Make sure that the cloches are firmly anchored into the soil and wash glass if the surface becomes grimy. The time will come when the weather is mild enough for the cloches to be removed — increase ventilation for a few days to harden off the plants before removing their protection.

HARVESTING

You may be surprised at some of the harvesting stages recommended in this book — turnips the size of a golf ball and carrots no longer than your finger. Picking at such a miniature stage would be uneconomical for the farmer, but they are the times of peak flavour and tenderness. Not all vegetables need be picked at an early stage — the flavour of swedes, parsnips, celery, etc. does not decline with size.

With some crops, such as marrows, cucumbers, peas and beans, it is essential to pick regularly as just a few ripe fruits or pods left on the plant can bring cropping to an end.

Carelessly tearing off pods can damage the stems of pea plants — pulling out roots by their foliage can leave part of the crop in the ground. Read what to do on the appropriate page before you begin to harvest a vegetable.

STORING

Nearly all vegetables can be kept for a few days or even a week or two in the refrigerator, but if we take growing seriously then there will be times when long-term storage will be necessary. With beans there is always a sudden glut, and it is far better to pick them at the tender stage for storage rather than trying to extend the harvest period to the time when they will be tough and stringy. Maincrops of roots are generally lifted in autumn for storage indoors as layers between sand or peat (beetroots, carrots, etc.) or in sacks (potatoes) in a frost-free shed or garage. It is possible to let the vegetable plot act as the vegetable store for some roots — swedes, parsnips and turnips can be lifted as required.

In the pre-refrigeration era storage methods had to be devised so that a winter supply of vegetables could be provided. Beans and peas were dried and then shelled. Onions and cabbages were hung up in bags or laid out on open trays. Runner beans were salted; onions and beetroots were pickled in vinegar.

Long-term storage, however, has been completely transformed by the advent of the home freezer. This is the ideal storage method for so many vegetables, including the leafy ones which cannot be kept satisfactorily by any other method.

The routine is to blanch, cool, drain and then freeze. A word about blanching. For the various vegetables described in this book which are recommended for freezing you will find a blanching time of several minutes. This involves immersion in boiling water — ¼ lb to 1½ pints of water. Bring quickly back to the boil and begin timing. When the blanching time is reached immerse the produce immediately into ice-cold water. After blanching, drain thoroughly and freeze. Use freezer-grade plastic bags, boxes and other containers and as much air as possible should be excluded before sealing.

GETTING THE MOST FROM YOUR PLOT

SUCCESSIONAL SOWING

Several vegetables, such as lettuce and radish, cannot be stored for later use. To avoid gluts and then famines it is necessary to sow short rows every few weeks. A boon for the gardeners who are not willing to do this are the 'mixed seed' packets offered by many suppliers. The mixture of early-and late-maturing varieties gives a long harvesting period from a single sowing.

CATCH CROPPING

Purple-sprouting broccoli will have come to the end in April or early May — early peas will be finished by late June or July. Catch cropping is the answer to summer-long bare ground. Fork over the area and level the surface with a rake. Sow a quick-maturing crop such as spring onions, radish, dwarf lettuce, beetroot, turnips or french beans. The crop will be harvested before the time for autumn digging and the rotational plan will not be disturbed.

INTERSOWING

Intersowing is a useful dual-purpose technique which involves mixing the seed of a compact and quick-growing crop such as radish or Tom Thumb lettuce with a slow-to-mature crop such as parsnips or parsley. The radish or lettuce seedlings emerge quickly and mark out the row —an important advantage at hoeing time. Thin out as normal. The radish or lettuce will be ready long before the parsnips have developed to the stage of needing the space occupied by the quick-growing marker plants.

INTERCROPPING

A neater method than intersowing of making the maximum use of land used for a slow-growing crop. Between adjacent rows of notorious slow developers such as brussels sprouts, leeks, parsnips, etc. is sown a row of a crop which will be harvested in summer before the prime crop needs the space. Popular intercroppers are radish, early peas, early carrots, spinach and dwarf lettuce. Make sure that the intercropping vegetable doesn't make a nuisance of itself by making the space between the rows too narrow to allow easy passage. If necessary, widen the recommended row spacings of the main crop if you plan to sow an intercrop.

CHAPTER 8

HERBS

There are several reasons why herbs are grown. Once they were widely cultivated for their medicinal or tonic properties, but this practice has declined with the advent of modern pharmaceutical products. Sweet-smelling leaves and flowers in various fresh and dry mixes to mask evil odours indoors is another use which has decreased — modern sanitation has made them desirable but no longer necessary. Both these applications for herbs are touched on in this chapter and so are herbal teas, but nearly all of the plants described here are culinary (pot) herbs which are grown for adding to food. They differ from vegetables by adding flavour or providing a garnish rather than being a dish in their own right. Once the use of herbs and spices in the kitchen was all-important in order to mask the taste and smell of meat, poultry and fish which were beginning to decay, but such uses are no longer necessary and so their role has declined. It is generally agreed that too little use is made of herbs and spices in British cooking nowadays, but there is no general agreement on the difference between herbs and spices. Some authorities use the word 'herb' for a flavouring plant grown in a temperate zone and restrict 'spice' to the seed, root, leaf, etc. from a plant grown in a tropical region. Others have a simpler idea — if it is green and is either a stem or a leaf then it is a herb, otherwise it is a spice.

The definition chosen here is even simpler — a herb is a flavouring plant which we traditionally think of as a herb and not as a spice, and in the following pages the most popular home-grown types are described. Nearly all are quite easy to grow, and the standard requirement is for some sun during the day, a well-drained soil, fairly regular picking to keep the plant compact and the replacement of perennials every three or four years using divisions or rooted cuttings. The herb bed should be weeded regularly and in spring it should be trimmed to prevent invasive herbs such as mint from taking over.

One of the joys of herb growing is that it is for everyone. If you don't have a garden, pots of basil, thyme, chervil, marjoram, parsley and mint can be grown on the windowsill. You can be more expansive with a herb trough or growing bags if there is a balcony or patio, but for those of us blessed with an outdoor garden we can create a herb bed — the ideal home for these plants.

The choice of species is, of course, completely up to you providing the conditions are suitable, but there are one or two rules concerning siting and design. The first point is to construct the bed as close as practical to the house — herb gathering tends to be neglected in wet weather when the bed is situated at the far end of the garden. Wherever possible, grow each type of herb in a separate pocket — you can do this the old-fashioned way by dividing the bed into distinct compartments ('knots') with a dwarf hedge of lavender or box. You can bring the idea up to date with a cartwheel design, using bricks or paving stones as the dividers, but perhaps the best plan is to cover a rectangular bed with small concrete slabs and then lift some in an irregular pattern to form planting pockets. In this way each herb can be easily reached, encroachment is kept in check and replanting can take place without disturbing surrounding herbs.

Most types can be raised from seed but it is more practical to buy them as small plants in pots from the garden centre. With shrubby herbs such as bay and rosemary you will only need a single plant but with smaller herbaceous herbs like parsley and chives you will require several specimens.

Harvest at the proper stage of growth — pick your requirements for immediate use when the plants are actively growing in spring, summer and autumn and also pick some for drying. Most herbs can be dried for winter use, but whenever possible basil, parsley, mint, chives and chervil should be used fresh. Dry herbs by hanging them in bunches or spreading them on a tray at about 85–90°F for a day or two. The airing cupboard or a greenhouse is a suitable spot — after this initial warm treatment they can be kept at ordinary room temperature for about a fortnight, turning them daily, until they are cornflake-crisp. Crush, discard chaff, and store inside an airtight container in a cool and dark place.

Deep freezing has revolutionised the preserving of soft-leaved herbs with the ice-cube method. Fill the cups of an ice-cube tray with chopped and blanched herbs and top up with water. Freeze, then store in polythene bags in the freezer. To use, drop a herb cube in the dish while cooking.

Remember to use herbs sparingly — their purpose is to enhance the flavour of the main ingredients, not to dominate them.

HERB GARDENS

A group of pots containing herbs is ▷ well worth considering if you use only a few different types and the amount you require to pick is small. Site the pots near the kitchen.

◁ Some herbs (sage, thyme, mint, etc.) are available in different colours so that you can make an attractive bed in various shades. A problem here is that the invasive types soon spread and swamp the more restrained ones.

△ *The best way to grow herbs is to create a system of pockets into which a single variety is sown or planted. You can create your own scheme in a paved area by removing some slabs or you can buy a preformed herb wheel as illustrated above.*

DICTIONARY OF HERB USES

BOUQUET GARNI

A bunch of several sprigs of parsley, a sprig of thyme and a bay leaf tied with fine thread. Tarragon or marjoram may be added. Place the bouquet garni in stock, stews or casseroles during cooking — remove before serving. If dried herbs are used it is necessary to place them in a muslin bag before putting in the pan.

FINES HERBES

A mixture of finely-chopped herbs with a delicate flavour. Three or more are required — popular ingredients are parsley, chives, chervil and tarragon. The mixture is used fresh or dried and is mainly associated with egg dishes.

HERB BUTTER

Butter in which finely-chopped herbs have been incorporated. The herbs should have a strong flavour — examples include garlic, thyme, chives, rosemary and sage. Mix about a tablespoon of herbs to ¼ lb of softened butter — beat until they are evenly mixed. Let the herb butter stand for a day or more before serving and then put into a mould or place in the refrigerator before cutting into cubes. Cream cheese can be flavoured in the same way.

HERB OIL

Oil in which one or more herbs have been steeped. Olive oil, sunflower oil, etc. are being increasingly used for salad dressings, marinading and stir frying, etc. these days and these oils can be given a flavour boost by adding sprigs of herbs. Leave the mixture to stand for about a month and then strain before bottling the oil. A favourite herb oil for Italian cooking is basil-flavoured olive oil, but there are others to try — fennel, marjoram, savory, etc.

HERB PILLOW

With modern sanitation the need for herb pillows is less than it used to be, but a sachet of sweet-smelling herbs inside the pillow case can still be a welcome and soothing touch. The favourite plant materials are the ones which smell of newly-mown hay when dried — examples include woodruff and melilot. Hops are another popular material as they are reputed to have sleep-inducing properties.

HERB TEA

A drink made by steeping herb leaves, flowers or fruits in hot water to produce a tisane (tea made with unfermented plant material). Mint and chamomile are the favourite herbs — use fresh or deep frozen leaves (see page 127) rather than dried ones if you can. Pour boiling water over the leaves and allow to stand for 5–15 minutes before serving. Use 3 teaspoons of chopped fresh herbs (1 teaspoon if dried) per cup of water.

HERB VINEGAR

Vinegar in which one or more herbs have been steeped. Bruise the leaves of a few sprigs of the chosen herb and place in a jar — pour 1 pint of tepid wine vinegar over them. Cover tightly and place the jar in a warm place for about 2–3 weeks — shake occasionally. Strain the vinegar and then bottle — include a sprig of the herb. Suitable herbs include mint, dill, rosemary, chervil, bay, basil and thyme — use alone or in combination.

MIXED HERBS

A mixture of chopped herbs with a stronger flavour than *fines herbes*. Popular ingredients include sage, thyme, marjoram and parsley. The mixture is used fresh or dried and is recommended for fish and meat dishes.

PESTO

An Italian sauce which has become popular for use with pasta, steak and poultry. It is a blend of two herbs (basil and garlic) with parmesan cheese, pine nuts and olive oil.

POT-POURRI

A mixture of dried flowers and leaves which remains fragrant for a long time. There are many recipes — below is a typical example. Collect petals from colourful flowers (marigold, rose, delphinium, cornflower, etc.) and place on a mesh-bottomed rack together with leaves from aromatic herbs — mint, lavender, pineapple sage, geranium, bergamot, etc. Place in an airing cupboard for a week or two, stirring occasionally until cornflake-crisp. You now need to add a mixture of spices (to enrich the fragrance) and a fixative (to stop the fragrance from disappearing in a short time). A basic recipe is 1 oz dried orris root, ½ teaspoon allspice and ½ teaspoon cinnamon to a quart of dried flowers and leaves. Keep in a tightly-closed container for about 3 weeks before placing in bowls around the house. Add a few drops of flower oil (rose or violet) when fragrance fades.

SALAD FLOWERS

Flowers from herbs and a few other plants which can be used to both decorate and add flavour to salads and other cold dishes. Examples include rose, chives, nasturtium, basil, thyme and pot marigold.

TUSSIE MUSSIE

A small nosegay or posy made with fragrant herbs surrounding a central flower. This central flower is usually a rose bud with a ring of other flowers (e.g violets, honeysuckle, pinks) round it. The outer leafy ring is composed of lavender, scented geranium, thyme, etc. Ribbon is tied around the leaf stalks to keep the posy in place.

ANGELICA

This short-lived perennial has no place in the average-sized herb plot. It will grow to 6 ft or more with a spread of 4–5 ft, so it belongs at the back of the border in a partially shady spot. After a few years the flower-heads appear — creamy balls of tiny blooms on top of branching stems.

Sow angelica in early autumn where it is to grow — if you do have to transplant then move the seedlings in spring before the tap root has developed. Some protection from the wind is necessary and so is regular watering in dry weather.

Angelica is a herb with several uses. The leaves and stalks can be cooked with tart fruit such as rhubarb to reduce the acidity, and candied stems are an old favourite for decorating cakes and jellies. The flower-heads are attractive in the border and dried flower-heads are useful material for indoor displays, but there is a price to pay — the plant will die if it is allowed to flower and seed.

BALM OF GILEAD

Most of the plants in this section can be found in the standard textbooks on herbs and many are available from your local garden centre. Balm of Gilead (Cedronella canariensis) is different — you will have to look for a specialist nursery or seedsman for plants or seed. It is a shrubby short-lived perennial, but as it can stand only a few degrees of frost it is more usual to raise it from seed.

Sow the seed in a propagator in spring and plant out when the danger of frost is over. The site should be well-drained and in full sun — pinch out the tips of young plants to induce bushy growth and water thoroughly in dry weather.

Balm of Gilead is a plain-looking plant which will grow about 3 ft high by the end of the season — treat it as a half hardy annual, so take cuttings to overwinter under glass or begin again with seed next year. Small pink flowers appear in summer, but it is grown for its leaves. These are used in pot-pourri for their heavy fragrance which is similar to the scent of the true balm of Gilead mentioned in the Bible.

BASIL

The strong, clove-like flavour of basil is an essential feature of many Italian recipes and its traditional partner is the tomato — spaghetti sauce, pizzas, tomato sauce and tomato salad all call for basil.

This tender annual cannot stand frost. Sow under glass in a peat pot in March or April and plant out in early June in a well-drained, sunny spot. Space plants about 1 ft apart and pinch out the growing tips regularly to produce a bushy plant with pale green, aromatic foliage. During the summer gather leaves as required — preserve by the ice-cube method (see page 127) and not by drying which destroys much of the flavour. The best way to have basil in winter is to lift plants and pot up in September, placing the pots on the kitchen windowsill.

Apart from its use with tomato dishes, basil is recommended for flavouring soups, salads, minced beef and sausages. Remember to use it sparingly.

BAY

The sweet bay is an evergreen, laurel-like shrub or small tree which is often grown in containers and trimmed as a cone, pyramid or 'lollipop'. It is not really happy in an English winter — in the south cold winds will burn some of the leaves and in the north the whole of the top growth may be killed by frost. In spring new growth will appear from the base.

Buy a pot-grown specimen and plant in spring — the requirements are a site sheltered from easterly winds and a soil or compost containing some lime. Water regularly in summer. Pick young leaves for culinary use and dry some at room temperature for winter use.

It is the basic ingredient of a *bouquet garni* but it has other important uses. Bay leaves should be added to fish dishes (especially salmon), custards, stews and rice dishes. Tear the edges before use and remove before serving. A word of caution — laurel hedge leaves may *look* like bay leaves but never use them … they are poisonous.

1 in. = 2.5 cm, 1 ft = 30 cm, 1 oz = 28 gm, 1 lb = 450 gm

BERGAMOT

You are more likely to find this hardy perennial in the herbaceous border than in the herb garden. The flower-heads of tubular blooms are borne on top of 2-3 ft stems from June to September. White, pink and red are available — buy pot-grown specimens from your garden centre in spring and plant at 2 ft intervals in moisture-retentive soil. Lift, divide and replant the clumps every 3 years and cut the stems back to just above ground level in autumn.

You will find this plant under its latin name Monarda at the nursery — as a herb it is sometimes listed as bee balm. The downy mint-like leaves have an orange-like flavour and can be used in salads or desserts — the round flower-heads make an attractive feature on top of trifles, jellies, fruit salads and so on.

Another use for the dried leaves is to produce a tisane with boiling water — see page 129 for details. It is not, however, the same as the 'bergamot' which gives the characteristic flavour to Earl Grey Tea.

BORAGE

Borage has long been a favourite plant in the herb garden — its drooping flower-heads provide a decorative touch all summer long and its leaves and flowers are used where a cucumber-like flavour is required. The plants grow about 2-3 ft high and the small star-shaped flowers are blue.

Sow the seeds between April and July — the preferred situation is light soil and full sun. There is a strong tap root so borage does not like transplanting — sow in the herb garden and thin the seedlings to about 1½ ft. Allow self-sown seedlings to develop at the end of the season to provide next year's plants. Staking is usually necessary.

The main use for borage is as a garnish or flavouring agent in cold drinks — wine, long summer drinks, fruit juices, etc. Leaves, small stem sprigs or flowers can be used. Another use for the leaves and flowers is as an ingredient for salads and sandwiches — chop the leaves finely. A word of warning about the leaves and stems — they are covered with bristly hairs which can irritate the skin.

CARAWAY

With caraway nothing is wasted. In the first season you can pick some of the leaves and at the end of the second season both the seeds and the roots are harvested. The leaves of this biennial are carrot-like in appearance and the small pink flowers are borne on 2 ft high stems.

Autumn is the best time to sow seeds and both partial shade and heavy soil are tolerated. It hates transplanting — sow caraway where it is to grow and thin to about 6 in. It readily self-seeds so continuity is not a problem.

Leaves can be cut during the growing season and used in salads — the flavour is much more like parsley than 'caraway'. The caraway flavour is obtained from the hard curved seeds. To harvest them cut the seed heads when they are ripe — the seeds will have begun to turn brown. Put these seed heads in a paper bag and leave in a warm place. The dry seeds can be used in many ways — in cakes, coleslaw, soups, bread made with rye flour, meat dishes, etc. The long carrot-like roots can be cut up and cooked like parsnips but there is not much flavour.

CHAMOMILE

The variety to grow is the double-flowered C. nobile Flore Pleno. This is the English or Roman chamomile — a creeping perennial which grows about 6 in. high with a 1-2 ft spread. Yellow-centred white flowers appear above the feathery leaves so it is a decorative as well as a useful herb. Alternatives include the non-flowering variety Treneague used for making chamomile lawns and the annual Matricaria recutita which grows about 2 ft high.

Plant clumps or sow seeds of English chamomile in spring or autumn — the distance between plants should be about 9 in. The plants spread quite rapidly once they are established and should be trimmed back if they become invasive. Lift and divide the plants every 3 years.

Chamomile is not used in food preparation but it does have several other uses. Its most popular role is in chamomile tea — a long-established cure for digestive and nervous troubles. The flowers and leaves are used for pot-pourri and the open flowers were once widely employed for making hair rinses.

1 in. = 2.5 cm, 1 ft = 30 cm, 1 oz = 28 gm, 1 lb = 450 gm

CHERVIL

Chervil has several delicate features, ranging from its ferny parsley-like foliage and its short life-span in hot weather to its subtle aniseed flavour which can easily be lost in cooking. Despite this apparent lack of robustness, it grows quickly and the first leaves can be picked about 8 weeks after sowing. It is also hardy, so you can pick chervil in winter when the top growth of plants such as mint has succumbed to frost.

Sow chervil where it is to grow. A March sowing will provide a summer crop and an August sowing will provide leaves from autumn to spring. Thin so that plants are 6 in. apart and water regularly in dry weather. Remove leaves from the outside of the plant when gathering for the kitchen. At the same time remove most (but not all) flower-heads — leave a few to produce seeds for a self-sown crop next year.

Make sure that you do not lose the delicate flavour. Add finely-chopped leaves to soups, fish and egg dishes just before serving. Garnish salads with it, but put it on the plates at the last moment.

CHIVES

The mild-mannered member of the onion family — its grass-like stems can be cut from March to October to improve the flavour of many dishes. Much of its value is lost by drying — for winter use grow a pot or two indoors or freeze by the ice-cube method (see page 127).

Chives can be raised from seed sown in March but it is easier to plant pot-grown specimens in spring or autumn. Space the clumps 9 in. apart and divide every 3 or 4 years. Water the plants regularly — the ideal situation is moist soil and full sun. For the kitchen cut the grassy leaves to within an inch of soil level — never snip off the tips and never leave the flower-heads to open if you want a regular supply of leaves.

A herb with many uses — add finely-chopped chives to potato salad, stuffed eggs, soups, salads, omelettes, cream cheese and sauces. Obviously a herb which everyone should grow.

COSTMARY

Many of the herbs in this section are known by everyone and are found in most herb gardens — mint, thyme, parsley, etc. Costmary is different — you won't find it in many plots and you may have to search for a supplier. This hardy perennial is not worth growing for its appearance — it is a sprawling plant with small daisy-like flowers. It is the fragrant oval leaves which earn this plant a place in the garden.

Buy container-grown plants and set them at 2 ft intervals. It is not too fussy about soil conditions and will soon produce clumps of greyish-green toothed leaves which emit a unique aroma when crushed — a mixture of mint and citrus. Remove creeping stems if the plant becomes invasive —use these runners for propagation.

Costmary comes into its own in winter when the leaves serve as an alternative to mint which will have died down. Minty but different — some people find the flavour rather bitter so do not add too much. Other applications are fresh leaves for costmary tea and dried leaves for pot-pourri.

CURRY PLANT

You will find the curry plant in many herb catalogues and books, and it is sold by most garden centres. It is therefore included in this book, but as explained below it does not have a role to play in the kitchen. Grow the curry plant for its decorative value in the border — the narrow silvery leaves and masses of yellow button-like flowers are a welcome foil against dark-leaved plants and the curry-like aroma around this herb is remarkably strong.

Choose a sunny spot and plant out pot-grown specimens or rooted cuttings at 2 ft intervals. This evergreen perennial is reasonably tolerant of cold conditions but a winter cover of peat, straw, etc. is advisable if your site is in a frost pocket. Cut back the stems in spring to prevent the plants from becoming leggy.

It smells like curry but it is *not* curry. Some books recommend the use of leafy sprigs to give a mild curry-like flavour to stews, soups, etc. but it is not a good idea. Cases of very mild poisoning have been reported. The dried leaves can be used in pot-pourri if you like a spicy aroma.

DILL

Countless British children received their first taste of herbs with the dill contained in gripe water. It has attractive feathery foliage, and the 2 ft plant bears flat plates of small yellow flowers in July. The leaves have a distinct flavour which is retained after drying, and the lightly crushed seeds have an even stronger taste.

Dill hates disturbance. Sow the seeds in April where the plants are to grow and thin to 12 in. apart. Pick a sunny, well-drained spot and keep the ground watered in dry weather. To harvest the seeds cut the stems when the flower-heads have turned brown. Tie a paper bag over each flower-head and hang the stems upside-down in bunches.

Gather leaves for immediate use and for drying whilst they are still young. Use as a garnish or in the cooking of all types of fish, especially salmon. The chopped leaves can also be used in yoghurt, meat and vegetable dishes. The main use of the seeds is in pickling vinegar for cucumbers, but they can also be added to cakes, bread, fish and rice dishes.

FENNEL

Common fennel is an attractive perennial growing up to 5 ft high with blue-green feathery foliage and yellow flowers. It has sometimes been called the grown-up dill — taller, perennial and with a more pronounced aniseed flavour. Do not confuse it with florence fennel (page 113) — an unusual vegetable grown for its swollen stem bases.

Choose a sunny, well-drained spot — common fennel is more at home in the herbaceous border than in the herb bed. You can sow seed in spring but it is much easier to buy a pot-grown plant from the garden centre or a specialist nursery. Pick leaves in summer as required — harvest the seeds in the way described for dill.

Fennel is interchangeable with dill — use the chopped foliage for fish, salads, vegetables and soups. The seeds are highly recommended for cooking with oily fish such as mackerel.

FEVERFEW

This short-lived perennial has been grown in cottage gardens for generations where its yellow-green feathery leaves and daisy flowers have provided colour and its foliage has been used for a variety of medicinal purposes. The common form has yellow-centred white blooms but you can buy all-white double-flowering ones as well as the golden-leaved variety Aureum. Feverfew grows about 2 ft high.

You should be able to buy pots of the basic species Tanacetum parthenium at the garden centre but you may have to raise plants from seed if you want one of the more colourful varieties. Sow seed or plant out cuttings in spring or autumn — space at 1 ft intervals.

Feverfew is a medicinal rather than a culinary herb and has been used for all sorts of things in the past. Despite its name it is used for migraine and not fever relief these days. Feverfew tea is sometimes recommended but the usual form is the feverfew sandwich. A few leaves as a filling is not particularly tasty but is effective for some people.

GARLIC

Until quite recently scientists smiled at all the wonderful medicinal powers claimed for garlic, but recent research has shown that there is some truth in a few of the old wives' tales.

Any well-drained spot will do for this herb. Buy a head of garlic from the greengrocer or supermarket and split it up into individual cloves. Plant them 2 in. deep and 6 in. apart in March. Apart from watering in dry weather there is nothing else to do until the foliage turns yellow in July or August. Lift the bulbs and allow to dry under cover, then store in a cool, frost-free place.

If you are a beginner with garlic, you must use it very sparingly or you will be put off for ever. Rub a wooden salad bowl with a clove before adding the ingredients. Rub the skin of poultry before roasting and then you can try dropping a whole *unskinned* clove into a casserole or stew, removing it before serving. If by then you have lost a little of your garlic fear, you can try using crushed (not chopped) garlic in meat, etc. as the Continentals do.

1 in. = 2.5 cm, 1 ft = 30 cm, 1 oz = 28 gm, 1 lb = 450 gm

HOP

Hops are not generally regarded as a herb — one immediately thinks of their role in flavouring beer. But they do have a place in the home plot. The twining stems can be used to cover a fence or wall at the back of the herb garden and they are often used to clothe arches in a potager.

Choose a female variety and remember the plant will take up a lot of space — the stems and large lobed leaves may cover 10 ft x 10 ft in a single season. The growth dies down in winter, so cut the stems just above ground level in early spring. Mulch around the base with compost in May and tie the shoots as they develop to the support. A word of warning — hop stems bear bristles which can cause an irritating rash.

Hops have several uses. The young leaves can be blanched for boiling or steaming as a vegetable but it is the cone-like flower-heads which are the important part. They have been used as a sleep-inducing herb for centuries — pour on boiling water to make a tisane or use the dried flower-heads for stuffing a herb pillow.

HORSERADISH

Horseradish sauce is the traditional accompaniment for roast beef and so this herb earns its place in this section, but you would need to be a horseradish devotee to plant it in your garden. The problem is that you cannot just leave it. If allowed to stay in the ground for a few years then a new weed will have appeared in your garden — horseradish.

In March make a 6 in. deep hole with a dibber — these holes should be 2 ft apart. Drop a 6 in. piece of root into each hole and fill with soil. The secret of preventing horseradish from swamping the area is to lift *all* the plants in October. Store the roots in sand.

Grating horseradish is an eye-watering job — use the shredder attachment of a food processor. Grated horse-radish can be used in steak tartare and also as a garnish for fish. It is more usually mixed with vinegar and a little milk to produce horseradish sauce or folded in with whipping cream, salt, sugar and a little vinegar to make horseradish cream. Serve with beef, ham or trout.

HYSSOP

A pretty plant for the middle of the herb bed, a container or as a low hedge instead of lavender. The shrubby growth of this perennial has narrow dark leaves and spikes of flowers in late summer. The usual colour is blue but both pink and white varieties are available.

Hyssop does best in a sunny, non-acid site. Sow seed in spring if you need many plants — set out the seedlings or rooted cuttings 1 ft apart for hedging or 2 ft apart in the herb bed. Pinch out the growing tips and cut back hard in early spring every year.

The semi-evergreen leaves of hyssop have been used as a medicine since Old Testament times and hyssop tea is sometimes recommended to relieve bronchitis and catarrh. These days it is the culinary value of the leaves which is more important. The flavour is strong and is usually described as sage-minty or bitter-minty. They are used in salads, soups and stews to provide a spicy touch and are also used to flavour pork. Use the flowers as a colourful garnish.

LAVENDER

You may not recognise hyssop or lovage but you will certainly know an ordinary variety of lavender when you see it. The grey-green needle-like leaves and spikes of fragrant mauve flowers are known to everyone, but there are other types with green leaves and white, pink or purple flowers.

Lavender needs a sunny, well-drained site. It grows 1–3 ft depending on the variety, so choose to suit the space available. Buy pots of rooted cuttings rather than trying to start from seed and set them 1 ft apart. Prune the shrub once the flowers have faded but do not cut back into the old wood. After a few years they generally become leggy so replant every 5 years.

The main use for lavender leaves and flowers is as an ingredient for pot-pourri. Another popular use is to dry the flower-heads at the bud stage and then sew them in small muslin bags. Lavender tea is supposed to have a restorative effect if you are tired but this herb has little or no use in the kitchen. The flowers are occasionally recommended as a garnish but there are much better herbs for this purpose.

LEMON BALM

Lemon (or bee) balm is an old cottage garden plant which has no special sun or soil requirements. It is a bushy perennial growing about 3 ft high, and as it can spread like mint it may have to be kept in check. The small white flowers are not significant — it is grown for its oval leaves which emit a strong lemon aroma when crushed.

You can start from seed in spring but it is much easier to use small plants in pots from your local garden centre. Remove the flowers to promote vigorous leafy growth and at the end of the season cut down the stems to a few inches above ground level. Lift and divide clumps in spring or autumn if you want more plants.

There are a variety of uses for lemon balm. Chopped fresh leaves can be added to salads, fish dishes, stewed fruit, etc. and dried leaves can be added to a stuffing mix where a lemon flavour is required. Lemon balm tea is an old remedy for feverish colds and dried leaves make a good ingredient for pot-pourri.

LEMON VERBENA

Like lemon balm this herb has leaves which emit a strong lemon aroma and there are small summer flowers which are of no herbal value. The similarity ends there. It is a rather tender shrub which can grow up to 10 ft high and it requires a sheltered site which is both sunny and well-drained. Frost protection may be necessary in winter.

You will need only one or two plants so buy pot-grown specimens from the garden centre. Lemon verbena makes a good pot plant and it can be trained against a sheltered south-facing wall.

Lemon verbena is reputed to have the most intensive aroma of all the 'lemon' herbs so be careful not to use too much. Pick a few fresh leaves for use in salads, sweets, etc. where a lemon flavour is required. Lemon mint tea is made with a mixture of lemon verbena and mint leaves — perhaps the most refreshing of all herbal tisanes. Gather and dry the leaves when they fall in autumn — use them in pot-pourri.

LOVAGE

Lovage is one of the giants of the herb world and is easy to recognise. It looks like a giant celery plant and may reach 7 ft or more when established. In summer heads of greenish flowers appear but these have little ornamental value and should be removed unless you plan to save the seed.

You can raise this plant from fresh seed but it is more usual to buy a few plants from a supplier and set them out 2 ft apart in spring. The plants need a humus-rich soil and should be watered copiously in dry weather. The stalks die down in late autumn — cut them off at ground level and apply Growmore around the plants when new growth appears in spring.

Lovage is generally used as young fresh leaves — drying is not really successful. The taste of this foliage is like celery with a touch of pepper — use finely-chopped leaves as a celery/pepper substitute in soups, stews, salads, etc. Lovage tea is an old remedy for indigestion and the dried seeds can be used as a substitute for celery seed in cooking and baking.

MARJORAM & OREGANO

There are many varieties of Origanum — most are called marjoram but O. vulgare is usually referred to as oregano. The usual type in the herb garden is sweet marjoram, a bushy plant grown as a half-hardy annual. Seeds are sown under glass in March and planted out in a sunny spot at the end of May, setting the plants about 9 in. apart. Gather leaves as required — for drying, pick foliage before the flowers open. In autumn lift plants and pot up to provide an indoor supply of leaves for winter use.

Pot marjoram is much easier to grow — all you have to do is buy a pot-grown specimen in spring and plant in the garden where it will grow as readily as mint. This dwarf shrub is a perennial, although the leaves may fall in winter.

The prime use of chopped marjoram is for sprinkling over meat or poultry before roasting. It can also be sprinkled on soups before serving, and both fresh and dried marjoram are widely used in stuffings and rissoles.

1 in. = 2.5 cm, 1 ft = 30 cm, 1 oz = 28 gm, 1 lb = 450 gm

MELILOT

This biennial is one of the more unusual types in this catalogue of herbs and you may have to go to a herb nursery to buy seed or plants. It is worth the effort if you like attractive plants and not just useful ones, as melilot produces long spikes of yellow pea-like flowers in summer — these blooms act like a magnet for bees. The bushy stems grow about 2 ft high.

Melilot can be raised like any other hardy biennial — sow in late spring and leave to overwinter for flowers in the following early summer. It is quite practical, however, to treat it as an annual by sowing in March for flowers in mid-late summer of the same year.

It is the clover-like leaves and not the flowers which are used. You can make a refreshing tea with them or chop them finely for adding to stuffing — the flavour is often described as honey- or almond-like. This almond-like fragrance remains when the leaves are dried so they can be used as an ingredient for pot-pourri or herb pillows.

MINT

Every country has its favourite herb — in Britain the honours are shared between parsley and mint. Mint will thrive in most garden soils — in fact it usually thrives too well and becomes a nuisance. Keep it in check by growing in a container, sinking metal or plastic sheets into the soil around the plants, or by simply lifting and replanting every year. There are several types — spearmint (garden mint) is the usual one, but Bowles mint is the variety most highly recommended for mint sauce, and apple mint (round-leaved mint) combines fragrance with a true minty flavour.

Plant pieces of root 2 in. deep and 9 in. apart in autumn or spring. Top dress with compost in autumn if the plants are not lifted annually.

Sprigs of mint are added to the water when new potatoes and peas are boiled, but its most popular use is as the basic ingredient in mint sauce or mint jelly served with roast lamb.

PARSLEY

You will find several varieties listed in the seed catalogues — the curly-leaved ones are the most decorative and the plain-leaved types have the most flavour.

Sow seed ½ in. deep in April for a summer and autumn crop and again in August for winter use. Germination is slow — it may take up to a couple of months. Rich soil in semi-shade is ideal, and the seedlings should be thinned to 9 in. apart. Water in dry weather, and cover overwintering plants with cloches or straw. Remove flowering stems as they appear but a few can be left in the second season to provide seeds for self-sown parsley plants. Pick regularly to ensure a continuous supply of fresh leaves — for drying dip the sprigs in boiling water for 2 minutes and then place in a cool oven until crisp. Crush and store as soon as the leaves are cool.

The garnish *par excellence*, of course, and an ingredient in *fines herbes* and a *bouquet garni*. White sauce with chopped parsley is popular, but for something different try parsley fried until crisp and served with fish.

POT MARIGOLD

There are few annuals which are easier to grow than pot marigold and not many herbs can provide such a bright splash of summer colour. The species Calendula officinalis has small yellow flowers which are single, but you can buy varieties with double flowers in yellow or orange.

Sow the seed in spring where the plants are to grow — thin seedlings to 6 in. apart. They will thrive under a wide range of conditions but for a really good display of flowers you will need a sunny, well-drained site. Dead-head faded flowers to prolong active growth and prevent excessive self seeding.

Pot marigold was once quite widely grown as a vegetable, but the leaves have a bitter taste and this use has declined, although you can try very young leaves in a salad. It is the flowers which are employed as a herb — used fresh as petals or whole heads they provide colour in salads, soups, egg dishes, etc. Dried flowers can be crushed and used as a substitute for saffron to provide yellow colour and a little flavour to a variety of dishes.

ROSEMARY

This attractive but slightly tender evergreen shrub needs well-drained soil in a sunny, sheltered spot — grow it in the shrub border, herb garden or in a tub close to a south-facing wall. Regular picking and spring pruning should keep the bush about 2 ft high, with both its needle-like leaves and blue flowers being highly aromatic and suitable for kitchen use.

You can sow seed in May but it is much more convenient to buy a pot-grown plant in spring. There are several decorative variegated types, but they are less hardy than the ordinary green rosemary. Winter frosts and icy winds in early spring may kill some of the shoots but new growth will appear from the base.

The most important thing to remember is that rosemary is strong flavoured and should therefore be used very sparingly. It is a traditional flavouring for lamb, pork and veal — insert a few sprigs before roasting and remove before serving.

SAGE

Sage is an attractive bush — its grey-green leaves and spikes of blue flowers are just as useful in the shrub border as in the herb garden.

A single plant should satisfy your requirements — plant a pot-grown specimen in spring in a sunny, well-drained spot. Gather leaves regularly and prune the bush lightly in July after flowering. Collect foliage for drying before the plant has flowered — sage takes a long time to dry, but will keep for up to a year in a closed container.

Sage has a very strong flavour. Its main role is to accompany onions in the traditional stuffing for duck and goose — it also makes an excellent accompaniment for veal and pork. It goes into sausages, kebabs, some cheeses and into bean and tomato dishes, but you really must be careful not to use too much because it is our strongest-flavoured herb.

SALAD BURNET

This member of the rose family is an evergreen perennial which can be used as an all-the-year-round edging for a herb bed. It has a neat and fern-like appearance with ranks of toothed, oval leaves along the stalks. In summer small heads of reddish flowers appear on long stalks — these have little ornamental value and are best removed.

Salad burnet is not too fussy about soil or situation but it seems to prefer non-acid soil. It can be raised quite easily from seed sown in spring to produce transplants which are set out at 1 ft intervals, or you can buy pot-grown plants at your garden centre. The rosette of leaves is quite low-growing but the flower stalks may reach up to 2 ft.

This herb is grown for the cucumber flavour of its leaflets — pick these off the stalk and chop for use. There is no cucumber smell, but the flavour is quite strong and can be used anywhere you would normally use its flavour taste-alike. Examples include long summer drinks, cream cheese sandwiches, soups, salads and yoghurt.

SAVORY

Savory does not appear in the top ten list of herbs, but it does provide a welcome alternative to the popular ones, such as sage, which we all know. There are two types from which to make your choice. Summer savory is an annual, sown ¼ in. deep in fertile soil and thinned to 6 in. apart. The plants grow about 1 ft high and leaves should be gathered before the pink flowers appear. Cut back after flowering and a second crop of leaves will develop.

Winter savory is an evergreen perennial, and the ideal site for this low-growing shrub is a light, well-drained soil in full sun. Plant in April and trim back in early spring each year. The experts tell us that the flavour of winter savory is not as good as the summer variety, but it has the advantage of being available all year round.

Both types of savory are used in the same way — they are the traditional flavouring for broad beans and lentil soup. Add fresh leaves to salads and egg dishes.

1 in. = 2.5 cm, 1 ft = 30 cm, 1 oz = 28 gm, 1 lb = 450 gm

SWEET CICELY

You will need space and an area of humus-rich moist soil for this perennial — after a few years the soft fern-like leaves may be over 1½ ft long. In late spring flat heads of tiny white flowers appear and these flowers are followed by elongated seeds which are dark brown when mature. Remove the flower-heads unless you want to harvest the seeds.

Seed can be sown in autumn but it is easier to buy pot-grown plants from the garden centre — because of its size it is doubtful whether you will need more than one or two in the garden. At the end of the season remove the stems when the leaves have turned brown — new growth will appear in early spring.

The leaves and also the seeds at the green stage taste of aniseed. Chopped leaves can be used in salads and the seeds can be sprinkled over desserts — note that ripe seeds have no flavour. Leaves and chopped stalks can be used to remove the tartness of fruit such as gooseberries when cooking and the roots can be boiled as a vegetable. A herb with many uses.

TARRAGON

Make sure you buy french tarragon, which has been described as the king of herbs, and not russian tarragon which is practically tasteless. This herb spreads like mint, its underground runners producing a fresh crop of leaves each year. It is not completely hardy, so cover the plants with ashes or straw in late autumn.

Tarragon needs well-drained soil in a sheltered position. Plant a pot-grown specimen in March — remove flowering shoots to maintain the supply of fresh leaves on the bush. The leaves should be picked from June to October for immediate use — the surplus can be dried or preserved by the ice-cube method (page 127).

Tarragon is used in many classical chicken and fish dishes. Chopped leaves are steeped in wine vinegar to produce tarragon vinegar, chopped leaves in butter are served with steak and fresh leaves are used in omelettes, salads, etc.

THYME

Thyme is a low-growing shrub which is delightfully aromatic. It is evergreen, so fresh leaves can be picked all year round and there is no need for drying. The flavour will depend on the variety you choose — common thyme is the strongest, lemon thyme is less pungent with a citrus flavour which makes it an excellent ingredient for custards, and caraway thyme has a unique pine/caraway aroma.

Plant pot-grown specimens 1 ft apart in a well-drained sunny spot in spring. Pick the leaves as required. Divide the plants every 3 years and replant. If you do not have a garden, thyme will grow in a pot on your windowsill.

This herb is the traditional partner for parsley in the stuffing for poultry. On its own it can be used for rubbing onto meat before roasting and it can also be added to fish dishes. Add thyme to soups and stews, but always use sparingly.

WOODRUFF

For maximum growth many of the herbs in this section require a sunny spot, but not this woodland perennial. It is a spreading plant which grows about 1–1½ ft high and makes an ideal ground cover under trees and shrubs. The small star-shaped flowers which appear in early summer are white and fragrant.

Propagate by digging up and dividing established plants which have become invasive. Plant clumps in spring or autumn — it is not an easy plant to raise from seed. The plant dies down in winter so cut down the stems once the leaves have died.

Woodruff is grown for the decorative effect of its white flowers under shrubs and also for its leaves which emit the smell of new-mown hay when dried — this aroma is retained for a remarkably long time. These dried leaves are used in pot-pourri and herb pillows. Woodruff has an age-old connection with drinks of various types. The dried leaves can be used to make a tisane and fresh leaves can be added to wine to provide a 'herby' taste.

CHAPTER 9

SHOP-BOUGHT VEGETABLES

Gardening magazines delight in telling us how by careful selection and skilful planning we can be self-sufficient in vegetables all year round. This is a counsel of perfection, as very few of us can (or would wish to) devote the time and space required for such a task, and freezer capacity is usually limited. So we regularly turn to the greengrocer to supplement our home-grown produce, even though the leaves, roots, pods, etc. we buy could easily be raised in the garden.

Labelling of shop produce has greatly improved in recent years, so you know exactly what you are getting. Of course, no one can tell you which vegetables to buy, but there are a few general rules for the shopper. Never buy more than you can store properly or eat immediately — there is nothing like eating vegetables which have been kept at room temperature for a couple of weeks to build up a life-long prejudice against them! Check freshness whenever you can — one up for the supermarkets or open stall where you can inspect the produce before buying. In general choose pods and roots which are smaller than average and reject leafy vegetables which are limp and abnormally pale.

So we buy fresh peas, cauliflowers, carrots, cabbages, etc. as well as growing our own in the garden. Canned and dried produce are available, but it is the frozen food phenomenon which has expanded so dramatically. We now spend about £350 million each year on frozen vegetables, and the advantages have often been listed — out of season vegetables at a reasonable price, no preparation, no waste and so on, but it is still a pity that so much frozen produce is bought when the fresh vegetable is plentiful in both shops and garden.

The vegetables described in this chapter are ones which are not grown in the home garden. It may be that our requirement is so limited that we are not prepared to devote greenhouse space to them (okra and chilli are examples) or their cultivation may be quite impractical — watercress is the outstanding example. Most of them, however, will not grow here and are imported from tropical or sub-tropical regions. All the ones listed are available from one or more of the large supermarket chains and the photographs illustrate typical specimens to be seen on the shelves. One or two of these exotic vegetables, such as the avocado, are reasonably popular, but most of them are unfamiliar. In the shop they are usually placed alongside other commercial oddities such as

mangetout peas (page 79), radicchio (page 50), mooli (page 87), scorzonera (page 89) and celeriac (page 46).

The shop-bought exotics illustrated on the next three pages are not a complete list of the unusual vegetables you can find these days. To sample the complete range you will have to visit the ethnic shops and ethnic areas of large supermarkets catering for the many different racial and national groups who live in Britain. In Chinese stores you will find Oriental mushrooms and tins of water chestnuts. Here and elsewhere you will find a range of vegetables from the Far East — lemon grass (a citrus-flavoured substitute for chives) and kuichai (a somewhat peppery alternative to the familiar spring onion). Look for plantains, so easily mistaken for bananas but which are always cooked before eating. You can boil and mash them or slice and fry as fritters.

You will occasionally find strange relatives of our vegetable marrow in stores catering for African or West Indian communities. There are the dudi, which looks like a cucumber, and the calabaza pumpkin with its squash-like appearance.

This chapter deals with the vegetables, both ordinary and exotic, which you can find in their fresh state in stores in Britain, although you may have to search to find some of the more unusual ones. Exotic vegetables which can be bought in cans or in the dried state are not included, as the range here is vast indeed. Canned water chestnuts have already been mentioned, and with them you will find bamboo shoots, palm hearts, etc. Leaving the canned vegetables you will find an even greater variety of dried produce — the legumes from all over the world. Large white butter beans, tiny brown haricot beans, black-eyed peas, chick peas, brown lentils (which remain intact when cooked), red lentils (which break up when cooked), red kidney beans … the list is far too long to complete.

No good gardener would want to rely solely on shop-bought vegetables. On several occasions there has been a firm recommendation in this book that you should devote the vegetable plot mainly to those types which the family enjoy but to spare a little space for the unknown in order to expand your experience of the range of vegetable tastes. The same principle should apply to shopping — satisfy the family's basic requirements with well-known vegetables but do try one or two of the oddities, following the preparation instructions provided on the following pages.

AVOCADO

The popularity of the avocado has increased greatly since its introduction as a basic starter on restaurant menus throughout the country. Its delicate buttery flavour blends well with shellfish, but the experts recommend plain *avocado nature*, served with an olive oil vinaigrette.

The fruits in the supermarket will be either smooth and bright green (South African) or rough and dark (Israeli). They are ready for eating when the flesh is yielding to gentle pressure — store for a few days if the flesh is firm. In the kitchen cut in half and remove the stone — coat the cut surface with lemon juice to prevent discoloration. Fill with prawns or crabmeat as they do in the restaurant, or be more adventurous by mixing with pineapple or grapefruit. Avocados can also be baked (15 minutes at 380°F) or mashed with chillis, onions and garlic to produce the fiery Mexican dip known as *guacomole*.

CHAYOTE

The chayote was once solely a feature of sub-tropical cookery — the Creoles of New Orleans, the Aztecs of Mexico, the Australians in the Outback and so on. But now these pear-like squashes have begun to appear in our own supermarkets.

It is not surprising that a vegetable which is now grown right around the globe should have acquired a number of names — choko, christophene, chow-chow, mirliton etc., but there is nothing complicated about its use. Slice, dip in butter and fry like a courgette or cut in half, fill with a meat or shrimp stuffing and bake for 20 minutes at 400°F. It has a definite advantage over the common-or-garden marrow — the flesh remains firm and not watery after cooking. Boil them if you wish — cook for 30 minutes and serve hot as a vegetable or allow to cool and add chunks to a salad.

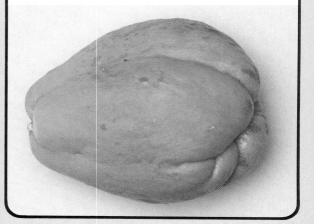

CHILLI

Take care — these hot peppers can make your throat burn, eyes water and skin sting if you are not used to eating or handling them. So a few general rules before you start — the smaller and redder the chilli, the hotter it will be, and removing the seeds plus blanching in hot water before use will remove much of the fire.

Don't eat them raw — don't even try a small piece unless they are part of your heritage. Use them in cooking to give a spicy taste to potatoes, rice, soups, stews, eggs, sweet corn etc. You will need one chilli per pound of meat or chicken, but the old American favourite *chili con carne* is not made with fresh chillies — it is a mixture of ground beef, garlic, tomatoes, vinegar, sugar, onions . . . and chili powder. Drying and crushing chillies produces cayenne pepper, not the chili powder you can buy in the shops.

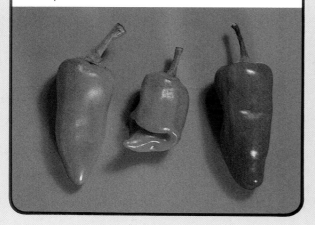

COLOCASI

You may find colocasi (or cologasi) in your supermarket if it offers a wide range of vegetables, but you will certainly not find it in your cookery books. Unlike okra, chayote, chilli, etc. with their near-universal appeal in sub-tropical and tropical areas, colocasi is grown and traditionally eaten in a tiny area of the world — Cyprus.

The large and bulbous tuber is borne at the base of the stem and is used as a potato substitute. There are differences — the skin is tough and the flesh is dense, which means that you have to peel thickly and then break the white tubers into pieces with the point of a knife. The basic cooking method is to boil until tender and then mash with butter and nutmeg. Alternatively you can parboil the pieces of tubers and then place them around the Sunday roast in place of potatoes or parsnips. The Cypriot favourite is *chirino me colocasi* — pork stewed with onions, celery, tomatoes and colocasi.

CORIANDER

Coriander has a long, long history in Europe and the Middle East. It was mentioned in the Old Testament, used to preserve meat in Ancient Rome and employed as an aphrodisiac in Persia. Yet it has become associated with Chinese and Indian cookery, with the alternative name chinese parsley. The delicate fern-like leaves of this annual are used as a parsley substitute. The flavour is different — there is a citrus-like taste which is missing from ordinary parsley.

The best-known part of coriander is the seed — it is the major ingredient of curry powder. The pale brown seeds are strongly aromatic when crushed and can be added to potatoes, salads, stews and cocktails. If the Ancients are to be believed, coriander will help your digestion, longevity and love-life.

EDDOE

Eddoe is the African name — it is taro in the Pacific Islands and America, and kandalla in Sri Lanka. The tubers are rather similar to thick-skinned potatoes, but the moisture content is appreciably lower and both the starch and protein content are higher. The flavour, usually described as nutty, is more pronounced than with our bland domestic potato.

Peel and use any standard potato recipe — bake, boil, fry, roast etc., as long as you remember that cooking times may have to be increased because of the lower water content. In their native home large eddoes are sometimes stuffed with chopped meat — bake at 350°F until tender — a recommended dish if you can find roots which are large enough. Definitely not recommended is the Hawaiian *poi* made by straining boiled and mashed eddoes and then leaving the liquor to ferment into a potent brew.

OKRA

Okra is eaten in all 5 major continents — a part of the staple diet in some nations and a rarity in others. It is still in the rarity class in Britain, although it now frequently appears in supermarkets and larger greengrocers. It is worth a trial, but do choose carefully in order to avoid disappointment. The pods ('lady's fingers') should be 2–4 in. long, crisp, bright green and free from shrivelling and discoloration. The pod should snap cleanly when bent.

Parboil in salted water for 8 minutes. Drain, dry each pod with a paper towel and then fry in deep fat until tender. Include in soups and stews as the Eastern Europeans do or add to curries as in India. One of the best known of all okra dishes is the chicken gumbo of the Southern United States — a stew of chicken, ham, tomatoes, onions, cayenne pepper and okra.

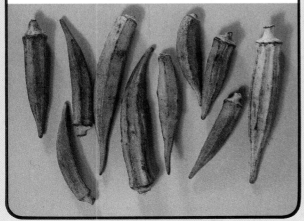

ROOT GINGER

Our ancestors used large quantities of ginger to flavour their food, but nowadays this tropical root only appears in biscuits, gingerbread, crystallised candy or occasionally on melon. Until recently we had to make do with the powdered dried root, but fresh root ginger has now begun to appear in the shops. Thus we have the opportunity to see if the *real* taste of ginger appeals, as the grated or finely chopped root has a much richer flavour than the powder. Love it or hate it, root ginger is worth a trial.

Scrub the root and peel off the outer scurfy coat. Grate or chop finely, and add to biscuits, fish or meat dishes. Follow a gingerbread or ginger snaps recipe using the grated root in place of powder, and add it to home-made ice cream. Root ginger is perhaps most at home in curry dishes, and chunks will help to liven up chutney. Shop-bought root ginger can be kept in the refrigerator for a couple of weeks.

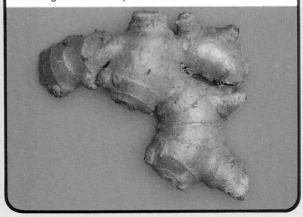

SWEET POTATO

Many American vegetables, from runner beans to juicy tomatoes, have been readily accepted in Britain, but not so the sweet potato. Most people on this side of the Atlantic find its sugary flavour unacceptable as an accompaniment to meat and poultry, but then many who have tried them have cooked them incorrectly.

Try again with the sweet potato (N. America), kumara (New Zealand) or batata (S. America) which are now featured in large supermarkets. Scrub (do not peel) and wrap in silver foil with a little butter and salt. Bake for an hour and serve. Alternatively boil in salted water until tender and then remove skins and mash with a little milk, butter and seasoning. Serve with pork or turkey — you might change your mind about sweet potatoes. An interesting point — this vegetable belongs to the bindweed family and is quite unrelated to the potato.

VINE LEAF

Throughout the Middle East you will be offered *dolmas* (or *dolmades*) — vine leaves which have been rolled around a herb-enriched rice and meat mixture. Nowadays you need not travel to the other end of Europe — they are standard fare at the many Greek restaurants which have appeared in Britain.

Until recently we had to use cabbage leaves to make *dolmas* at home, but fresh vine leaves in brine are now available in neat plastic bags at some supermarkets. The first task is to blanch the leaves — pour boiling water over them and leave to stand for 15 minutes. Wash several times and the leaves are ready for filling. Prepare a mixture of boiled rice, minced beef or lamb, mixed herbs, chopped onion and garlic, seasoning, lemon juice and a little olive oil. Put a dessertspoonful on to each leaf, folding over and tucking in the ends. Place the *dolmas*, tightly packed, in a pan, add a cup of water and simmer for an hour. Serve hot or cold.

WATERCRESS

Unlike many of the vegetables in this section, watercress is neither unusual nor exotic. It is a native British plant which is bought rather than grown because of its need for free-flowing fresh water in the bed.

Cut off the base of the stems, remove discoloured leaves and wash thoroughly. Shake off any remaining water and the sprigs are ready for eating. The standard uses are as a garnish around meat or fish, in a salad or occasionally as a sandwich filling.

There are other ways of using this nutritious plant. Sauté in a little butter for 10 minutes and serve as a hot vegetable or use it to make one of the delicious watercress soups which you will find described in your cookery books. Finely-chopped watercress will give a distinctive taste to mashed potatoes, dumplings, white sauce etc. Watercress quickly deteriorates on storage but you can keep the sprigs in a polythene bag in the refrigerator for up to 2 days.

YAM

The Americans sometimes loosely refer to sweet potatoes as yams, but the true yam is quite a different vegetable. The flesh of the yam is orange and not yellow, and the texture tends to be oily rather than floury. The tubers tend to be much larger than those of the sweet potato — yams weighing 100 lb or more have been recorded.

Yams are the staff of life for millions in the tropical regions of the world. Many types are grown — the large ones have little taste, the small varieties are generally very sweet. The best way to use a large yam is to either boil or fry it — use small ones for roasting. Baking is an excellent cooking method for potatoes and sweet potatoes, but not for yams. On the other hand there are uses for this tropical vegetable which are out of the question for our domestic potato. You can try candied yams, yams casseroled with orange juice and also curried yams — a true taste of the Orient.

1 in. = 2.5 cm, 1 ft = 30 cm, 1 oz = 28 gm, 1 lb = 450 gm

CHAPTER 10
VEGETABLE & HERB INDEX

Acknowledgements

The author wishes to acknowledge the painstaking work of Gill Jackson, Paul Norris, Linda Fensom and Angelina Gibbs. Grateful acknowledgement is also made for the help received from Joan Hessayon and Colin Bailey. A special word of thanks is due to Suttons Seeds Ltd for their provision of transparencies — other photographs were received from Pat Brindley, Harry Smith Horticultural Photographic Collection, London Express News and Feature Services, and Unwins Seeds Ltd.

Artwork for this book was produced by the late John Woodbridge, Deborah Mansfield and Henry Barnett.